how to garden

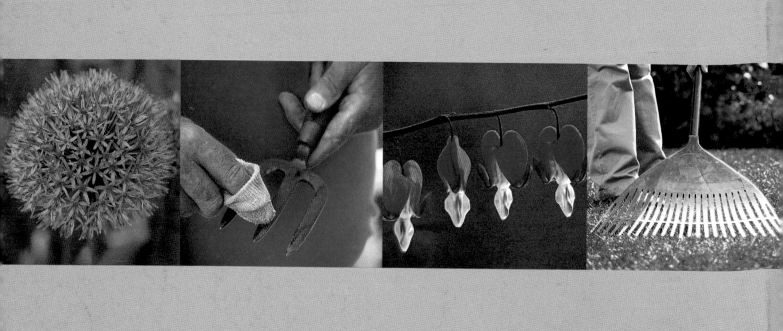

how to garden

hamlyn

First published in Great
Britain in 2004 by
Hamlyn, a division of
Octopus Publishing Group Ltd
2-4 Heron Quays,
London E14 4JP

ISBN 0 600 60837 9

A CIP catalogue record for
this book is available from the
British Library

Printed and bound in China

10 9 8 7 6 5 4 3 2 1

contents

6   7   8   9   10   11

Introduction

Some people regard gardening as nothing more than a necessity; others see it as a positive joy. But no matter how you feel about it, it's likely you'll want to – or have to – have a go at one time or another because we all want to have a pleasant outside space for relaxation and entertaining. And what begins as a chore may also turn into an absorbing pastime.

Many people get an enormous thrill when they see the first seeds they've sown germinate and develop into mature plants, but others are struck with panic at the thought of failure because there seems to be so much to learn. It's often difficult to persuade new gardeners that it's mainly a matter of common sense. You're bound to make mistakes – people who have been gardening for years have their own horror stories - but this book will be somewhere you can turn to for the answers whenever you need help. It will not only enable you to pinpoint the cause of a problem and put it right but also, more importantly, steer you in the right direction so that you avoid problems from the outset. Your plants will still need some tender loving care. Treat your plants as individuals and keep an eye on them so that you notice when they are not growing well. Then you can take the appropriate action. And don't forget: if something goes wrong, there's always next year to try again.

Whether you have a small patio garden, a large plot or just a windowbox or two, there are almost limitless options. If this is your first garden, try to be original. Most gardeners stick to traditional ideas when it comes to planning their garden or combining plants into a display, more out of fear of trying something new than a lack of imagination.

This is especially true when it comes to annuals and containers: just look around you at the displays in your neighbours' gardens and in public plantings this summer. How much more fun it would be to have containers with a different colour scheme each season, as if you were decorating a room. Try combining shades of pink and lime green, or blues and oranges, or use all white for a different look. Your garden will be far more personal as a result. Even if, occasionally, a display for which you had high hopes looks terrible,

top Growing your own plants from seed and cuttings can be immensely satisfying, and it is a very economical way of filling a garden. Even roses can be raised this way.

left Planting up containers allows you to ring the changes without disturbing permanent planting: hot hues one summer, cool pastels the next.

right Tulips in a sea of forget-me-nots create a classical spring scene against a backdrop of fresh new foliage.

you can always try again with different plants. And every now and again you'll produce something wonderful.

Some people find the fact that things don't happen instantaneously in the garden frustrating. In fact, it is a positive advantage. There's something satisfying about taking your time and watching the seasons unfold and the plants develop at their own speed. There are particular times of the year when certain tasks have to be done and there are specific methods to be followed for others, but most jobs in the garden are a matter of following your own judgement and finding the best and most convenient ways for you.

Most plants do best in bright light – though not necessarily direct sun – and in well-drained soil that has been enriched with plenty of well-rotted manure or compost. Most gardeners, though, are faced with terrible soil, plenty of deep shade and generally difficult conditions, especially if you have recently moved into a new house where the garden is nothing more than turf laid over builder's rubble. Don't worry. You will find plenty of suggestions here for ways you can improve the conditions you have as well as plants that will thrive in inhospitable spots. Sometimes, of course, no matter what you try, plants just won't seem to grow, but you can give them the best possible chance by making sure they are in an appropriate position and in the sort of soil they like. The key to successful gardening is to choose the plants that will grow in the conditions you can provide – it's no good trying to grow the moisture-loving plants that you might see around a natural pond if you are gardening on very sandy, fast-draining soil. You will waste your money and your time.

Gardening can be very rewarding. It allows you to create a personal space that can be truly yours. And creating a beautiful grden is quite different from decorating a room, for it will change with the seasons and evolve over the years Gardening also provides good, regular exercise and the opportunity to spend time in the open air. For many, dealing with growing and propagating plants is a fascinating pastime, and here lies one of the main problems – it can become addictive; you have been warned!

Thinking about your garden

For most people, the process of raising and tending plants is a means to achieving an attractive outside space, a place in which they can relax, spend time with their family and friends, play games and enjoy meals outside. Before you rush out to get your hands dirty, though, take the time to consider the garden as a whole. You should ask yourself if it fulfils all your needs or do you need to make sweeping changes before it can meet all your requirements?

How much time have you got?

One of the most important questions to ask yourself before you even begin to think about redesigning and planting up your garden is how much time you can devote to it. Although no garden is entirely maintenance free, it is possible to create one in which chores are minimized. If you have a busy life with many commitments outside the home or if, frankly, you'd rather be sitting in the garden with a book or drink in your hand than tending it, don't design a garden that revolves around bedding plants and annuals. Think instead about a design with plenty of paving or gravel and with low-maintenance trees, shrubs and perennials. You could also include some artefacts rather than plants to provide the main decorative features. A few containers will begin to make the space look even more like a garden, but the amount of time you will need to spend looking after it will still be minimal.

If you have more time to spend on gardening, the area of hard surfacing could be reduced to a minimum and the number and size of the beds and borders and the amount of plants increased.

Your ideal garden will probably lie somewhere on this spectrum. Think carefully about it and be honest with yourself about deciding how much time you can devote to planting, weeding, grass cutting, pruning and the like. Match this to the type of garden you would like. There's no point in overestimating how much time you will find to spend outside – you will only end up with a messy space that you never seem to get straight.

top Gravel gardens repay the care needed to create them by being easy to maintain and requiring little watering.

right Space for the children to run around and play is a vital consideration when planning a family garden.

Choosing a style

Your garden should reflect your own interests and lifestyle. It is not a static object and can be changed from time to time, although you will need to allow time for it to mature. Don't forget, though, that your garden surrounds your house and should complement the style of the building and the main materials used.

There are so many different styles from which to choose. Looking at books and television programmes will generate some ideas, but it's often easier to see what you do and don't like by looking at other people's gardens.

One of the main decisions is whether you prefer a formal or informal look. Formal gardens tend to be symmetrical and to have clipped hedges, geometrically shaped beds and internal areas divided by neat paths. Gardeners with families often choose an informal style, as do people who want a contrast from their ordered, busy lives. Others, however, may prefer to have a more ordered, uncluttered garden in which lines are crisp and clear rather than indistinct and understated, as they frequently are in an informal garden. Many gardens are not so clear-cut and have small areas of each style within the overall garden.

In many respects, the actual size of a garden is irrelevant. It is what you do with it that is important. Two people with similar, small town gardens may well treat them in totally different ways, one choosing a minimal approach, with elements sparely ordered and a few choice plants, while the other prefers to fill the space with hundreds of plants. It is surprising what can be done with even the smallest patch.

What features do you need?

One of the most important steps when you are planning a garden is to sit down and draw up a list of what you and everyone in your family needs from the garden. You should then try to rank these requirements in order of priority, because it's almost certain that there won't be room for them all or that some uses may conflict with others. For example, making room for children's games, such as football, is likely to conflict with a desire to have a beautifully manicured lawn. You might, however, be prepared to forgo the lawn for a while. There'll be time enough

when the children have left home to transform the space allocated for games into a dream lawn.

Next, consider whether, realistically, you are going to have the time and money to achieve what you want. It is very easy to take on more than you can manage and end up with a part-finished garden, which becomes more of a nightmare than a pleasure.

Making a plan

Although it sounds dull, it is a good idea to draw up a scale plan, marking in the fixed features, such as trees, an existing pond or a shed, that you would like to retain. Also include areas of permanent shade and maximum sun, and any other relevant details, such as inspection covers. Then see if you can fit in what you want to achieve. When you have finished, go out and try to visualize whether it will work. Mark out areas with string or hosepipe and see what the finished design might look like on the ground. Live with the idea and the plans for a few weeks, looking at the garden in different light levels and weather to see how it will work. Only when you are satisfied is it time to start getting your hands dirty.

right This flower-lover's garden will attract bees and butterflies and, as the season progresses, the seed will be collected to provide new plants to grow and give away.

How to get started

Analysing the conditions in your garden is one of the first things that you should do when you are starting out. All plots are different; even if they are exactly the same size and in the same road, each will require a different approach. Take time to study your plot and to assess both its positive and its negative aspects.

Assessing the site

Before you start planting your garden, you need to look at your specific plot and work out its advantages and disadvantages. Its location will affect many of your planting choices. The whole of a neighbour's garden, for example, may be bathed in sunshine all day long, while a tall tree plunges part of another, similar garden into deep shadow in the afternoon. Winds may make it necessary to install a windbreak in one garden, while in another breezes may be hardly noticeable. Each plot must be judged on its own characteristics. The type of vegetation already growing in a plot is often a good indicator of the nature of the soil. If your garden is filled with rhododendrons and azaleas in spring and there is an abundance of heathers throughout the year, you can be sure that the soil is acid. On the other hand, if the surrounding countryside supports a large population of plants that enjoy alkaline conditions, the soil is almost certain to be chalky. If you are starting a garden from scratch it is a good idea to buy an inexpensive soil-testing kit. Test the soil in several places all over the garden – you might find that it proves to be acid in one spot and alkaline at a point only a few metres (yards) away. Because some plants are lime-haters while others cannot thrive in acid soils, your planting scheme choices will be constrained by the soil. See pages 22–33 for more details.

A preponderance of marsh plants among the wild plants will give a good indication of waterlogged soil. If the whole plot shows signs of being wet, it's possible that the entire area needs to be drained. Such a spot in only one part of the site, however, will provide the opportunity to have a bog garden or a natural pool as a special feature. At the same time, make a note of any places where the soil appears to be exceptionally dry, so that you can organize the planting accordingly.

left Serenity on a summer's morning: consider where and when your garden gets the sun and when parts of it are shady.

top Planning is important, but sometimes you just need to get down and work with the soil for a while to trigger ideas.

What grows where

Fortunately, although some plants may prefer a particular kind of soil, most will tolerate a wide range of conditions, happy anywhere reasonably fertile that is neither too wet nor too dry.

Exposure to both wind and temperature extremes will influence growth. There are gardens on hillsides or near to the sea where it is almost impossible to develop a planting scheme until prevailing winds have been moderated by shelter belts of evergreen trees and shrubs and carefully sited fences that filter the wind. Before you buy any plants, look in neighbours' gardens and note what grows well.

Aspect

The way the site is positioned in relation to the sun and shade – its aspect – is the next consideration. The aspect determines how much sun the garden enjoys and at what time of the day certain parts of the area are in sun or shade. In some cases, such as beside the sea, aspect determines what particular spots in the garden are exposed to strong winds and so need to be screened.

In an ideal world, your back garden should have a sunny aspect. A little shade, or a shaded area, is welcome during the summer, but will benefit from receiving as much light as possible during the winter, while being sheltered from cold winds.

The worst aspects for a garden are when only a limited amount of sun shines directly on the garden or where there is shade during the afternoon. Prevailing winds are often strong and biting, and if the site is in a particularly open position this could have a damaging effect on plants. Gardens that receive sun during at least the afternoon are much more favourable to plants, which tend to benefit from a certain amount of warmth, shade and moisture.

Once you have assessed your site and know what you are dealing with, you will be able to get an idea of what plants will do well in your garden. Use the information in this book to guide you through the stages of buying new plants, getting them off to a new start and keeping them happy thereafter.

Getting started

If you are a first-time gardener, take time to think about what you really want to achieve and keep the following guidelines in mind as you assess the possibilities of your new garden:

- Don't be over-ambitious – start small and work your way up slowly so that you don't take on more than you can cope with.

- Start with popular plants, which tend to be widely grown because they are adaptable and accommodating.

- Containers are good practice. Cut your gardening teeth on temporary displays, which will be changed during the next season anyway.

- Spend time with your plants. The more you observe them, the more you will learn about them and the sooner you will detect a problem.

- Tackle mundane tasks – weeding, for example – in small, regular batches. An hour an evening will seem less daunting than a whole day. Remember that weeds are easier to deal with when they are small, so don't let them take over.

- Don't feel you have to do everything from scratch. A display of bought petunias will look just as good as those you have grown from seed.

- Have fun, regardless of what the neighbours may think. Create a garden you like and you will want to spend time perfecting it.

right Annuals such as these vivid poppies flower best on poor soil and will provide colour in the first season until shrubs and perennials establish themselves.

the basics

What is a plant?

In order to keep plants happy and healthy, you need to understand them – to know what they like and what they don't like. It also helps to understand how they work, what they need to function properly and what conditions they are used to in the wild.

Plants are an enormously diverse group – compare an oak tree with a crocus – but they all have the same constituent parts and work in much the same way. They are made up of roots, usually below ground, and stems and leaves, usually above ground. They also need a means of reproducing themselves, and the majority of garden plants do this by their flowers which, after they are fertilized, produce seed.

Roots

The roots are the lower parts of a plant and are designed to take up water and nutrients. They are usually found below ground because they normally take up moisture from the soil, but in some environments – rain forests, for example – there is so much humidity in the air that roots grow out of plant stems above ground and take moisture out of the air.

There are two types of roots. The thicker roots growing out of the plant stem are used to anchor the plant in the soil and to transport water and nutrients back to the plant. The fine hair roots, which grow out of the tips of these thicker roots, are designed to take up the water and nutrients from the soil.

Some plants develop taproots, which go straight down in search of water. Others have a comparatively shallow network of fine roots, which are close to the surface and can benefit from light rain or dew that does not penetrate down into the soil.

We are most aware of these different root systems when it comes to weeding: dandelions send down deep taproots, whereas the short mass of roots on buttercups makes them much easier to prise out. Some plants, such as parsnips and dahlias, have roots that act as storage organs for the energy made by the leaves.

Stems

Stems form the framework of a plant and hold the leaves and flowers in the most beneficial positions, the leaves to receive maximum sunlight, the flowers to be in the most advantageous position for pollination, whether this is done by wind, insects or animals. Stems on some long-lived plants – notably trees and shrubs – become woody with age and create an even stronger framework to support the weight of the foliage.

Stems also act like blood vessels, carrying water and nutrients up to the leaves from the roots, and plant foods down from the leaves where they have been manufactured, to feed the rest of the plant or to be stored in the roots.

left Most plants, however different in appearance, consist of the same basic structure of roots, stems and leaves.

top We are drawn to flowers for their beauty, but from the plant's point of view flowers are fashioned to attract pollinators.

Leaves

Leaves are rather like solar panels. They use a process called photosynthesis to convert energy from the sun, carbon from the air and water drawn up from the soil into food for the plant. These plant foods are used for growth or may be stored in the roots or stems for later use. Photosynthesis relies on a green pigment called chlorophyll, so, in general, greener leaves are more efficient at making use of the available light. This is why many shade-loving plants have such green leaves – they have adapted to survive in shady conditions by making the best use of the available light.

Water is released through pores on the undersides of the leaves where it evaporates. This process draws more water up through the plant's leaves, stems and lastly the roots where water is taken up from the soil.

Flowers

Although we appreciate flowers for their decorative qualities, they have an important practical role for plants. Flowers are the means by which most plants reproduce. The male part of a flower, the stamen, produces pollen. This is transferred, by one means or another, to the female part of another flower to fertilize it. This flower then produces fertile seeds, which will eventually ripen, germinate and grow into new plants.

If you look closely at a flower, you will see it is made up of several different parts. In the middle is the stigma, which is on a little stem that leads down to the ovary. These are the female parts of the flower. The stigma is designed to catch pollen from another flower to fertilize the ovary, where the seeds will form.

Around the stigma are a number of anthers. These bear pollen, which is transferred to another flower to fertilize it. Pollen is transferred by different means in different plants. Some make use of the wind; the pollen is literally blown from one plant to another. Others use insects to transfer pollen; they lure insects into the flower by providing them a meal of sweet nectar. While the insect is feeding, pollen will be transferred to its back from the anthers of one flower and then it will be carried to the next flower, where it will be deposited on the stigma for fertilization.

The petals are usually the most obvious parts of a flower, and they have evolved to have bright colours and patterns to attract insects. Plants that are pollinated by wind rather than insects usually have less conspicuous petals.

Most flowers have both male and female parts, but some plants have separate male and female flowers. *Betula* spp. (birch), for example, have male 'catkins' as well as female flowers. Other plants have male and female flowers on different plants, so you need both a male and a female plant nearby. This is why you only get berries on some *Ilex* spp. (holly) plants and not others – they only form on female plants and only when they have been fertilized by a nearby male plant.

left above and below Reflective silvery skins and furry or waxy leaves protect plants from overheating and prevent them losing too much water in hot, sunny climates.

How do they grow?

From just water, air, soil and sunshine, plants manage to make their own food and everything they need to grow. If they are to perform at their best, they need a fine balance of the right 'ingredients', so you need to provide the best possible growing conditions for all your plants according to their specific requirements.

Light

Plants use sunlight to make the energy they need to work effectively by a process called photosynthesis. Some plants need more light than others; some have become adapted to living in shady conditions in the wild. These shade-lovers have evolved so that their leaves can make maximum use of the available light, and they will scorch and shrivel if they get too much sunshine. On the other hand, a plant that grows in sunny places in the wild will become lanky and drawn if you plant it in a shady part of the garden because it will try to grow into the light.

Some plants have adapted to living in really hot, bright places and can defend themselves from the sun's harsh rays. Some have glossy, waxy or silvery leaves to reflect light; others have hairy or furry foliage to shade the leaf's surface. It goes without saying that these plants will not be happy in a shady place because they just won't receive enough sunlight to function.

Water

All plants need water. They draw it up through their roots, and it passes up through all parts of the plant and is then released onto the surface of the leaves where it evaporates, causing the plant to draw up more water to replace it in a continuous cycle. In this way, water acts rather like blood in an animal as it transport gases and nutrients to the parts of the plant where it is needed.

In hot weather the cycle speeds up as water evaporates more quickly from the leaves. If the supply of water to the roots is reduced or if it is simply too hot to keep up with demand, the pores on the leaves that release the water are closed and the system shuts off. The plant stops growing until conditions return to normal. This is why plants become stressed in dry conditions. When the temperature drops or the plant receives more water at its roots, the system starts

top Give young plants a good start in life and they will be less likely to prove problematic later. This young clematis is being encouraged to climb.

left Unless you have consciously chosen drought-resistant plants, the garden will need watering in dry spells.

right Garden compost is a marvellous soil conditioner – and costs nothing.

up again. If, however, the temperature doesn't drop or the roots remain dry, the plant will wilt and eventually die.

The flow of water through the plant obviously depends on the roots doing their job efficiently. Newly planted plants need to be kept well watered until they can grow new roots out into the soil to seek moisture more effectively from a wider area.

A supply of water is also needed by plants because it contains hydrogen, which is used in the process of photosynthesis.

Nutrients

Just as we need a balanced diet to grow healthily, plants need a range of nutrients, which they take up from the soil in moisture. There are about 30 different nutrients that plants need, most in only tiny quantities. The three main nutrients needed for plant growth are nitrogen (N), for leaves, phosphorus (P), for roots, and potassium (K), for flowers and fruit. Plants also need lesser amounts of magnesium, calcium, sulphur, carbon, hydrogen and oxygen. The minor, or trace, elements that plants need include iron, manganese, boron, molybdenum, zinc and copper. They are found in most soils but need to be replaced regularly as the plants use them up. A plant lacking any of these elements will either not perform well or show signs of distress in the form of discoloured foliage.

Any organic matter that you remove from the garden – grass clippings, weeds, dead flowerheads – also contains nutrients, and this is why it makes sense to make your own compost from this material so that you can return the nutrients to the garden rather than removing them and throwing them away.

Occasionally plants will suffer from a deficiency disease brought about by a lack of a certain nutrient, but more often they will be short of a whole range of nutrients together and will benefit from the application of a general fertilizer.

Soil

Soil is a mixture of rock dust, broken down over millions of years, and organic matter formed from decaying plant material. Soil is important to plants in a number of ways, perhaps most obviously in providing them with the means to anchor themselves to the ground. Plant roots grow out into the soil and hold the plant upright. While they are there, the fine hair roots that grow from the main roots draw up water and nutrients from the soil.

What is not so obvious is that soil also contains air, which plant roots need if they are going to function properly. This is why soil type is so vital. Sandy soils contain relatively large particles, so the air gaps between them are large. Clay soils contain smaller particles, which pack more closely together, making the air gaps between them smaller. But it's not just the air content that matters to the plants. The size of the air gaps affects how easily water can pass through the soil – quickly through sandy soils with big gaps and much more slowly through clay soils, which can become waterlogged.

Air

Air provides plants with carbon and oxygen, which they need as part of the process of photosynthesis by which they convert sunlight into energy. Air is also a source of nitrogen, one of the most important plant nutrients. Plants take up nitrogen through their roots, and it gets from the air into the soil where the plants can get to it in several ways. The first is by the action of nitrogen-fixing bacteria, which are found in great numbers in healthy soil. The second is by bacteria that are found in the root nodules of nitrogen-fixing plants, such as peas and beans. The third way is by the action of lightning during thunderstorms, which enables nitrogen to dissolve in rainwater.

Describing plants

Different plants are described in different ways, and becoming familiar with some of these everyday terms is useful to understanding what you are buying and how a plant will behave. Buying plants can otherwise seem quite unnecessarily daunting.

Annuals

Annuals are plants that are grown from seed, flower and die within a single year. They are used to provide a blaze of short-term colour in borders and containers. There are two main types of annual.

Hardy annuals

Plants such as *Calendula* spp. (pot marigold) and *Nigella damascena* (love-in-a-mist) can spend their entire life out of doors. They can be sown directly in the positions in which they are going to flower. Sow in early spring for summer flowering, or in the previous autumn for slightly earlier flowers.

Half-hardy annuals

Some plants, such as petunias and *Moluccella laevis* (bells of Ireland), will not germinate from seed in cold conditions, so they must be raised by sowing seeds in a greenhouse or on a windowsill. They cannot be put out into the garden until all risk of frost has passed (usually in early summer), and they must be gradually hardened off as young plants before they are set outside.

Biennials

Biennial plants are those that are raised from seed in one year for flowering the next. As most of them are hardy and are used as bedding plants, the seeds are usually sown outdoors during the first summer in a seedtray or in a spare area of soil. The young plants develop and are planted in their flowering positions in autumn or the following spring. They flower in the second summer and then die. Among the most widely planted biennials are *Digitalis purpurea* (common foxglove) and *Myosotis sylvatica* (forget-me-not).

top *Papaver orientalis* (oriental poppy) is a long-lived perennial that bursts into glorious colour early each summer.

right Lilies are rewarding bulbs. This is a short-stemmed variety called 'Enchantment', a popular choice for pots and tubs.

Perennials

All plants that live for more than two years under the right conditions are called perennials, but gardeners usually use the word perennial to mean the herbaceous border plants that die down after flowering, remain dormant over winter then throw up new stems and leaves in spring. Hardy perennials are generally herbaceous and can remain in the garden all year round. Half-hardy or tender perennials cannot withstand cold temperatures and need some protection in winter. Most of them, including pelargoniums and many fuchsias are, in fact, treated as bedding plants and discarded at the end of the season or moved under cover in winter.

Bedding plants

A bedding plant is a flowering or foliage plant that is set out in a border or container to give a few months' display of colour. Bedding plants are used mainly in spring and summer. After flowering, they are lifted and discarded (if they are annuals or biennials) or given winter protection (if they are tender perennials).

Bulbous plants

These have fleshy roots, stems or underground stems that act as food storage organs. Above-ground stems, leaves and flowers grow out of these organs at certain times of year. The leaves generate more food from sunshine, and the food is stored in the storage organs the leaves die down again. Bulbous plants can be divided into true bulbs, such as *Narcissus* (daffodil), corms, such as crocuses, rhizomes, such as irises, and tubers, such as dahlias, but, from a gardener's point of view, there is little difference between them, and they are usually referred to under the general term 'bulb'.

Shrubs and trees

Herbaceous plants have soft stems, but shrubs and trees develop woody stems and branches, which live throughout the year. Trees differ from shrubs in their growing habit. Most trees develop a single main stem (trunk) that branches out at some height above ground; a shrub, on the other hand, has branches near or even below the soil's surface.

Evergreen or deciduous

Deciduous plants are those that shed their leaves in autumn, remain bare through the winter and grow new leaves in spring. Evergreens are clothed in leaves throughout the year. It is a mistake to think that evergreen plants never shed leaves; they do, but they lose a few at a time throughout the year so it's not noticeable. Some plants are described as semi-evergreen, which means that they will keep their leaves in a mild winter, or if they are in a sheltered position, but lose them in a cold spell.

Climbing plants

Climbers differ from other plants in that they have a built-in means of clinging to a support. Climbers can be woody shrubs – *Hedera* spp. (ivy) and some forms of *Lonicera* (honeysuckle), for example – which produce a permanent framework of stems, or they can be herbaceous perennials – *Humulus lupulus* (hop), for example – which dies down below ground in winter and produces a new set of stems in spring.

Latin names

Although they appear rather off-putting at first, Latin plant names do make life easier for gardeners. Common names vary so much from place to place that it can be impossible to know which plant someone is referring to unless each plant has a unique and internationally recognized name.

Latin names start with the genus name, such as *Thymus* for the thymes. Members of the genus, the species, have a different second name – common thyme or garden thyme is known as *Thymus vulgaris*, for example, and caraway thyme is *Thymus herba-barona*. Because common thyme also sometimes has white flowers, you can have a third name, *Thymus vulgaris* f. *albus*, to refer to the white-flowered form. Plant breeders develop new forms of certain species (called cultivars), and these are written in a different way to the naturally occurring variants – for example, *Thymus vulgaris* 'Silver Posie' has been bred for its white-edged leaves. In some cases, the parentage of a plant is so confused that it is simply known by the genus and cultivar names, such as *Thymus* 'Doone Valley'.

The genus name is often shortened to its initial when several species are being described. You might, therefore, find references to *Thymus ciliatus*, *T.* × *citriodorus* and *T.* 'Hartington Silver' – all types of thyme.

The Latin name can also be a useful guide to the type of habitat a plant prefers. The specific (second) names of *Caltha palustris* (marsh marigold) and *Thelypteris palustris* (marsh fern) indicate the plants' liking for marshy ground. Other specific names are descriptive: *Muscari azureum* (grape hyacinth) has azure blue flowers.

Choosing tools

A selection of good-quality, basic tools is indispensable for any work in the garden. Choose your tools with care, selecting the right size and type for your particular needs. Although a good spade or fork is not cheap, with care it will probably have as long a life as its owner.

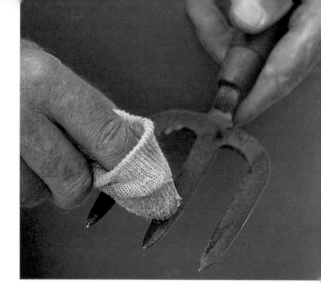

Always select a tool that will perform the task that it is meant to do efficiently. It is also wise to take into account how frequently it is likely to be used, as this could determine the amount you are prepared to spend on it. As a rule, spend as much as you can afford, because well-designed and well-made tools are a pleasure to use and will last a lifetime. Cheap tools will soon break or rust.

Spades

Spades are available with shafts of different lengths and blades of different sizes. The standard spade blade measures about 29 × 19cm (11½ × 7½in), smaller spades are 25 × 17cm (10 × 6½in), and a border spade is 23 × 14cm (9 × 5½in). Choose whichever is most comfortable to use and bear in mind that heavy digging will probably be easier with the middle size. Choose a shaft length to suit your height. The shaft of the spade should have a gentle crank to allow maximum leverage, and the strapped or tubular socket should be securely attached to the shaft. Metal treads welded to the upper edge of the blade make digging heavy soil less painful to the foot.

Spades that have stainless steel blades are far more expensive than those with blades of forged steel, but they are long lasting and cut into the soil much more easily than ordinary steel spades.

An essential tool for digging, the spade is also efficient for skimming weed growth off the soil before cultivation begins. Always hold the spade upright when cutting into the soil so that the ground is cultivated to the full depth of the blade. A spade is also useful when you are planting trees and shrubs, and for mixing compost.

Forks

A garden fork is just as useful as a spade and is similarly manufactured. The four tines (prongs) may be square in cross-section, as in the general-purpose or digging fork, or flat, as in the potato fork, which is designed to avoid damaging tubers at harvesting time. The head of the digging fork measures 30 × 19cm (12 × 7½in), and that of the smaller border fork is 23 × 14cm (9 × 5½in). Both stainless and forged steel types are available.

A fork is easier to use than a spade for digging heavy soil. It is essential for breaking down roughly dug soil and for lightly cultivating well-worked ground before seeds are sown and young plants are put into the ground. A smaller border fork can be used to cultivate the soil among herbaceous plants and shrubs, and a larger fork is useful for moving compost and manure. Both can be used to aerate lawns.

top Looking after your tools will extend their working lives.

above Digging is not all about brute force: find a technique that doesn't strain your back or legs, and don't try to lift over-heavy loads in an effort to save time.

Trowels

This invaluable planting tool usually has a wooden or polypropylene handle, 10–15cm (4–6in) long. Versions with longer handles are available, but they may be less comfortable to use. If you can, buy a trowel with a stainless steel rather than a forged steel blade because it will be much easier to use, will be less likely to bend and will not rust.

A trowel can be used like a shovel or flour scoop and also as if it were a digging claw – use it whichever way is comfortable and effective for you to plant bedding and herbaceous plants, vegetables and bulbs.

Hand forks

A hand fork will probably be the first thing you buy. Choose one that sits comfortably in your hand and spend as much as you can afford. Forks are the same size as trowels, but with three or four prongs, and are made in the same way.

Use your fork for transplanting seedlings, for working among tightly packed plants, such as alpines in the rock garden, and for intricate planting and weeding. It is an invaluable tool.

Rakes

The most popular type of garden rake has a steel head, about 30cm (12in) wide, fitted with teeth 5cm (2in) long. The shaft should be about 1.5m (5ft) long and smooth to allow a good backwards and forwards motion. Larger wooden rakes are useful for gathering up leaves, grass and debris, which get clogged in the teeth of steel rakes, but they are not essential.

The main use of the rake is to level soil that has been previously broken down to a reasonable tilth (fine, crumbly texture) with a garden fork. Although the rake will make the soil texture even finer, it should not be over-used or the soil will be inclined to compact. Move the rake backwards and forwards over the soil in a sweeping motion, first in one direction and then at right angles to ensure an even finish.

Hoes

There are many different types of hoe, but the two most important are the Dutch hoe and the draw hoe. Both are equipped with handles about 1.5m (5ft) long and forged or stainless steel blades. The head of the Dutch hoe has a flat blade, 10–12cm (4–5in) long, designed to cut almost horizontally through the soil. A draw hoe's head is of a similar width, but rectangular or semicircular and attached at right angles to the handle. It is used with a chopping or scraping motion.

The Dutch hoe is perhaps the best tool for general weeding, as the gardener skims it backwards and forwards just below the surface of the soil while walking backwards. In this way the cultivated ground is not walked over and the weeds (severed from their roots) are left to dry out in the loose soil. The Dutch hoe is also used for breaking up surface pans.

With the draw hoe the gardener must move forwards, chopping the soil and pulling it towards them slightly or scraping the weeds off the surface. The draw hoe (despite its disadvantage of forcing the gardener to walk over the cultivated soil) is safer to use among closely spaced plants than a Dutch hoe. Both types of hoe can be used to create seed drills against a taut garden line, and the draw hoe is used to earth up (mound soil around) vegetables, such as potatoes, leeks and celery.

Wheelbarrows

You will need a wheelbarrow only if your garden is large or if you have a vegetable plot, when it will save you a lot of time and energy. Always check the weight distribution of a barrow before buying it – as much of the load as possible should be placed over the wheel so that the barrow, not you, takes most of the weight. Barrows are available with large, inflated, ball-shaped wheels, and these are especially useful if the ground is particularly soft. Small, two-wheeled barrows can be easier to load, unload and push than single-wheeled types. Models with solid tyres are adequate where the ground is hard enough for sinkage not to be a problem. Make sure that the chosen barrow is large enough but is not too heavy.

If you have a wheelbarrow you will be able to move compost, manure, soil, sacks of fertilizer and all manner of equipment around the garden. Stand the barrow upright against a wall or under cover when it is not in use.

These are the basic digging and planting tools that you will need. You will also require tools for cutting back, pruning and clipping your plants once they have grown (see pages 162–3).

all about soil

What soil have you got?

The importance of soil cannot be overestimated. Good soil will support strong, healthy plants, and probably the most useful thing you can do before you do anything else in your garden is to get to know your soil. Then, if it needs it – and most soils do – you should find out how you can improve it.

Know your soil

From the gardener's point of view, soils are classified according to the amount of sand or clay particles they contain. They are also described according to their acidity or alkalinity.

Clay

Clay soils are difficult to cultivate because they are slow to drain and have little air penetration. They are sticky when wet, hard when dry, slow to warm up in spring and described as heavy. They are usually rich in nutrients, however, because the flow of water running through is limited, so few nutrients are washed away.

To find out if you have clay soil, squeeze a moist sample between your finger and thumb. If the particles slide readily and the soil looks shiny and sticky, it has a high clay content. If you squeeze a handful of clay soil, it will form a dense ball.

The addition of organic matter, such as well-rotted garden compost, will greatly improve a heavy clay soil, allowing water and air to pass through it more readily. Adding lime will cause the particles to bind together, forming larger air spaces between clumps.

Sand

Sandy soils drain rapidly and there is ample air for plant roots. They are easy to cultivate and quick to warm up in spring, but they dry out easily and, because of the rapid drainage, nutrients are quickly leached (washed) away.

To find out if you have sandy soil, squeeze the particles between your finger and thumb. If the sand content is high the particles will both look and feel rough. If you squeeze a handful of sandy soil, it will not form a ball because it is too crumbly.

You can improve sandy soil by the addition of organic matter, such as well-rotted garden compost. This will help the soil to hold moisture and, therefore, enhance the nutrient levels.

Silt

Silty soils have particles that are intermediate in size between sand and clay. They are sticky and fairly heavy and can be difficult to cultivate. You can improve the texture of a silty soil by applying large amounts of organic material.

Loam

This is the ideal soil to which most gardeners aspire. Loam contains a mixture of clay, sand and silt, plus organic matter and plant nutrients. It is easy to cultivate, retains moisture and nutrients, yet is well drained. Loam may be classified as light, medium or heavy, depending on the clay-to-sand ratio – you will also hear expressions such as 'sandy loam'.

Peat

Made up of partially decomposed organic matter, peaty soils are inclined to be acid and poorly drained. They are dark and fibrous, with no sand or clay particles. To improve a peat soil, add lime, nutrients,

top Feeling your soil and becoming familiar with how it reacts when wet or dry will help you tell what type it is and which plants will grow best in it.

coarse sand, grit or weathered ashes. In extreme cases, you may also need to construct a drainage system to dry them out.

Life-giving humus

The dark brown, crumbly, organic matter within the soil is humus. It consists of plant and animal remains in various stages of decomposition and ensures the continued survival of bacteria, which are essential if a soil is to be fertile. Humus also retains moisture, keeps the soil well aerated and is a source of plant nutrients. On cultivated ground, humus breaks down more quickly than it would if it were left undisturbed. It is, therefore, important that the soil is amply and regularly replenished with well-rotted manure, garden compost, leaf mould or other humus-forming material whenever possible.

Drainage

Both water and air are necessary in the soil if plants and soil organisms are to thrive. A lack of air inhibits a plant's uptake of minerals from the soil, and in poorly drained soils a plant's roots tend to stay in the top layer of soil where there is more air. However, a plant with shallow roots cannot anchor itself firmly or search far for nutrients and will not, therefore, grow so well.

Soil life

Earthworms, insects, burrowing animals, slugs, snails, bacteria and many other forms of life contribute to the organic content of the soil, and unless their presence is a severe nuisance they should be encouraged.

Acid or alkaline

The amount of lime in soil dictates its acidity. A soil rich in lime or chalk is said to be alkaline. One that lacks lime is described as acid or sour. The degree of acidity or alkalinity is measured on the pH scale, which runs from 0 to 14. A soil with a pH above 7 is called alkaline; one with a pH below 6.5 is called acid. Soils with pH readings above 8.5 and below 4.5 are rare. Most plants prefer a soil with a pH between 5.5 and 7.5; 6.5 is ideal.

Soil profile

In most temperate climates, a cross-section of the soil (known as a soil profile) will show five separate layers. The topmost layer (a) will consist of humus. If the ground has recently been cultivated, this layer will have been incorporated in the topsoil (b). The most important layer as far as the gardener is concerned is the topsoil. Ideally this should be 60–90cm (2–3ft) deep. It should contain adequate supplies of plant nutrients and organic matter and should be well drained and aerated. Below the topsoil is the subsoil (c), which consists of partially broken-down rock. It is infertile but can contain useful nutrients. A layer of fragmented rock (d) may occur between the subsoil and the solid parent rock or bedrock (e).

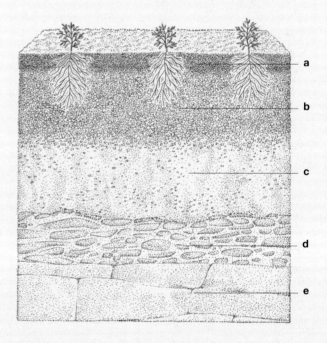

a topmost layer
b topsoil
c subsoil
d fragmented rock
e bedrock

Get to know your soil

Few people are lucky enough to have a perfect loam soil. However, help is at hand. There are many materials that can be used to improve soil and, with a bit of work, turn it into the best possible home for a wide range of plants.

Altering pH

Some plants need acid soil; others prefer a chalky, alkaline soil. To test the pH of your soil, buy a simple soil-testing kit and follow the instructions on the packet. It is a good idea to test the soil in a number of places around the garden because there may be underlying rocks or stone that affect a particular area, or a previous owner might have brought in masses of soil from somewhere else.

It is possible to adjust the pH value of your soil, but it will only be a temporary change. To raise the pH value – that is, to increase the alkaline balance of the soil – add hydrated lime, ordinary ground limestone or chalk (calcium carbonate). Follow the instructions on the packet to the letter and work on a still, dry day. Spent mushroom compost is also strongly alkaline. To lower the pH of your soil – so as to make it more acidic – begin by enriching the soil with a peat substitute and other acidic organic matter, such as leaf mould made from pine needles. Then apply flowers of sulphur. Test the soil every month and reapply as necessary.

Rather than going to all this bother, however, you will be much better off growing plants that will thrive on the soil you have. Most plants are fairly tolerant of a range of soil types and few soils have extreme pH values, so most of us will not be limited in our choice of plants. If you really want to grow rhododendrons and you have strongly alkaline soil, it is far easier to build a raised bed or grow them in containers, where you can give them the ericaceous (acid) soil they need, than to try to change the underlying nature of your soil.

top Soil testers are inexpensive and easily available, and knowing your soil pH is a helpful guide to choosing suitable plants.

left If plants like this wild *Rhododendron ponticum* grow locally, it is a good indication that your soil is acid.

right Adding a little lime to the soil every few years will make it more alkaline, which some plants will appreciate.

Using fertilizers

There are two basic kinds of fertilizer – organic and inorganic – and both are equally valuable in the garden (see page 159).

All organic fertilizers contain carbon and have been derived from living organisms. Before organic fertilizers can be absorbed by the plant they must be broken down in the soil by bacteria and fungi into inorganic chemicals, so organic fertilizers encourage soil bacteria and thus increase fertility. They are slowly released for plant use over a long period of time.

Inorganic fertilizers do not contain carbon. They cannot improve the texture of the soil and do not add any humus, but they are often quick-acting and richer in nutrients.

Fertilizers are labelled to show the nutrient content in terms of nitrogen (N), phosphorus (P) and potassium (K). Some fertilizers are described as 'straight', which means that they supply just one of these nutrients; others are called 'compound', and these supply varying quantities of all three nutrients. They will also contain trace elements, which are minerals vital to plant health but only needed in minute quantities.

Inorganic soil improvers

If you have a heavy soil you can use a wide range of inorganic soil conditioners to help make it easier to cultivate the soil. Try weathered wood and fuel ashes, coarse sand, grit, sawdust, wood shavings and pine needles, all of which help to open up the soil, allowing in air. They are, however, best applied in combination with organic matter.

Organic soil improvers

Bulky organic materials improve the texture and structure of soil. Organic matter makes the nutrients in the soil more accessible to plants, which improves its fertility and makes it easier for the plant roots to grow down through the soil. It is also often rich in trace elements, which may be lacking in fertilizers, and they release their nutrients relatively slowly. Most plants thrive in soil that has been dressed with well-rotted manure, garden compost or leaf mould before planting, and this material can also be used after planting as a mulch to ensure that the soil remains moist and to help control weed growth.

Choosing organic materials

Your choice of organic soil improvers may be limited depending on where you live, but until you get your own compost heap working well, you will need to find a good source of at least one of the following.

Manure

Animal manures are valuable in the garden because they improve soil structure and provide nutrients. Most are mixed with bedding materials, such as straw or sawdust, then left to rot before use. Never add fresh manure directly to the soil before it has had a chance to decay, because in its fresh state it gives off harmful ammonia. In addition, until bacteria work on the manure, the nitrogen is not available to plants. Rotted manure is odourless and pleasant to work with.

Garden compost

Garden compost is a valuable alternative to animal manures. It consists of a wide variety of garden and kitchen waste, which has been rotted down over a period of several months. It is relatively rich in nutrients and is a good soil conditioner. It may be applied as a mulch or dug into the soil. See pages 32–3 for details on making your own compost.

Leaf mould

Leaf mould is simple to make and is a good soil conditioner, although it provides few nutrients. It will make the soil slightly more acidic and makes a good mulch for beds and borders. *Never* take leaf mould from the wild; you will disrupt the natural lifecycle of the plants and trees.

Peat

Peat has been used by gardeners for many years, but not only is it not very effective – it needs to be replaced regularly – it is now ecologically undesirable to extract it from irreplaceable habitats. Don't use peat. There are alternatives, such as coir and bark, which make perfectly good substitutes and should be used instead. Also, avoid bagged proprietary composts that are peat based.

Coir

Coir (coconut fibre) can be used as a soil conditioner or a potting compost. It contains few nutrients but increases the acidity (reduces the pH) of the soil, so it is only appropriate for acid-loving plants. You can buy it in bags from garden centres.

Seaweed

Seaweed contains plant nutrients, particularly potash, and it decomposes quickly. It can be dug straight into the ground while it is wet or composted with garden waste and applied when partially broken down. Dried seaweed meal can be bought from garden suppliers, and most gardeners will find it easier to get hold of in this form.

Spent mushroom compost

Although they vary in their nutrient value, the spent composts sold by mushroom growers are well worth using to boost the organic content of your soil. They usually contain animal manure, loam and chalk in varying quantities and can be used in all soils, except those that are being used to grow plants that love acid soil.

Worm compost

This material is beneficial as a plant food and soil conditioner, and it can be used as a potting compost. It can be applied wherever feeding is needed and is ideal for adding to hanging baskets and planters and for top-dressing pots. Scatter the compost thinly on to the soil and mix it into the top layer. You can make it yourself with a wormery or buy it ready bagged at a garden centre.

Cultivation techniques

Digging

There are two methods of digging, single digging and double digging (see pages 30–31). It is best to dig heavy soils in autumn and winter so that frost, wind, snow and rain can gradually break down the clods of earth. However, you should never work on soil when it is frozen or waterlogged as it is all too easy to damage its structure and compact it.

Light soils will not present such problems and can be cultivated at any time in winter and early spring, provided they are allowed to settle for two or three weeks before you sow or plant.

Raking

The main reason for raking is to level a piece of ground, either for sowing seeds, planting or laying paving materials. Rakes can also be used to cover seeds after sowing and to collect leaves and other garden debris. Raking is satisfyingly rhythmic – use long, steady movements of the arms, drawing the rake to and fro and supporting it so that its teeth sweep over the surface and do not dig in.

left A compost bin doesn't have to be fancy, and in time will turn both kitchen and garden waste into rich compost.

Forking

Use your large garden fork if you have stony or heavy ground or if you are cultivating the bottom of trenches during double digging. The disadvantages of using a fork for the entire digging operation are that you won't be able to slice cleanly through surface weed growth and light soils may fall through its tines.

Hoeing

Hoeing serves two useful purposes: it keeps down weeds and so reduces the competition for light and nutrients, and it relieves compaction and allows vital air into the soil. It is also claimed that a layer of fine soil on the surface of the ground acts like a mulch and prevents excess water loss.

The Dutch hoe (see page 21) is the most versatile type of hoe and can be used for weeding between plants and making drills for sowing seeds. When you are weeding, hold the hoe so that the blade is parallel to the ground and pull it along the ground to uproot the weeds. To make a seed drill, hold the hoe at an angle, with the corner pointing downwards, and drag it along, so leaving a small V-shaped drill.

No-dig gardening

This may sound too good to be true, but some gardeners believe that digging is harmful to the soil because it disturbs the activity of bacteria and earthworms and upsets the natural balance. Non-diggers prefer to apply thick mulches of well-rotted compost or manure to the surface of the soil in spring and in autumn and let earthworms and other organisms incorporate the material into the soil. Seeds are sown in the surface compost and subsequent mulches are applied while the plants are growing.

Mulching

Mulching means covering the ground with a layer of material, which may be organic and biodegradable, such as leaf mould, bark and compost and even newspaper or cardboard, or inorganic, such as plastic or polythene sheeting. Both types help to discourage weeds by preventing light from reaching the soil surface, which weed seeds need to germinate. Mulches also have several other important uses:

- They help to keep the soil moist.
- They help to keep the soil warm in winter and cool in summer.
- They protect the topsoil from heavy rain.

In addition, organic mulches improve the structure of the soil and supply plant nutrients because they are eventually incorporated into the soil.

Before you apply a mulch, make sure the soil is moist and warm. This is because the mulch will prevent water percolating into the soil and will act as an insulator, so preventing the soil from warming up quickly.

top Forking the soil puts less strain on your body than digging, and can be a better option on heavy or stony soils.

right This crop of potatoes is being grown through plastic sheeting, which keeps down weeds and conserves moisture.

Single digging

Most ordinary soils of reasonable depth that do not overlie an intractable subsoil can be cultivated by single digging – that is, the soil is cultivated to the depth of one spit (the length of your spade's blade). If the plot is wide, divide it in two lengthways and take out the first trench on one half of the plot, depositing the soil at the same end of the other half. Now work down the first strip of land and back up the second, throwing the soil from the current trench into the last one.

1 Take out a trench one spit (the depth of the spade blade) deep and 30–50cm (12–20in) wide across one end of the plot. Pile the soil at the opposite end of the plot (it will eventually be used to fill the final trench). If the soil is to be manured as it is dug, throw the manure or compost into the bottom of the trench at this point and mix it in well.

2 Use your spade to dig another trench next to the first. Lift up a comfortable spadeful of soil and throw it forwards into the first trench, turning it upside-down as you go. Watch out for perennial weeds and remove any roots that you come across. Work along the second trench, throwing the soil over and forwards into the first trench with your spade until the second trench is complete.

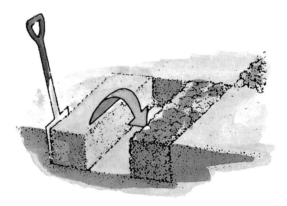

3 More manure can be added in the bottom of the second trench and the operation repeated. Dig a third trench and use the soil to fill the second trench and so on.

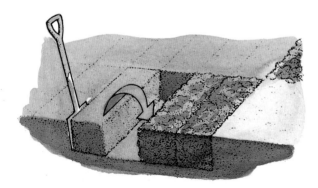

4 When you reach the end of the plot, use the soil from the first trench to fill the last one.

Why cultivate the soil?

We cultivate the ground for several reasons:

- To control weeds
- To incorporate manures, composts and fertilizers
- To relieve compaction and improve the texture of the soil
- To allow in air

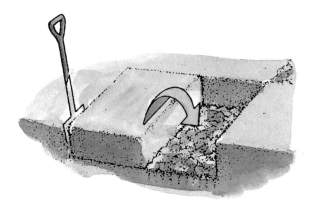

Double digging

If you decide to double dig your garden, you will be cultivating the soil to a depth of two spits. This is hard work but is useful on land that has not been cultivated before or if a hard subsoil layer impedes drainage and the penetration of plant roots.

1 Take out a trench 60cm (2ft) wide and one spit deep at one end of the plot. Position the soil alongside the spot to be occupied by the final trench. Divide the plot in two if it is large.

2 When all the soil has been removed from the first trench, break up the base to the full depth of the tines of your garden fork. Fork compost or manure into the lower layer of soil.

3 Start to dig a second trench and throw forward the soil into the first trench, following the same procedure as for single digging. Make sure that the soil is turned over and remove perennial weeds as you go.

4 When you have completed the second trench, the first will be full of soil. Break up the soil at the base of the second trench, to a spit's depth, and fork in more compost. Continue until the entire plot of soil has been dug to a depth of about 50cm (20in).

Digging tips

- Remember to keep your spade vertical because a slanting cut achieves less depth. Always keep your back straight.
- Drive the spade in at right angles to free the clod of earth and allow it to be lifted cleanly.
- Lift up small spadefuls of soil that are light and easy to handle.
- Dig a little ground at a time on a regular basis. Cultivate a 1m (3ft) strip every day rather than attempting to dig the entire plot at once.

Compost and leaf mould

All soils benefit from the addition of home-made garden compost and leaf mould – add them when you are digging or planting or use them as a mulch. Both are straightforward to make and, what is more, they don't cost a thing. It is also satisfying to collect garden waste and eventually return it to the soil, along with its nutrients, so that nothing is wasted.

Making compost

Garden compost is a valuable source of bulky organic matter, and a compost heap will cheaply and quickly turn garden and kitchen waste into soil-enriching material. When it is well made, compost is deep or medium brown, crumbly, slightly moist and sweet smelling, and none of the original ingredients should be identifiable.

To make good, crumbly compost the heap must be properly constructed so that the organic material can decompose rapidly and not just turn into a pile of stagnant vegetation. Air, moisture and nitrogen must be present if bacteria and fungi are to break down the raw material efficiently. Air is allowed in through the base and sides of the heap. Water should be applied with a can or hose if the heap shows signs of drying out, and moisture can be kept in by covering the heap with sacking, old carpet or polythene sheeting. Nitrogen must be provided in the form of grass mowings, young nettles or manure, or you can add a proprietary compost activator.

Site the heap in a sheltered and shady place but not under trees or where tree roots could grow into the compost. It must be protected from the drying sun and wind. Allow ample time for decomposition.

Compost bins

You will need something to contain the compost heap – either a proprietary bin or a home-made one, such as a timber or wire-netting enclosure. One of the problems of a small garden is that it takes quite a long time to fill a compost bin. Rather than having one large bin, you might find it easier to have two smallish bins, so that you can fill one and leave it to break down while you add to the other one.

top When well composted, garden and kitchen waste is transformed into a homogeneous compost that will enrich the soil and improve its composition.

left Garden compost can either be forked into the soil to improve its structure or spread over the surface to form a thick mulch.

right Green manure, like this white mustard, is dug into the soil in early autumn, where it decomposes and provides an excellent soil enricher.

To make a wire compost heap, erect a square cage of wire netting supported by four stout posts driven into the ground. Make the front removable so that you can easily remove the rotted compost.

Compost bins are also easily constructed from spare timber. Erect four stout corner posts as before, then screw or nail planks to the posts to make the sides. Leave spaces between to allow air to penetrate the heap. Again, make sure the front can be removed to allow access to the compost. If you make a large bin, make a false floor by placing a layer of twiggy branches or brushwood in the base, or support a few short planks on bricks to allow air to permeate the compost.

Some bought wooden compost bins come with tops, but old carpet, sacking or polythene will do just as well, held down with bricks to keep in the moisture.

Compostable materials

Almost any garden and kitchen waste can be turned into good compost if properly mixed. However, you should never add meat or fat – you will only attract rats and other vermin.

One of the secrets of ensuring rapid decomposition is not to allow large quantities of one particular material to build up in the heap. All the following materials may be composted if they are properly mixed together: animal manure and urine, annual weeds, crushed eggshells, dead flowerheads, lawn mowings (unless the lawn has been treated with hormone weedkillers), vegetable peelings, soft hedge clippings, tea leaves, tree and shrub leaves and vegetable leaves, stems and pods. Do not use woody material or any vegetation that has been sprayed with herbicides or is affected by diseases and pests. Also avoid perennial weeds and annual plants that have set seed.

Constructing the heap

Layer the material and lightly firm it down with the head of a rake or the back of a fork. Add a proprietary compost activator if necessary, although young nettles or comfrey do just as well. Continue until the bin is full. Keep a cover over the top of the heap, and, if the compost becomes dry, take off the cover and water it to encourage the rotting process.

When the bin is full, you can spread a 5cm (2in) layer of soil over the top instead of using sacking or polythene. (If you do this, think about growing a courgette plant in the top.) Leave the compost to rot and, if possible, start to fill a second bin.

Using the compost

When the compost is brown and crumbly it is ready for digging in to enrich the soil or to be spread over beds as a mulch. Use only well-rotted compost as a mulch, because partially decomposed material may contain weed seeds that will germinate and become a nuisance. Any unrotted material that is still recognizable should be left to form the basis of the new heap.

Making leaf mould

Leaves of deciduous trees and shrubs can be rotted down on their own to make leaf mould, which is rich in plant foods, especially nitrogen. A wire-mesh bin similar to one for compost will be a suitable container. A fast, space-saving alternative is to pack the leaves in black polythene sacks that have been perforated to allow in air. Tied at the top and stood in an out-of-the-way corner of the garden, the sacks will form good leaf mould, which can be used the following spring. Leaves that are kept in open bins may take longer to decay.

Green manure

Some plants, known as green manures, can be grown on a patch of poor soil to help improve it. The plants grow quickly and are dug into the soil just before they flower and set seed. As they rot, they enrich the soil, provide a source of nitrogen and improve the texture of the soil. Rape, annual lupins, vetches, mustard and perennial rye grass can all be used. Sow the seed quite thickly in spring or early summer and then rake it in. Dig the plants into the soil, leaves, stems and all, just before they come into flower. This is a useful way of dealing with a vacant part of the vegetable plot if you are leaving a section fallow as part of a crop rotation.

growing new plants

Buying plants

Most people buy plants from garden centres or nurseries, but they are also available from DIY stores, florists and even supermarkets, and, if you decide that you want something a little out of the ordinary, then you can order plants by mail order or over the Internet.

Container-grown plants

Container-grown plants – sometimes called containerized plants – are those that are growing in pots, polythene bags or anything else that allows all the roots and the soil around them to be transported and planted with the minimum of disturbance. Although they are more expensive than bare-rooted or balled plants, they can be planted at just about any time of year, provided they are hardy and the soil is in a suitable condition. Plants can even be bought in full flower and planted as soon as you get home for an instant effect.

Bare-rooted plants

Bare-rooted plants are usually less expensive than container-grown equivalents, but usually only trees and shrubs are available in this form. Bare-rooted plants are lifted from a nursery bed and most of the soil is shaken from around their roots. They should be transplanted only in autumn and winter when the plants are dormant or nearly dormant.

Balled plants

Balled plants, usually trees or shrubs, are lifted with as much soil as is practicable, and the rootball encased with sacking or polythene. Balled plants are more expensive than bare-rooted ones, but if treated carefully they have a better chance of survival. The planting season is a little longer than that for bare-rooted plants, and balled evergreens are often moved in early spring or early autumn.

Trays of plants

Buying trays of seedlings is an economic way to buy plants for your spring and summer displays. The plants can vary enormously in quality, so check they have not dried out or are so far advanced that the roots are growing out through the base of the tray; pick sturdy, compact plants that are growing evenly and just in bud. Ask if the plants have been hardened off (acclimatized to outdoor conditions): plants that look soft and lush may have just come out of a warm greenhouse and planting them out straight away would be a big shock (see page 44).

top Check whether plants are container-grown or are bare-rooted ones that have been recently moved into containers for sale (containerized).

left A more economical alternative to buying container-grown shrubs is to buy them bare-rooted, usually in the autumn.

Seeds

One of the great advantages of buying seeds is that you can get a far greater range of annuals and biennials than if you are depending on the selection of pre-grown plants offered in your local nurseries and garden centres. Read the instructions on the packet carefully to make sure that this is the plant for you. Many people believe that plants will flower from seeds in a short time, but this is true only of annuals (see page 18). Most of the more beautiful plants that you can grow from seeds need a whole year, during which they must be transferred from their initial growing place into containers, before being planted out into their flowering positions the following year.

Bulbs

Many bulbous plants – a term that applies to bulbs, tubers, corms and rhizomes – are sold as dry 'bulbs', either loose or in small bags. Choose heavy bulbs that feel firm and show no signs of damage, mould or wrinkling. Plant bulbs as soon as you can after getting them home. An exception to this general rule is *Galanthus* spp. (snowdrop). Try to get these 'in the green' – that is, in late winter or early spring while the leaves are present – because they are more likely to become established than bulbs that are planted in autumn.

Plug plants

Plugs are a sort of halfway stage: very young plants rooted into individual pots, usually about 3–5cm (1–2in) in size. The plants should have developed at least a couple of pairs of true leaves. They will have to be potted on and acclimatized, but save the trouble of raising plants from seed when you only need a few.

Recognizing quality

Most garden centres and nurseries sell good-quality plants, and the plants are well cared for while they are waiting to be sold. Even so, it pays to inspect plants carefully before you buy.

- Make sure that plants are not loose in their containers, which could indicate that they have not long been planted in the container and may not transplant well when you get them home.

- Check to see if there is a little root showing through the bottom of the container, which will indicate that the plant is well established. However, if there are too many roots hanging out of the bottom of the pot, it means the plant has been cramped in the pot too long. Pot-bound plants are not likely to be growing well and are more susceptible to disease.

above A plant's rootball should fill its container (left), but the roots should not have become so overcrowded (right) that the plant is likely to be under stress.

- Make sure that the compost in the container is moist. If plants have been allowed to dry out their growth may have been checked and they may later lose their leaves.

- Make sure that there are no weeds or moss growing on the compost surface. This shows neglect and the plant may be stressed.

- It goes without saying that plants should be completely free from any signs of pests or disease. They should look healthy and vigorous.

- Plants should appear to be growing sturdily. Avoid thin, spindly plants and any that appear to be etiolated (pale from lack of sunshine).

- Foliage should look healthy, without brown spots, marks or other discoloration. It should not be yellowing or have brown edges, unless, of course, you are buying a deciduous plant in autumn.

Planting

Planting is a fairly simple operation, but there are a few things you need to do to make sure your plants get the best start and grow quickly without check. Proper planting can really make the difference, whether it's a single shrub or a border.

When to plant

Container-grown plants (see page 36) can be planted at any time of the year provided the soil is not too wet or frozen. Spring and autumn are the best times for planting because the soil is usually moist and fairly warm. If you plant in summer you will probably have to keep watering the plant to make sure the soil stays moist. In winter the soil may be too wet or simply frozen solid, and standing on waterlogged or frozen soil will damage its structure.

Bare-rooted and balled plants, which are available from late autumn to early spring, should be planted straight away to prevent the roots from drying out. If the soil is not suitable for planting, either pot up bare-rooted plants in containers or wrap the rootballs in a plastic sack or sheet of hessian packed with moist potting compost or coir.

Whenever you plant, you must make sure that the soil does not dry out until the plant has been able to develop a decent root system. Keep a check for at least a year, particularly during hot weather or during a spell of desiccating winds, and water when necessary (see page 156).

Storing plants

Small plants can be easily stored in a temporary trench dug in a spare corner of the garden. This technique, called heeling in, should also be used for bare-rooted shrubs and container-grown plants that are not to be planted immediately.

Thrust a spade vertically into the ground to a spit's depth and pull it back, while still in the earth, to form a V-shaped trench. You can then lay the plants against the upright side of the trench and replace the soil loosely to protect the roots.

Staking trees and shrubs

Most trees and some large shrubs benefit from a stake to support the stem of the plant while the roots grow. This is especially important in windy sites, because the wind can rock the plant and stop the roots getting established or even blow the whole thing over.

So that you don't damage the roots when the plant is *in situ* drive the stake into the bottom of the planting hole before you plant the tree or shrub. Make sure it is firmly anchored – remember it has to support the head of the tree or shrub with all its wind resistance – then plant the plant next to it (see page 160).

The stake should be relatively short to allow the stem of the plant some movement, which will help to strengthen it. You are aiming just to stop the rootball moving around in its hole. For added strength, drive in the stake at an angle and attach the stem to the stake with an adjustable tie, which can be relaxed as the stem expands.

top Velvety dark varieties of *Hemerocallis* (daylily), scabious, verbena and achillea combine to create a scheme with the richness of a Renaissance painting.

Container-grown or balled plants

1 Dig a hole just a little larger than the container and break up the soil at the bottom. Add a good handful of organic matter, such as well-rotted garden compost or manure, and lightly fork it in (see page 27). To remove the plant from its pot turn it upside-down and tap the pot while carefully holding the plant so it does not fall to the ground or snap off. Cut away the wrapping from balled plants at the edge of, or actually in, the hole, to minimize root disturbance.

2 Slip the plant into the planting hole. The plant should be planted to the same depth it was in its pot, so if necessary remove the plant and adjust the soil level. Back-fill the hole with a mixture of soil and more organic matter. Mix a little slow-release fertilizer, such as blood, fish and bone, into the soil to give the plant a boost if the soil is poor (see page 159).

3 Firm the mixture down around the rootball, using your fingertips, fist or heel, depending on the size of the plant. Water well to settle the soil around the roots.

Bare-rooted plants

1 Dig a hole large enough for all the roots to spread out naturally in it, with room at the top for a covering of 2.5–5cm (1–2in) of soil over the uppermost roots. Look for a dark soil mark on the stem or stems, which indicates where the soil came to in the nursery bed. Mix the soil from the hole with a good quantity of organic matter and a sprinkling of slow-release fertilizer. Stand the plant in the hole and work the soil mixture around and between the roots.

2 Once the hole has been filled, firm the soil down with your heel or fists and add more soil to fill the hole again. Water well to settle the soil around the roots. It is essential that the soil around the roots of bare-rooted plants does not dry out until the plant is well established, so water regularly in dry spells for about a year.

Planting large bulbs in grass

Large bulbs, such as daffodils, have to be planted individually. Scatter the bulbs randomly over the area to be planted to achieve a natural effect.

1 Plant with a trowel or a bulb planter. A bulb planter will take out a core of soil, but is not as flexible when it comes to hole size and depth.

2 Insert the bulb in the hole and replace the turf. It may be necessary to remove some soil from the base of the core.

Planting small bulbs in grass

Small bulbs, such as crocuses and snowdrops, are best planted by lifting a small area of grass. Make an H-shaped cut, then slice underneath and roll back the turf. You do not need to bury the bulbs deeply – simply scatter them on the bare soil and roll the turf back down to cover them.

1 Loosen the compacted ground with a fork, incorporating a slow-release fertilizer at the same time.

2 Scatter the bulbs randomly, then plant individually where they have fallen. Level and compress the loosened soil, then roll the grass back down and firm flat. Remove or add soil if necessary to reinstate the former level. Water thoroughly.

Planting bulbs

Bulbs, corms and tubers are usually bought in a dormant state, so they are easy to deal with. Dig a hole three times the depth of the bulb and slip the bulb in, replace the soil, firm and water well. Try to make sure that the bulbs are planted the right way up, although most can cope with being upside-down. This is easy with true bulbs, which tend to taper towards the top, so plant them with the flat end down. You will probably be able to see some dried roots coming out of the base anyway, so it should be obvious. With corms and tubers, try to identify the place where the roots and shoots emerge and plant the roots down and the shoots up.

Unless you are using them in a formal bedding display, plant bulbs in random groups for a natural effect. Dig a flat hole large enough to take a group of bulbs and arrange them randomly in the hole and replace the soil. Like any plants, bulbs benefit from the addition of organic matter and slow–release fertilizer at planting time, so add some of this when you replace the soil.

Some bulbs, especially tulips and some lilies, are susceptible to rotting. If your soil is heavy and holds water, mix some sand (sharp sand as sold in garden centres, not builders' sand) into the planting holes to improve drainage.

Planting in open-mesh bulb baskets can be useful where you will want to lift the bulbs after flowering, either to make way for a formal summer scheme or because the bulbs will benefit (many tulips survive better from year to year if lifted and left to dry and ripen out of the ground).

Planting distances

The distance at which you should space individual plants and bulbs so that they have enough space to develop is given in books, on garden-centre labels and on seed packets. As a rule, set plants at a distance equal to half their mature height; bulbs can be set one-third of their mature height.

Planting bulbs in grass

One of the most attractive ways to grow bulbs is naturalized in grass. Choose the bulbs carefully, because some popular bulbs, especially tulips, do not naturalize well. Others, however, including daffodils, snowdrops and crocuses, are ideal. Grassy banks are particularly suitable for naturalized bulbs, but you can even find a corner of a small lawn for dwarf bulbs, such as crocuses. Remember that you must allow the leaves to die down naturally, and you should not mow the grass until this has occurred. Among the best bulbs for naturalizing are:

- *Anemone blanda*
- *Colchicum autumnale* (meadow saffron)
- *Crocus* spp.
- *Cyclamen hederifolium*
- *Fritillaria meleagris* (snake's head fritillary)
- *Galanthus* spp. (snowdrop)
- *Narcissus* (daffodil)

below Crocuses naturalized in short grass.

Growing plants from seeds

This is an enjoyable – and economical – way of getting a host of new specimens for bedding displays and permanent borders. Seeds will germinate whenever and wherever the conditions are right, and with a little nurturing they will soon make an impact in your garden.

Potting composts

A compost is a soil substitute used for propagating and establishing plants in containers. The compost must be well aerated, and it must be able to retain water and hold nutrients, and able to conduct warmth. Many proprietary brands are available for different purposes. Look for peat-free products, which are more environmentally friendly.

Seed compost

This type of compost is designed to provide enough air and moisture for the seeds to germinate and the roots to develop. It contains some nutrients to help the seedlings on their way.

Cuttings compost

A compost for rooting cuttings really needs only two attributes: the retention of sufficient moisture and the provision of an aerating agent.

Multipurpose compost

This type of compost can be used for just about any purpose, but it does have its disadvantages. Multipurpose composts are fibrous and usually black or dark brown. They are composed primarily of peat or a peat substitute and can be difficult to rewet once they have dried out. They also hold rather too much moisture for plants that are susceptible to rot, such as alpines or cuttings that take some time to root. These plants are better off with a compost that contains loam (known as soil-based composts). Multipurpose compost is, however, fine for sowing seeds, but keep a check on moisture levels and make sure it does not dry out.

Soil-based composts

These contain, primarily, loam, which has a steadying and controlling influence on both water and nutrients that peat does not provide. They are sharper and less fibrous than multipurpose composts and usually dark grey. They are well suited to establishing and growing on young plants, because the compost must contain enough water and nutrients, have the correct pH value and be moisture-retentive. Soil-based composts are also better for permanent container plantings.

Sowing seeds in pots

Apart from hardy annuals (see page 18), most seeds should be sown in pots so that you can keep an eye on them and control the amount of light, heat and moisture they receive. You can raise just about any plants like this, but for the home gardener it is likely to be mainly half-hardy annuals, which are too tender to be raised outside. Some people raise hardy annuals such as *Lobularia maritima* (sweet alyssum) and pansies in the same way to make sure that they are as advanced as other bedding plants by planting time.

A greenhouse is a distinct advantage, but you can raise a small number of plants on a windowsill. Bear in mind that the young plants will need much more space as they move into larger pots, so don't be over-ambitious with the number you try to raise indoors.

When sowing in containers, use a specially formulated seed compost and choose a container large enough to allow the seedlings space to develop.

top Germinated seedlings will soon crowd out their first pot or tray and will need pricking out to give them space to grow.

1 Fill a seedtray with a special seed compost. Remove any excess potting soil, then level it with a board or piece of stiff card. Firm gently to leave a level surface for sowing.

Sowing half-hardy annuals

The key to raising plants successfully from seeds is to give them the best possible start in life. Most seed germinates easily, but it is important that the seedlings' growth is not checked, so keep an eye on them and prick them out as soon as they are ready.

2 Large seeds can be scattered directly from the packet. Scatter thinly, first along the length of the seedtrays, then across. Mix very fine seeds with fine sand before scattering them to give even coverage.

3 Most seeds should be covered with a thin layer of sifted soil (cover with about the depth of the seed), but check the packet because some are best left uncovered.

4 Use a sprinkling-type watering can if the seeds are large enough not to be washed around. For fine seeds, stand the tray in a shallow bowl of water and let it seep through.

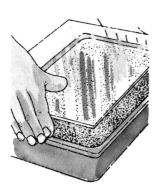

5 Unless you have a propagator, cover the seedtray or pot with glass or enclose it in a plastic bag, then top with some newspaper until the seedlings emerge – but, again, check the packet because some seeds need light. Keep warm.

6 When the seedlings are large enough to handle, prick them out into individual pots or space them out into seedtrays. Loosen the potting soil before lifting the seedlings.

7 Use a small dibber or a pencil to make holes deep enough to take the roots, and always hold the plant by its seed leaves (the first ones to open). Keep them in good light.

The developing seedling

After sowing, monitor the seedtray regularly and, as soon as the seedlings emerge, both paper and glass should be removed. The container should then be placed in a well-lit area, but out of direct sunlight to avoid any risk of scorching. If the seedlings are to be kept in their container for some time they should be given a liquid feed, diluted according to the manufacturer's instructions. This is because many seed composts contain only a phosphate fertilizer.

Pricking out

As soon as the seedlings are large enough to be handled, transplant them into a more suitable compost, leaving enough space for the unrestricted development of the young plants.

You should have 24–40 seedlings in each tray. Fill a container with a soil-based compost, such as John Innes no.1 or similar, and firm to the base with the tips of your fingers. Strike off the compost level with the rim. Lightly firm with a presser board so that the compost is 1–1.5cm (about ⅛in) below the rim of the container. Hold the plantlets by their seed leaves and transfer them to the compost, using a pencil or dibber to make the hole.

Hardening off

After the seedlings have been pricked out, they have to be gradually weaned to a stage at which they can be planted out and survive cool temperatures, fluctuating water conditions and the effects of wind without their growth rate being affected. Once the pricked-out seedlings have re-established, move them to a cooler environment. For this purpose there is no real substitute for a cold-frame, which should be kept firmly closed. Over the course of a few weeks increasingly air the frame during the day by raising the lid, until the frame is continually aired during the day and night – the lid can even be completely removed during the day if it is warm. Eventually, the lid can be discarded altogether.

If you don't have a cold-frame, put the seeds in a well-ventilated area indoors and gradually introduce them to the garden by putting them outside for a few hours each day in warm weather. Increase this until they are out all day. Don't leave them out overnight until all risk of frost has passed.

Watering and feeding

Regularly check the seedlings in the cold-frame to make sure that they are not drying out excessively. Do not give them too much water, though. It is much better to err on the side of dryness rather than risk them becoming waterlogged.

Another aspect of seedling management is feeding. Feed seedlings regularly using a proprietary liquid fertilizer at intervals as indicated by the manufacturer on the packet. Take care not to over-feed, however, because this produces over-vigorous plants, which will check growth on transplanting.

Sowing seeds outside

Hardy annuals can be sown in the garden where they are to flower, and for many people this is the best way to treat them as they receive the least setback to growth. Mid- to late spring is a suitable time for most kinds to be sown, but check the packet first. The sequence shown opposite assumes you are sowing a bed of hardy annuals, but, if you just want to sow a few plants to fill some gaps in a border among the perennials, sow just a pinch of seeds at the final plant spacing and then thin the young plants to one in each position if more germinate.

top It is easy to damage delicate seedlings, so it is important to handle them carefully by their seed leaves (the first pair of leaves to develop).

Sowing hardy annuals

Don't be in a rush to sow directly outside. Time and again early sowings are caught by an unexpected frost, while seeds started off later in warmer soil soon catch up.

1 Dig over the area and clear it of weeds, especially difficult perennial ones. Ensure that the large clumps of soil are broken down.

2 Then rake the soil level to get ready for sowing. A bed of hardy annuals looks best if the plants appear to be growing in bold drifts. Mark out the areas to be sown with the different types, using sand to draw the lines.

3 Use a trowel or the end of a stick or cane to mark out shallow drills where the seeds are to be sown. Consult the packet for the spacing between rows.

4 Sow the seeds as evenly as possible, sprinkling them along the rows between your fingers and thumb. If the seeds are very fine, mix them with fine horticultural sand first. Alternate the direction of the rows in each section to avoid creating a regimented appearance.

5 Make sure you label the sections, then rake the soil to cover the seeds. Water thoroughly after sowing, and whenever the soil begins to dry out. Thin out the seedlings to the spacing recommended on the packet in stages as they grow.

Taking cuttings

It is possible to propagate some plants by taking cuttings. This involves cutting off a piece of stem or root and growing it on in a separate pot. Shrubs grow surprisingly fast from cuttings, and many types are very easy to root.

Tools and equipment

The most important of the gardener's special tools and equipment for taking cuttings are a sharp knife, a pair of secateurs, a dibber, suitable compost and a selection of pots and seedtrays. It is essential to use the right tools to give the plant material the very best start in life. If the plant material is damaged, it will become a prime site for decay, which will infect the cutting.

If you are taking small numbers of cuttings a clear plastic bag and a windowsill will suffice, but results are quicker and better with an electrically heated propagator. A cold-frame is not essential when it comes to acclimatizing the young plants to outside conditions, but it helps. Alternatively, you can stand the pots outside for an increasing amount of time during the warmest part of the day; eventually you should be able to leave them outside over a mild night – but it is important not to rush the process.

Secateurs

Anvil secateurs have one cutting blade and a flat metal surface. Scissor secateurs also have one sharpened blade, but normally only the internal surface is ground flat. This blade cuts by rotating past the anvil blade as in a conventional pair of scissors. It is best to use scissor-type secateurs for propagation because they make a cleaner cut and cause less crushing and bruising in the region of the cut.

Knives

There can be no doubt that a knife is the most important piece of equipment you need for propagation, and, for most tasks, a medium-weight knife with a sharp carbon-steel blade is best. Use a knife with its blade set well back into the handle. For cuttings, a scalpel or craft knife with replacement blades will give the cleanest cut.

Rooting hormones

Some chemicals will promote or regulate growth responses in plants when they are used in minute doses, and they can be used by gardeners for plant propagation. The majority of rooting hormones are powders. In many cases fungicidal chemicals are also incorporated into the powders, and this helps protect against any rots that may develop in the cuttings.

Stem cuttings

There are several kinds, with the most popular being softwood, semi-ripe and hardwood cuttings. These are characterized by the woodiness of their stems.

Softwood cuttings

Hardy plants, including a wide range of shrubs, climbers, perennials and alpines, can be propagated by softwood cuttings. This also applies to many tender perennial plants, including fuchsias.

The cuttings are taken in spring, just as new shoots are beginning to harden but the growth is still soft. For shrubs, use a soft sideshoot (a tip cutting). It should be about 8cm (3in) long. For perennials take a new, young basal shoot (a basal stem cutting) about 5cm (2in) long. This means taking a cutting that has a piece of the woody stem attached to it.

Semi-ripe cuttings

Take semi-ripe cuttings in summer when the stems are firmer and woodier. Take a main shoot and cut off the sideshoots for propagation. Each cutting should be 10–15cm (4–6in) long.

top Pelargoniums take easily from stem cuttings: use a sharp knife to cut just below a leaf node and have a pot prepared.

right Hardwood cuttings of shrubs are taken during autumn and winter, when the stems have had a chance to ripen.

Hardwood cuttings

These cuttings are taken from autumn to spring, when the wood is at its hardest. There are two types: broad-leaved evergreen cuttings and leafless deciduous cuttings. The cuttings should be 15–23cm (6–9in) long; you should cut just beneath a bud at the base of the plant and just above a bud at the top if the tip is soft.

Preparing and planting stem cuttings

Cut across the stem just beneath a leaf node (joint). Make the cuttings with a razor blade or scalpel, knife or secateurs, depending on the hardness of the stem. Remove the lower leaves from the cutting to leave just the top few. If the leaves are very large, cut them in half to reduce the amount of moisture lost from the cutting. To help the cuttings strike (produce roots), you can wound the flesh by taking out a sliver of bark from the lowest 2.5cm (1in) of the cutting.

Fill a pot with cuttings compost and make a hole with a dibber or pencil. Plant the cutting with a bud about level with the compost surface. Firm sufficiently to prevent rocking. Label and water in. You can plant several cuttings to a pot, but make sure that the leaves do not touch as they are more likely to rot.

Place hardy cuttings in a cold-frame and less hardy cuttings in a well-lit, more protected environment, such as a mist unit or propagator. Plant hardwood cuttings straight into the ground outside.

Heel cuttings

Heel cuttings can be taken at any time of year and are an alternative to softwood and semi-ripe cuttings. Taking a stem cutting with a heel gives the cutting a firm base so that it is well protected against possible rot because you are letting it tear off naturally rather than cutting into the wood. The other reason for a stem cutting is that it exposes the swollen base of the current season's growth, which has a good chance of producing roots.

Taking a heel cutting

When taking a heel cutting, a young sideshoot is stripped away from its parent stem so that a heel – a thin sliver of bark and wood from the old stem – also comes away at the base of the cutting.

1 Hold the bottom of a sideshoot between your thumb and forefinger. Pull down sharply.

2 Neaten the long tail on the heel and any leaves. Dip the basal cut in a rooting hormone. Make a hole in the compost and plant the cutting. Water in.

Taking a root cutting

Before propagating from root cuttings, prepare the parent plant itself so that it will develop roots that will have a high capacity to regenerate stem buds and so produce new plants.

1 Lift a healthy, vigorous plant from the ground during the dormant season.

2 Wash the roots in a bucket of water or hose them clean.

3 Use a sharp knife to cut off some of the root close to the crown.

4 Return the plant to its position in the garden and leave it to re-establish itself during the growing season.

5 Cut off any fibrous side roots that you see on an undamaged young root.

6 Make a right-angled cut on a root where it was severed from its parent.

7 Cut away the thin root end at the appropriate length, using a sloping cut.

8 Fill a pot with compost and make a hole with a dibber. Plant the cutting vertically in the compost. Plant the remaining root cuttings 2.5–4cm (1–1½in) apart.

9 Cover the pot with grit. Strike off the grit until it is level with the rim. Label and leave the cuttings to develop. Do not water until the roots have appeared, then feed.

Root cuttings

Root cuttings are taken during the dormant season from young, vigorous roots that are usually about the thickness of a pencil.

The length of a root cutting depends on the temperature of the environment it is left to grow in. Usually, the warmer the environment, the quicker the cutting will grow and the smaller it can be. No cutting should, however, be less than 2.5cm (1in) long. If you are going to leave the cuttings outside, they should be at least 10cm (4in) long because they will need to survive for some 16 weeks before they are likely to root. A cold-frame or cold greenhouse provides a warmer environment, and the cutting should root in about eight weeks; these cuttings need be only just over 5cm (2in) long. In a warm greenhouse or propagator, where the temperature is 18–24°C (65–75°F), regeneration time is reduced to four weeks, so root cuttings need be only about 2.5cm (1in) long.

Layering

This is a method of propagation in which a stem is encouraged to produce roots so that a new plant is formed while it is still attached to and nourished by the parent plant. Some shrubs layer themselves naturally, and you can simply lift them from the soil, cut them from the parent plant and replant them.

The simplest way to propagate by layering is to select vigorous young shoots and peg them down around the parent plant. First, dig over the soil around the main plant and prepare the shoot by cutting a notch on the underside, halfway through, at a leaf node (joint) about 30cm (12in) from its tip. Treat the cut surfaces with a rooting powder and peg the shoot down so it is in contact with the soil. Check from time to time and pot up or transplant when roots develop.

below Encourage a layered stem to send down roots by firming it into the soil and holding it in place with a wire hook.

Plants to propagate from root cuttings

Alpines

- *Anemone* (some)
- *Geranium* spp.
- *Primula denticulata* (drumstick primula)
- *Verbascum* spp. (mullein)

Herbaceous plants

- *Acanthus* spp. (bear's breeches)
- *Eryngium*
- some forms of *Papaver* (poppy) and **phlox**

Shrubs

- *Chaenomeles* spp. (flowering quince, japonica)
- *Daphne*
- *Prunus* (some spp.)
- *Rhus* spp. (sumach)
- *Rubus*

Offsets and runners

An offset is a plantlet that has developed laterally on a perennial either above or below ground. They can be detached from the parent plant and grown on to make firm new plants. Many rosette-forming plants are propagated in this way.

A runner is a more or less horizontal stem that arises from a crown bud and creeps overground. The leaves are normally scale-like, and rooting may occur at the nodes. The lateral buds develop as new plants, and eventually the stem of the runner deteriorates, leaving a new isolated plant. Strawberries can be propagated from runners.

Dividing plants

Division is a common way of propagating many herbaceous perennials, and it is also used to rejuvenate favourite plants that are getting past their best to keep them vigorous and growing strongly. It is a simple and reliable technique.

Plants with fibrous crowns

Herbaceous perennials with fibrous roots and a relatively loose crown are best propagated by division. Normally, the central part of the crown becomes woody over the course of two or three years. Because this woody area does not produce many shoots and generally loses vigour, it is discarded and the remainder of the clump is divided into suitably sized portions for planting out and re-establishing a new crown. Smaller plants can often be divided by hand. Lift the plant carefully, shake off as much soil as you can and gently pull away sections with visible growing points or 'eyes'. It's usually best to discard the central section. If plants have become congested or rather woody, the easiest way to separate them is to put two garden forks back to back in the centre and force them apart.

The only variable feature of this form of propagation is timing. In general, the best time is directly after flowering, because this is when the new shoots are being produced and the new root system is developing. Spring division is preferable in late-flowering plants.

Plants with fleshy crowns

Many herbaceous plants develop a compact, fleshy crown that is not easy to pull apart and these, too, lend themselves to division. The size of divisions will depend on preference, but must include at least one developed shoot. Avoid latent buds, which do not always develop satisfactorily.

top A large clump of primulas is formed of several plantlets that pull apart easily.

Semi-woody herbaceous plants

Some perennials that have upright, sword-like leaves increase in size by producing a sort of offset. This develops into a large crown of individual shoots, each with its own individual root system.

In spring, lift them and shake out the soil, if necessary hosing or washing the crown clean. Pull the various pieces apart. Cut the clump with a spade or hatchet if it is hard and woody in the middle and replant the divisions fairly quickly so that the roots don't dry out.

Bulbous plants

Bulbs and associated plants (corms, rhizomes and tubers) can also be propagated by division.

- Bulblets are tiny bulbs that develop below ground on some bulbous plants. Remove the flower stem and bury it until bulblets develop in the leaf axils.
- Bulbils are tiny bulblets that grow on a stem above ground. These can be picked off and grown on.
- Bulbs such as lilies can be propagated by scaling. Take several scale leaves from the bulb, dust them with fungicide and place them in a plastic bag of damp peat and grit. Blow into the bag and seal it and place it in an airing cupboard. When bulblets appear on the scales, plant each scale leaf and collect the bulblets when the leaf dies.
- Divide corms – crocuses and gladioli, for example – by cutting them in pieces, each one with a bud. Dust these in fungicide, leave them in a dry place and plant them when they have developed a tough outer coat.

Dividing plants with fibrous crowns

The best time to propagate herbaceous plants with fibrous crowns is directly after flowering, but propagate in spring for late-flowering plants.

1 Lift the plant that is to be divided as soon as it has flowered. Shake off as much soil as possible. Wash the crown and its roots in a bucket. Shorten all tall stems above the ground to minimize water loss.

2 Break off a piece with at least one good 'eye' from the edge of the crown.

3 Divide any intractable pieces with an old carving knife or similar blade. Make a hole and plant the new clump. Firm the soil and label the plant. Water thoroughly, using a watering can that has a spray attachment.

Dividing plants with fleshy crowns

Propagate herbaceous plants with fleshy crowns towards the end of their dormant season.

1 Lift the plant to be divided.

2 Wash the crown well. Cut off a piece that has at least one developed bud.

3 Dust the cut surfaces with a fungicidal powder and replant the divisions immediately.

selecting plants

Plants for all occasions

The plants you choose will depend on a number of factors, including the size and scale of the garden and the effect and atmosphere you are trying to create. Plan the beds and borders before you go to the garden centre, so that you end up with harmonious displays, and try to avoid impulse buys.

Choosing plants

Before you buy anything, decide what you use your garden for. If you haven't already sketched out a plan (see page 9) now is the time to do so. Is your garden somewhere you spend relatively little time and do you use it principally to provide a view from the house? Or do you spend a great deal of time in it – every free moment you have available, in fact? Are you looking for somewhere to sunbathe, read a book and relax? Or do you do a lot of entertaining and want the

garden to be an extension of the house? Do you have children and need to provide a play area? Perhaps most important of all, do you want it to be somewhere you spend hours tending your plants or do you really want a low-maintenance garden that looks wonderful for minimum effort?

There's also your own personal preferences to consider. Everyone has their own favourite plants. Think about what it is that attracts you most about them. Do you like them to be fragrant, exotic, dramatic, pretty, colourful, graceful or unusual? Do you want them to provide a peaceful relaxing background or do you want attention grabbers? Do you want a working garden, which will provide fruit, vegetables and herbs for the kitchen, or do you want borders that will provide a supply of flowers and foliage for cut-flower arrangements?

top Brilliant red geums set among bronze-tinged grasses produce an arresting contrast of colour and form.

left Choosing silver-variegated foliage as a skirt for this white clematis has knitted together a coolly simple scheme.

right Cottage-garden classics – such as lupins, roses, irises – never fail to mix happily together.

All these considerations will influence your choice of plants, and in the rest of this chapter we will be looking at the different types of plants that are available and considering ways to choose among them and use them to their best advantage. The sheer number of plants that is available these days can be confusing, but, if you have assessed your garden and found out what type of soil you have, your choice can be focused on the plants that will do well in the conditions you can offer them. Look, too, at the lists of plants for special places on pages 146–53 for suggestions for plants that will do well in difficult sites or that can be used for particular purposes. Don't waste your money on something that will just not grow in your garden or that does not complement or play a useful part in your overall design.

Creative planting

Anyone who has waited at the garden centre check-out behind a long line of enthusiastic gardeners with carts loaded with enough plants to pack the car to the roof can be forgiven for wondering why there are not more stunning gardens to be seen. Sadly, however, once that cart-load has been planted, the impact is seldom as wonderful as hoped for. The usual reason behind this disappointing fact is that the plants have been bought on impulse and planted without an overall strategy and clear planting plan.

A successful bed or border, or even a rock garden, usually works because it is more than a collection of individual plants: it has a cohesion that comes from planning. The plants look right together because they have been grouped for pleasing associations.

The most successful gardens are also planted for year-round interest. Placing too much emphasis on, say, a spring

display or summer bedding can leave the garden looking rather bleak and uninspiring for many months of the year. By planting creatively and using a little imagination, all the seasonal delights can be enjoyed, without great stretches of time when your garden is colourless and unwelcoming.

Although we include many planting ideas and suggestions for complementary planting, avoid following any planting scheme too slavishly. The aspect or soil in your own garden may be unsuitable for some of the plants, and the size and dimensions of beds and borders should always suit the individual garden. Draw on other people's ideas, whether in books or in real gardens, as a source of inspiration, but modify and adapt them to suit your own garden and your own tastes and needs.

Foliage and form

It is hard to overestimate the value of foliage plants in the garden. Use them lavishly in the year-round border, where they will clothe the ground and remain attractive for many months. As long the soil is well covered, the area won't look neglected or unplanned.

Not all foliage plants are green, of course, and there are plenty of wonderful plants with silver and grey foliage. Some of these, such as *Artemisia* 'Powis Castle' or *Perovskia atriplicifolia* (Russian sage), are superb plants in their own right and will act as a bridge between colours and plants with different flowering times.

Purple foliage can look dull on its own, but partner it with light-coloured leaves to bring out the best in both. The purple leaves of the coral flower *Heuchera micrantha* var. *diversifolia* 'Palace Purple' will have a much greater impact partnered with a golden hosta, such as 'Midas Touch'. The almost black lilyturf *Ophiopogon planiscapus* 'Nigrescens' will go almost unnoticed on its own but will become a real feature planted in front of the variegated form of the golden Japanese rush, *Acorus gramineus* 'Ogon'; they go well together because both have grass-like leaves.

Stature and structure

Borders need height, and in a mixed border this can be provided by suitable shrubs. In a non-shrubby border a similar function is served by some of the taller grasses, such as *Stipa gigantea* (golden oats, Spanish oats) or *Miscanthus sinensis*. Grasses like this will remain attractive well into autumn, and some look extremely attractive when they are touched with hoarfrost in the colder months.

Cordylines and phormiums, with their spiky and usually coloured or variegated leaves, make excellent year-round border plants where the climate is suitable. Both are frost-hardy, but they will succumb in areas where there is prolonged freezing weather, so check whether they are suitable where you live.

Few plots are too small to accommodate a small tree, and this can immediately give stature and a focus to a planting (see page 58).

Long-life leaves

Whether they are used to edge a shrub border or included in a mixed or herbaceous border, evergreen but non-woody edging plants are particularly useful. Two that are remarkably tolerant of varying types of soil and will grow in sun or shade are *Ajuga reptans*

left It would have been a shame to obscure this beautiful slate wall with anything more than see-through grasses.

top *Heuchera micrantha* var. *diversifolia* 'Palace Purple' has lovely delicate flowers and boldly coloured leaves.

(bugle), best grown in one of its purple or variegated varieties as a ground-covering carpet, and bergenias (elephant's ears). The large, leathery foliage of some bergenias colours particularly well in winter, assuming shades or red or purple.

Foliage plants that die back in winter are still worth including if they look bright all summer. If you have reliably moist soil, look out for *Houttuynia cordata* 'Chameleon', which will keep its bright foliage right into autumn. *Alchemilla mollis* (lady's mantle) is often grown for its sprays of bright greeny-yellow flowers, but the dense mounds of the lovely, pale green leaves look wonderful in a shady border, especially when they are spangled with droplets of morning dew.

Filling gaps

Bulbs and summer bedding plants are ideal for creating interest and avoiding blank spots. Wherever possible, use bulbs that are hardy enough to be left in the ground, where they will make larger and bolder clumps with time. Never succumb to the temptation of cutting off the leaves before they start to die back naturally, otherwise future flowering will be jeopardized.

It's usually possible to plant summer bedding plants over the area where the bulbs were. Placing bushy plants slightly to one side of the bulbs will cover the area while the bulb foliage dies back without damaging the bulbs below ground. Alternatively, sow hardy annuals, such as *Calendula* spp. (pot marigolds) or *Eschscholzia californica* (California poppy). The seeds should be just scratched into the surface, so the bulbs won't be damaged.

above Winter colour is a prized commodity, and the stems of *Cornus sanguinea* 'Midwinter Fire' provide brilliance long before spring's first bulbs.

Planting for year-round interest

Design your garden for year-round interest as well as for clever colour combinations. This is especially important if you have only a small border that has to work hard to produce interest over a long period. A mixed border will work best if you incorporate several different kinds of plant, from bulbs and bedding plants to shrubs and herbaceous perennials. Choose plants to provide flowers, coloured foliage, berries or dramatic bark in every season of the year.

Garden trees

Trees bring height to a garden and impart a sense of permanence and maturity. They give a planting scheme a structure and provide a permanent backdrop against which the garden is viewed. Remember, though, that trees that are too large or in the wrong place will rob your other plants of light, moisture and nutrients, so choose with care – it is such a shame to have to lop or fell a tree just because not enough thought was given to how it was sited.

No garden is too small for at least one tree. There are fastigiate (narrow, columnar) forms for confined spaces, dwarf weeping trees and slow-growing cultivars that should not outgrow their welcome. You can even grow trees in large containers if you are really pressed for space.

Do take time to select the right tree for your garden. The trees we see growing in woods and parks, though beautiful in their own right, are usually not suitable for the majority of gardens. They need space for both their crowns and root systems to develop to the full. Tall trees cast shade and take nutrients and moisture from the soil, so choice and positioning should be part of the overall garden design. Bear in mind, too, that trees with questing roots could pose a hazard to drains or even the footings of nearby buildings.

Where to plant trees

Site garden trees where they will have room to develop unhindered, and avoid planting specimens that will outgrow the available space. Consider the habit of the trees as well as their flowers, foliage and berry colour, and plant them where you will be able to appreciate their form. A majestic, spreading *Cedrus libani* (cedar of Lebanon) is a wonderful sight – but not in a cramped back garden. When space is limited, choose an upright, columnar tree. Choose one with a spreading crown only if you have the space.

Do not underestimate the amount of water an established tree can extract from the subsoil, which can bring the risk of subsidence. It's a good idea to observe the general rule of never planting a tree

Tree forms

It is important to know the habit of a tree before planting it. Trees can be:

a **spreading**

b **weeping**

c **fastigiate** or

d **conical**

Check the eventual height and spread of the tree and allow it adequate space to achieve its mature dimensions when you are planning the garden.

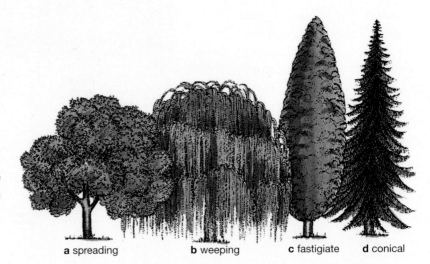

a spreading   b weeping   c fastigiate   d conical

closer to your house than the ultimate height of the tree. Thus, if you wanted, say, to plant *Betula pendula* (silver birch) for its graceful form, beautiful bark and long, yellow catkins, you should be aware that in ideal conditions the species can grow to 25m (80ft) tall. If your garden simply cannot accommodate a tree that you have to plant 25m (80ft) from your house, look for one of the smaller cultivars – the extremely attractive *B. pendula* 'Youngii' (Young's weeping birch), for instance, will get to about 8m (25ft) high.

Remember, too, that the ground under deciduous trees will have to be cleared of leaves in autumn. For this reason, do not position pools or sandpits under their canopies.

Space-savers

Space-saving trees are perfect for small gardens, of course, but they also come into their own for cramped corners in a large garden. Where you need the height and sense of permanence that only a tree can provide but where space or spread is restricted, try a tall, narrow tree. These trees are also useful even where there is ample space for a normal spread but you want to minimize the shadow cast on beds and borders.

Many weeping trees are ideal for a small garden where height has to be restricted but spread is less important. Although weeping trees can be grown in a border, they look best as specimen plants set in a lawn. To make mowing easier, protect the tree's bark and, to stop the grass taking moisture and nutrients from the tree, do not allow grass to grow right up to the trunk. Clear the grass from a circle around the base of the tree and apply a mulch of chipped bark, which you will need to replace every year.

top This weeping elm, *Ulmus glabra* 'Camperdownii', becomes a dense dome of green when in full leaf.

Top ten tall, narrow trees

Acer 'Scanlon'
A tall, columnar tree, to 15m (50ft) tall and 5m (15ft) across, this has leaves that turn it into a pillar of red in autumn.

Betula pendula 'Fastigiata'
This attractive cultivar of the silver birch has an upright, narrow habit, growing to 20m (70ft) tall and 6m (20ft) across. The green leaves turn yellow in autumn, and there are yellowish catkins in spring.

Carpinus betulus 'Fastigiata'
This upright hornbeam, to 15m (50ft) high and 12m (40ft) across, is grown for the texture created by the dense foliage. Although narrow when young, it broadens at the base with age and may be too large for a really small space.

Crataegus monogyna 'Stricta'
A small hawthorn, to 10m (30ft) tall but only 4m (12ft) across, this has erect branches clothed with white flowers in late spring.

Fagus sylvatica 'Dawyck'
This tall, slender beech, to 25m (80ft) tall, broadens with age, eventually getting to 7m (23ft) wide. It has good autumn colour.

above *Crataegus monogyna* 'Stricta'

Liriodendron tulipifera 'Fastigiatum'
This magnificent form of the tulip tree is narrow when young but broadens with age, ultimately getting to 20m (70ft) high and 8m (25ft) across.

Malus tschonoskii
An erect, small to medium-sized ornamental crabapple, to 12m (40ft) high and 7m (23ft) across, this has pink-flushed white flowers in spring, small, yellowish fruit in autumn and brilliant foliage in autumn, in vibrant shades of yellow, orange, purple and scarlet.

Prunus 'Spire'
One of the best small flowering trees, to 10m (30ft) tall and 6m (20ft) across, this has lovely pale pink flowers in spring. The upright *P.* 'Amanogawa' is also justifiably popular, forming a column, 8m (25ft) high and 4m (12ft) across, of fragrant, pale pink flowers in spring.

Sorbus aucuparia 'Fastigiata'
This small, rather stiff-looking tree, to 8m (25ft) tall and 5m (25ft) across, has the added attraction of red berries at the end of summer.

Ulmus minor 'Dampieri Aurea'
This elm is a good, compact tree, to 10m (30ft) tall and 5m (15ft) across, with a conical habit and golden leaves.

below *Sorbus aucuparia* in late summer

Multi-merit trees

Unless you have a large garden, the number of trees you can plant will be limited, so it makes sense to choose plants that have several features of merit whenever possible so that you get some colour and interest in every season.

Shrubby trees

If your garden is small, select trees that have a shrubby habit of growth and that can be kept under control by pruning. Look out, too, for smaller cultivars of some of the large growing species. You may not have room for *Ulmus glabra* (wych elm), which can get to an imposing height of 35m (120ft) or more, but you will probably have room for the attractive cultivar 'Exoniensis' (Exeter elm), with unusually twisted leaves, which achieves a more manageable 15m (50ft).

Amelanchier larmarckii (snowy mespilus) and the similar *A. canadensis* (shadbush) are often listed as shrubs, but they can be regarded as multi-stemmed trees and are sometimes sold in standard tree form, with a head on a single trunk. They will remain small enough for most gardens and stay looking good from first leaf in spring to last leaf in autumn. Masses of white flowers appear about the same time as the leaves open, creating a cloud of bloom. In early summer there may be a bonus of edible black fruit, and it says goodbye to autumn in a blaze of red foliage.

Catalpa bignonioides (Indian bean tree), which can get to 15m (50ft) high and across, is only suitable for a large garden, where its big leaves, white flowers in mid-

and late summer and slender 'bean pods' in winter provide a succession of interest. More suitable for a smaller garden is the yellow-leaved form *C. bignonioides* 'Aurea', which is one of the best yellow trees, to 10m (30ft) high and across, and it can be grown as a multi-stemmed plant that makes it more like a large shrub.

Flowers, fruit and foliage

Many ornamental trees are of value not only for their foliage and habit of growth, but also for flowers and fruit. *Cornus kousa* is one of these, and it is a tree that deserves to be more widely grown. It's a slow-growing plant and is not suitable for dry, shallow or chalky soil. However, it's well worth waiting for if you can plant it in moist but well-drained soil in sun or partial shade. The spreading branches are covered with star-like flowers – the 'petals' are actually bracts surrounding the true flowers – in late spring and early summer. If conditions are suitable, these are followed later by edible (but seedy and insipid) fruit that resemble strawberries in appearance. In autumn the leaves take on shades of crimson and bronze.

Crataegus spp. (hawthorn) are useful trees in small gardens, with flowers in late spring or early summer and red or orange fruit in autumn, which often persist into winter. Two of the most popular for showy flowers are *C. laevigata* 'Paul's Scarlet' and *C. laevigata* 'Rosea Flore Pleno', but for all-round performance choose *C. persimilis* 'Prunifolia', which has white flowers in early summer, is a blaze of orange and red leaves in autumn and produces bunches of rich red, long-lasting fruits. *C. monogyna* (common hawthorn) is not as good for autumn tints, but it flowers prolifically in late spring and the branches are usually laden with red fruit in autumn.

The ornamental crabapples, *Malus* spp., are invaluable multi-merit trees for a small garden. In mid- or late spring they are covered with blossom, which may be white, pink, red or purple. Purple-leaved forms, such as *M. × moerlandsii* 'Profusion', are colourful all summer, and most have very attractive, long-lasting red or yellow fruit in autumn. Some also have good autumn colour. The leaves of *M. tschonoskii* turn yellow, orange, purple and scarlet before they fall, which is why it is sometimes called the bonfire tree.

left Among the large leaves of *Catalpa bignonioides* hang the long pods from which it gets the name of Indian bean tree.

above right In early summer the foliage of *Cornus kousa* disappears under the showy bracts that surround its flowers.

Most forms of *Sorbus* (mountain ash, rowan) are neat, small or medium-sized trees, and those grown for their berries are at their best in autumn and early winter. The flattened heads of creamy-white flowers in late spring and early summer are unspectacular but a useful bonus. It's the autumn berries that bring these trees to life, and they come in shades of red, orange, pink and white, according to species and form. Many also have brilliant foliage colour to light up those autumn days.

S. 'Joseph Rock' is particularly useful for autumn colour, the leaves turning a fiery combination of orange, red, copper and purple at the same time as the berries deepen from creamy-yellow to amber gold.

Top ten deciduous garden trees

Amelanchier lamarckii (snowy mespilus)
This round-headed small tree or large shrub, to 10m (30ft) high and 12m (40ft) across, has bronze young leaves, which turn crimson in autumn, and masses of tiny white flowers in late spring, which are followed by blue-black berries.

Cornus controversa 'Variegata'
This is a fairly slow-growing tree, to 8m (25ft) high and across, with leaves that have bold creamy-white margins.

Fraxinus angustifolia 'Raywood' (claret ash)
This vigorous tree, eventually to 20m (70ft) high, has glossy green leaves that turn deep red-purple in autumn.

Ginkgo biloba (maidenhair tree)
This upright tree, to 8m (25ft) across, is slow-growing so is suitable for a small garden, although it can reach 30m (100ft) tall. The fan-shaped leaves are pale green in spring, turning yellow in autumn.

Gleditsia triacanthos 'Sunburst'
This popular form of the honey locust is a fast-growing tree, ultimately to about 12m (40ft) high and 10m (30ft) across. The foliage is golden-yellow as it emerges, turning to pale green and then turning yellow again in autumn.

Liquidambar styraciflua (sweet gum)
The maple-shaped leaves turn to rich shades of crimson before they fall. It grows into a shapely, pyramidal tree, rather narrow in proportion to its height, with an eventual height and spread of 25m (80ft) and 12m (40ft).

Prunus x *subhirtella* 'Autumnalis' (Higan cherry)
The mid-green leaves of this ornamental cherry, which gets to about 7m (23ft) high and across, turn orange-bronze in autumn, and the flowers, pink in bud, opening to white, appear from autumn (in mild areas) to spring.

Pyrus calleryana 'Chanticleer'
From early to mid-spring this narrowly pyramidal tree bears clusters of white flowers, sometimes producing a second flush in summer. It will ultimately get to about 15m (50ft) high with a spread of 6m (20ft).

Robinia pseudoacacia 'Frisia' (golden false acacia)
This popular tree, growing to 15m (50ft) high and 8m (25ft) across, has ferny leaves, with good autumn colour, and white, pea-like flowers in clusters in summer.

Sorbus 'Joseph Rock'
This excellent and good-value garden form of the mountain ash or rowan gets to 10m (30ft) high and about 7m (23ft) across, making a neat, upright shape. It has bright green leaves, turning vivid shades of red and orange in autumn. It also has white flowers in spring and yellow-orange berries.

below Ginkgo biloba (maidenhair tree)

Autumn colour

Make sure that the growing season goes out with some fireworks. Although the intensity of colour and the length of the display will depend on the weather, there are trees that can be depended upon to put on a good show.

Liquidambar styraciflua (sweet gum) has leaves resembling those of a maple, and really comes into its own in autumn, when they turn orange, red and purple. Sadly, this is a large tree, sutiable only for a large garden. Other large trees that give splendid autumn colour include *Quercus rubra* (red oak), which grows comparatively quickly for an oak, *Nyssa sylvatica* (black gum, tupelo) and the magnificent *Liriodendron tulipifera* (tulip tree), which gets its name from its unusual yellowish-green flowers in early summer.

Acers

This is a huge genus of trees, some dwarf enough for a large rock garden, others more suitable for a forest. Because they vary so widely in size and habit of growth there are sure to be some that are suitable for your garden, but do check carefully before you buy.

If you have space for only one tree and want something that will provide year-round interest, consider the slow-growing *Acer griseum* (paper-bark maple) – its cinnamon-coloured, peeling bark looks

especially good in autumn sunshine against the vivid foliage. Although *A. pseudoplatanus* 'Brilliantissimum' is a kind of sycamore, don't be deterred from planting it. The tree remains small, to 6m (20ft) high and 8m (25ft) across, and as well as having good autumn colour it looks spectacular in spring when the foliage opens shrimp pink.

One of the most reliable acers for autumn colour is *A. rubrum* (red maple, scarlet maple), whose common names tell you what you can expect. 'October Glory' lives up to its name, and 'Schlesingeri', one of the first to turn, creates an early splash of deep red.

Among the medium to tall maples, *A. cappadocicum* (Caucasian maple) turns clear yellow in autumn, while *A. rubrum* turns first red and green, then gold. The stately *A. platanoides* (Norway maple) can also be depended on for a good display of red and gold.

Among the most familiar acers are, perhaps, the cultivars of *A. japonicum* (Japanese maple), which slowly make small trees and are often grown as large shrubs. Two particularly fine forms for autumn colour are 'Aconitifolium', with ruby-red and crimson autumn colour, and 'Vitifolium', which turns a brilliant red.

left The lacy-fingered leaves of *Acer palmatum* 'Dissectum' have all the gorgeous autumn colouring of larger maples.

top Peeling bark on the trunk of a *Prunus serrula* reveals the rich satiny glow of fresh new bark beneath.

Interesting bark

Attractive bark is, of course, a year-round feature, but it comes into its own in winter, especially when the trunk of a deciduous tree can be seen in all its glory.

Plant a tree with decorative bark where the full beauty of the colouring and texture can be appreciated. A bold drift of winter-flowering heathers will look superb around the base of a white-barked birch, for example, and the green and white foliage of *Pachysandra terminalis* 'Variegata' will make an attractive contrast to the cinnamon-coloured bark of *Acer griseum*.

The trees suggested below are only a few of those with beautiful bark. Don't dismiss *Betula pendula* (silver birch), for example, and if you have a large garden there are delights to be discovered, such as *Arbutus × andrachnoides*, which has remarkably beautiful cinnamon-red trunk and branches. Remember that the colouring and markings may change as the tree ages, so don't judge the effect by a young sapling in a garden centre. Try to find a mature specimen in winter so that you can see what your tree will be like after a few years.

Snake-bark maples

These acers have reticulated or striated bark that resembles a snake's skin. *A. capillipes* is a small tree, to 5m (15ft), with branches that are striped with green and white. New shoots are coral-red, and the autumn leaf colour is good. *A. davidii* (Père David's maple) has green and white streaked bark, and good orange and yellow autumn leaf colour. *A. grosseri* var. *hersii* has beautifully marbled bark and excellent autumn leaf colour. The young stems of *A. pensylvanicum* (striped maple) are streaked with white and pale green. The cultivar 'Erythrocladum' has pink young shoots with pale striations in winter.

Flaking and peeling

Many birches have ornamental, peeling bark. *Betula albosinensis* var. *septentrionalis* (Chinese red-barked birch) has flaking bark, which is marbled fawn or orange-brown and pinkish-red, with a grey bloom. *B. nigra* (black birch, river birch) has shaggy, blackish bark, which is more attractive than it sounds. It must be grown in reliably moist but not waterlogged ground. *B. papyrifera* (paper-bark birch) has smooth white bark that peels like sheets of paper to show the orange-brown bark beneath. The pinkish or copper-brown bark of *B. utilis* (Himalayan birch) peels in horizontal bands, while *B. utilis* var. *jacquemontii* has dazzling white peeling bark.

Mahogany finish

Among the trees with glossy, red-brown trunks, seen at their best on cold winter days, are *Prunus serrula*, a small but vigorous tree grown for its red-brown bark that looks like polished mahogany when new and that peels in bands, and *P. maackii* (Manchurian cherry), which has golden-brown flaking bark that on young trees looks like polished wood.

Small trees to make a big splash

***Amelanchier lamarckii* (snowy mespilus)** and ***A. canadensis* (shadbush)**
These trees, which are often grown as large shrubs, have white flowers in spring and orange and red autumn leaves.

***Parrotia persica* (Persian ironwood)**
An uninspiring tree for most of the year, in autumn it comes alight as the deep green leaves change to fiery scarlet and gold.

***Prunus sargentii* (Sargent cherry)**
This ornamental cherry has pink flowers in early and mid-spring, and a rich display of orange and crimson autumn colour.

***Rhus typhina* (stag's horn sumach)**
This is grown for its very large pinnate leaves, which are one of the spectacles of autumn when they turn red, scarlet, orange and yellow.

Sorbus commixta
Another useful member of the genus, this compact tree, to 10m (30ft) high and 7m (23ft), has wonderful autumn colour, the dark green leaves turning shades of yellow, red and purple, white spring flowers and vivid red berries.

below Amelanchier lamarckii

Conifers

Small and medium-sized conifers can be the backbone of a garden design, providing structure, texture and colour all year round. Plant them lavishly if you have the space. Your garden will never look drab or boring if you mix colours and shapes, and they make an excellent backdrop for the rest of the garden.

Classic cedars

Cedrus spp. (cedar) are sometimes grown in small gardens, but they are at their best when they are given plenty of space and set into a large lawn. They are ideal conifers if you want a striking specimen tree as a focal point, but you will be planting for the next generation to enjoy, because they take many years to achieve maturity. Nevertheless, a respectably sized specimen can be grown within 10–20 years, and these younger trees are often more attractive because they are still well clothed with foliage to the base.

Cedrus atlantica Glauca Group (blue Atlas cedar) has silver-blue foliage, with statuesque ascending branches when young, spreading with age. *Cedrus deodara* (deodar) has a more graceful appearance, its drooping habit of growth and tiered branches making it an airy and unoppressive tree despite its size.

Talking-point trees

Ginkgo biloba (maidenhair tree) does not even look like a conifer. Its leaves are fan-shaped and not needle-like, and it sheds them in winter. It does not produce cones; instead it has small, yellow, plum-like fruit (although these are seldom formed on garden trees). It's the last survivor of an ancient family, the ancestors of which were growing in many parts of the world about 160 million years ago. It is regarded as a sacred tree in parts of the East and is often planted near Buddhist temples. It's a medium to large tree, not suitable for a small garden, but excellent as a specimen in a lawn. The foliage turns a butter-yellow before falling.

That old favourite of Victorian gardeners, *Araucaria araucana* (monkey puzzle, Chinese pine), is a stiff-looking tree with branches that look like thick, curved ropes as the triangular and pointed leaves clasp the stems. The common name is said to have originated

left Conifers have needles in a wonderful range of colours, from blue, green, grey and silver to bronze and gold.

top *Cedrus deodora* (deodar cedar) has a slightly drooping look when young but grows fast into a large, stately tree.

when someone at a ceremonial planting remarked that it would puzzle a monkey to climb such a tree. It's too often planted in small gardens – it will ultimately grow to 25m (80ft) – although it is comparatively slow growing, so you might enjoy it and leave it to the next owners of your garden to cut down.

Another tree that is too tall for all but the largest of gardens is the majestic *Metasequoia glyptostroboides* (dawn redwood). It is a magnificent conifer if you have the space and moist ground in which to grow it. At one time this tree was known only from fossils; then one was discovered in the grounds of a Chinese temple in 1841. Unusually for a conifer, it sheds its leaves in the autumn.

Golden foliage

Conifers have a reputation for being dull, dark green, but there are many golden forms that are worth seeking out. Even cedars can be found with rich yellow foliage. *Cedrus atlantica* 'Aurea' and *C. deodara* 'Aurea' look stunning and are not quite as tall as their dark green cousins.

The popular *Chamaecyparis lawsoniana* (Lawson cypress) has spawned a whole collection of golden varieties. Don't be misled by the name 'Ellwood's Gold', however, because it's only the tips of the shoots that are gold at certain times of the year. 'Lanei Aurea', 'Lutea' and 'Stewartii' are three medium-sized golden cultivars that won't disappoint, 'Lanei Aurea' being the brightest.

'Goldcrest' is an outstanding cultivar of *Cupressus macrocarpa* (Monterey cypress), but you should plant it in a sunny position for the best colour.

Blue-greys

Some of the most attractive conifers have blue-green or blue-grey foliage, introducing a completely different type of foliage into the garden and a marvellous foil for scarlet autumn leaves. Perhaps the lightest silvery-blue cultivar is the spruce *Picea pungens* 'Hoopsii', which is pyramidal to conical in outline and has broad, silver-blue needles, turning more silvery in winter. *P. pungens* 'Koster' is another popular choice. Among the cypresses, *Chamaecyparis lawsoniana* 'Pembury Blue' is a striking silvery-blue.

Conifers for autumn colour

Not all conifers are evergreen, and some have a change of leaf colour even though the needles are retained.

- The **Japanese cedar *Cryptomeria japonica* Elegans Group** has green summer leaves that turn reddish-bronze in winter.

- The leaves of the rarely seen ***Cunninghamia lanceolata* (China fir)** turn from green to brown in autumn.

- Unusually among conifers, ***Larix decidua* (larch)** sheds its leaves in autumn, but not before they turn gold.

- ***Metasequoia glyptostroboides* (dawn redwood)** also sheds its leaves in autumn, after they have changed to gold.

- Another deciduous conifer, ***Taxodium distichum* (swamp cypress)**, has pale green leaves that turn bronzy-yellow before falling.

below Metasequoia glyptostroboides (dawn redwood)

Shrubs

Shrubs are the essential plants of the garden. They provide structure all year round, and add an element of height that is needed in every garden, especially where there are no trees. If you decide that your plot really is too small for a tree, you will find that there are any number of shrubs that will fit the bill. There are shrubs for every season, from sweet-scented winter flowers to favourites that bloom all summer long.

As with trees, it is important to choose shrubs carefully and plant them with thought. They can take several years to become well established and look mature, by which time they are difficult to move or discard if you made the wrong choice. Borders dedicated entirely to shrubs can be difficult to accommodate in a small garden, but shrubs can be used creatively with other plants, especially bulbs and herbaceous perennials, in a mixed border, or as specimen plants to be viewed in splendid isolation. Some make excellent container plants. It is also among the shrubby plants that you will find some of the best year-round groundcovers.

Shrubs of all kinds make a year-long contribution to the garden scene that cannot be matched by other types of plant. Even deciduous shrubs, such as *Buddleja davidii* and *Hydrangea macrophylla*, which lose their leaves in autumn, have interesting branch patterns, and these are sometimes given added attraction by virtue of having distinctive bark.

Because they retain their leaves in winter, evergreen shrubs – *Viburnum tinus* (laurustinus) and *Ceanothus impressus* (Santa Barbara ceanothus), for example – can provide a useful foil to the deciduous kinds, a factor you need to take into account when deciding where to

Camellias

If you have acid soil you will want to have at least one of these handsome evergreen shrubs. If your soil is alkaline, buy the largest container you can afford and fill it with ericaceous compost so you can have one in your garden. There is an enormous range of cultivars to choose from, with flower colours ranging from purest white to deepest dark red. When you are choosing, remember that they are grouped according to flower type: single, semi-double, anemone-form, peony-form, rose-form, formal double and irregular double. The lovely blooms are produced above glossy green leaves.

Camellia japonica **'Alba Simplex'** has single white flowers with yellow centres.

C. j. **'Mathotiana'** has formal double red-pink flowers.

C. j. **'Rubescens Major'** is a formal double with deep pink flowers.

C. x williamsii **'Anticipation'**, a peony type, has dark pink flowers.

C. x w. **'Clarrie Fawcett'** has pale pink, semi-double flowers.

C. x w. **'Donation'** is a semi-double with mid-pink flowers.

locate them. Evergreens with leaves that are variegated with white or cream, such as *Euonymus fortunei* 'Silver Queen', or with yellow, such as *Aucuba japonica* 'Crotonifolia', can be particularly valuable in winter because they bring some welcome colour to the garden.

Some shrubs are grown primarily for the beauty of their flowers – *Syringa* × *persica* (Persian lilac), for example – and some for their berries or other autumn fruit – *Cotoneaster* × *watereri*, is a good example. Others are chosen for the colour of their foliage – the leaves of *Cotinus coggygria* 'Royal Purple' are dark reddish-purple. A few shrubs even combine two or more of these attractions. There is also great diversity in height and habit, from completely prostrate shrubs, such as some species of cotoneaster, to almost tree-like specimens, such as the lilacs.

Using shrubs

In the garden shrubs are commonly grouped either with other shrubs or with herbaceous plants and annuals, but some kinds look their best planted as isolated specimens and some can be trained against walls and fences, which is useful if space is limited. *Magnolia stellata* (star magnolia) is an excellent example of the former type, a plant that should be grown as a specimen, while *Pyracantha* spp. (firethorn), *Chaenomeles japonica* (Japanese quince) and ceanothus do well against walls, where their stiff branches may provide support for genuine climbers, such as the less rampant clematis.

Most shrubs take several years to attain their full size. Temporary plants, such as dahlias, annuals and herbaceous perennials, can be used to fill the space until the shrubs require it all.

top There are spring- and autumn-flowering ceanothus, with puffs of flowers that are mostly in a range of beautiful blues. This is the later-flowering 'Gloire de Versailles'.

Top ten shrubs

Abelia x grandiflora
This shrub has arching branches of pointed, deep green, evergreen or semi-evergreen leaves and small, fragrant, pink-tinged, white flowers. This is a useful shrub since it flowers well into autumn when little else is of interest. The cultivar 'Gold Spot' has yellow foliage.

Buddleja davidii (butterfly bush)
A favourite plant for attracting butterflies, buddleias have long panicles of blue-purple flowers. Look out for cultivars with different colours: 'Black Knight' (deep purple), 'Empire Blue' (violet-mauve) and 'Peace' (white).

Ceanothus impressus (Santa Barbara ceanothus)
This evergreen bush produces clusters of beautiful deep blue flowers from late spring right through to autumn.

Chaenomeles speciosa (ornamental quince)
This colourful shrub produces bright vermilion flowers in early spring, and they are sometimes followed by yellow fruit in autumn. The cultivar 'Nivalis' has white flowers, 'Moerloesii' has pink and white flowers, and 'Simonii' has semi-double crimson flowers, which are ideal against walls.

Cornus alba (red-barked dogwood)
The young shoots are bright red in winter, while the dark green leaves turn vivid shades of orange and red in autumn. Creamy-white, star-shaped flowers are produced in spring. 'Elegantissima' has white-edged, grey-green leaves; 'Spaethii' has yellow-edged, green leaves.

Cotinus coggygria (smoke bush)
This neatly mounded shrub has rounded or oval leaves which turn red or yellow in autumn, and plumes of pale greyish-brown flowers. The cultivar 'Royal Purple' has purple leaves, which turn shades of fiery red and orange in autumn, and pink flowers.

Cotoneaster frigidus
This deciduous cotoneaster has white flowers in summer and bright red berries in autumn.

Daphne odora (winter daphne)
This lovely evergreen shrub has glossy, dark green leaves and fragrant pink and white flowers from midwinter to early spring.

Kerria japonica
A graceful, suckering shrub, this has golden-yellow flowers on green shoots.

Viburnum x burkwoodii
This evergreen shrub produces fragrant pink then white flowers above glossy, dark green leaves. 'Park Farm Hybrid' has fragrant white flowers, which open from dark pink buds.

below Buddleja davidii 'Royal Red' (butterfly bush)

Scented shrubs

When fragrance is combined with the beauty of a flower, as with roses and lilies, all the senses are heightened and gardening really does seem a magical pastime. But don't overlook those scented shrubs that have less spectacular flowers.

Siting for scent

Take a little trouble about siting fragrant shrubs. If you have the space, spread them throughout your garden, because if you concentrate them in one place, such as a single border, the scents may conflict with each and confuse your sense of smell. Planting several of the same kind together will intensify the scent. Don't place them too far back in the border, especially if the scents are not especially strong, and put those with fragrant foliage, such as *Choisya ternata* (Mexican orange blossom) and *Rosmarinus* spp. (rosemary), where you can easily crush a leaf to release the scent as you pass.

Summer borders

If you have only ever come across *Elaeagnus pungens* at a distance, you may be surprised to find that this useful foliage shrub bears fragrant flowers in autumn once the plants are mature enough to flower well. The flowers are insignificant, however, and you will probably smell the fragrance long before you spot a flower. *Elaeagnus commutata* (silver berry) flowers in late spring, *E. angustifolia* (oleaster) in early summer, and cultivars of *E.* × *ebbingei* in autumn, so you can spread

the benefits of the fragrance by planting all four types.

Philadelphus spp. (mock orange) are famed for their scent. The single or double white flowers are produced in profusion in early and midsummer. Some of them grow large, but whenever possible allow them to overhang the edge of the border a little.

Lavenders make pretty front-of-border plants as well as aromatic dwarf hedges. There are several species and many cultivars, so you are sure to find a colour and size to please. A little further back in the border try planting *Romneya coulteri* (tree poppy, matilija poppy) or the cultivar 'White Cloud'. These both have fragrant flowers that resemble large white poppies with bright golden-yellow centres.

It's worth including the spring-flowering and clove-scented *Ribes*

top The small white flowers of *Elaeagnus* x *ebbingei* 'Gilt Edge' appear in the autumn and exude a heavy scent.

left *Philadelphus* 'Belle Etoile' is one of the larger mock oranges, whose fruity fragrance announces the arrival of summer.

right Beloved of perfumiers, lavender is the classic scented shrub. This is *Lavandula angustifolia* 'Hidcote Pink', a pretty variation on the more usual shades.

odoratum (buffalo currant) in any planting of fragrant shrubs. The bright yellow flowers are followed by black berries, and the autumn leaf colour is pleasing, too. Also flowering in spring are the beautifully fragrant *Osmanthus* × *burkwoodii* and *O. delavayi*, which produce masses of small white flowers.

The flowers of *Syringa vulgaris* (common lilac) span late spring to early summer and are almost indispensable in any collection of fragrant shrubs. As well as shades of lilac, they can be white, reddish-purple or even yellow. When you are growing common lilac in a shrub border, prune it hard back after flowering so that it does not outgrow its position.

Calycanthus floridus (Carolina allspice, common sweetbush) has unusual, star-shaped, fragrant, reddish-purple flowers in mid- and late summer, but it lacks impact in a border and is more likely to be appreciated as a specimen in a lawn. *Clethra alnifolia* 'Paniculata' (sweet pepper bush) is worth including for its late-summer flowers, which continue into early autumn. The upright spikes of white flowers, about 15cm (6in) long, are not especially beautiful, but they are sweetly scented.

Pineapple and honey brooms

The pineapple-scented *Cytisus battandieri* (Moroccan broom, pineapple broom) seldom fails to attract attention in early summer. The cone-shaped clusters of yellow flowers, borne on tall, grey-leaved stems, have a delicious pineapple fragrance. This is a plant that grows fast and tall – often to 3m (10ft) or more – but it needs a sheltered position. It is often grown against a tall wall, where the plant benefits from the extra protection it receives.

Spartium junceum (Spanish broom) has honey-scented, pea-shaped, yellow flowers all summer. Luckily, the fragrance is strong enough to be appreciated from a distance, for this is not a good plant for a small border: at 2.4m (8ft) or more it needs plenty of space.

Winter scent

There are many shrubs for winter fragrance, including the deliciously scented *Chimonanthus praecox* (wintersweet) and *Sarcococca hookeriana* (Christmas box, sweet box). *Lonicera* spp. (honeysuckle) is usually thought of as a summer-flowering climber, but there are winter-flowering, shrubby, non-climbing types with unexciting, small, white flowers but a lovely scent. As the name suggests, *Lonicera fragrantissima* is one of these, as are *L.* × *purpusii* and *L. standishii*, all of which flower from early winter to early spring. (See also page 71.)

Shrubs for winter interest

A well-designed garden will have pockets of interest in every month of the year, and shrubs play a vital role in helping to achieve colour at a time when the summer-blooming annuals and perennials are no longer on the scene.

Winter-interest shrubs should be planted with their winter role in mind and not simply as part of a mixed planting. Position them for maximum impact. The most spectacular winter shrubs can be used as focal points to take the eye to various parts of the garden, but low-growing ones or those with small flowers are best grouped together, perhaps with some winter-flowering border perennials, such as *Helleborus niger* (Christmas rose) and *Iris unguicularis*, and underplanted with bulbs, such as *Galanthus* spp. (snowdrop) and *Eranthis hyemalis* (winter aconite).

Finding a focal point

Choose a few large or particularly bold plants that look good in winter and position them in an otherwise uninteresting area. This will reduce the number of 'low' spots in the garden at this time and draw the eye towards a particular view across the winter garden.

Many winter flowers are small – some are usually described in reference books as insignificant – so rely on foliage to provide colour from a distance. A large *Elaeagnus pungens* 'Maculata', with its gold-splashed leaves, will look magnificent as the winter sun catches the variegation – especially effective if the surrounding plantings are uninteresting at that time of year.

A number of mahonias flower in winter, some with wonderfully scented blooms, and one of the more upright forms, rising almost aggressively with big spiky leaves, will make a bold statement. According to where you place it, *Mahonia lomariifolia* or *M.* × *media* 'Charity' will bring interest to the back of a border or a group of winter-flowering plants. Alternatively, place one of these tolerant and evergreen plants where it can stand alone to be a focal point when viewed across the garden. The fragrant yellow flowers bloom even during the gloomiest days.

Hamamelis mollis (Chinese witch hazel) takes a few years to become established and look its best, but it will bring light and life to an apparently dormant area of a lightly shaded part of the garden or an otherwise almost bare mixed border. A mature plant often looks its best in a sunny position in a lawn where it can be viewed against a dark background, such as a hedge. The fragrant yellow flowers are borne on leafless branches in midwinter, and the little blooms are often packed so tightly that its beauty can be appreciated even from a distance.

Grow *Garrya elliptica* (silk-tassel bush) where you can see the long and long-lasting catkins to advantage. On an established plant it will look as if they are dripping from the branches. In cold areas this shrub will benefit from the protection of a wall or fence, but it makes an attractive wall shrub and will benefit from the extra warmth it receives. The cultivar 'James Roof' has spectacular silvery-grey catkins, often more than 20cm (8in) long. Although this is not a colourful plant, it makes a wonderful specimen shrub or focal point.

left With its shiny dark evergreen leaves and spikes of yellow flowers, *Mahonia* x *media* 'Charity' is a dramatic presence all winter. As a bonus the flowers are very sweetly scented.

late autumn and continue through till early spring. It is usually grown against a wall, where its green stems can be trained against a trellis or a framework of wires.

Winter-flowering heaths – cultivars of *Erica carnea* and *E. × darleyensis* – look best in bold drifts, especially around the base of a deciduous tree with attractive bark, such as a white-barked *Betula* (birch).

Not all winter flowers are colourful or fragrant. *Viburnum tinus* (laurustinus) is an unassuming evergreen that grows to about 2.4m (8ft), with clusters of white or pink-tinged flowers, but it starts to bloom in mid-autumn and is usually still flowering in early spring.

Colourful stems

Choosing a shrub for the sake of its winter twigs and stems may not seem to be a priority, but anyone who has grown trees with attractive bark (see page 63) or shrubs with vivid winter stems will know that they are more colourful and longer lasting than almost all the winter flowers. In a large garden, a group of them makes a superb feature in winter sunshine, but even a single shrub is worth having in the border.

If you have space for a single shrub in this group, look at the dogwoods, *Cornus* spp., which are widely grown for winter colour. They are best pruned back to just above ground level every spring (or every second spring) to maintain a supply of young shoots, which have the most intense colours. Two of the brightest are *Cornus alba* 'Sibirica' (bright red stems and the bonus of red autumn leaves) and *C. sericea* 'Flaviramea' (greenish-yellow stems). The willow *Salix alba* subsp. *vitellina* 'Britzensis' can be pruned severely every second year and grown as a shrub; it has brilliant orange-scarlet winter shoots.

If there is space for its long, arching stems and vigorous growth, grow *Rubus cockburnianus* (whitewash bramble). Cut it right down to the ground every spring: the new arching canes that arise from the ground have a white bloom, which make them a real feature whether or not the sun is shining.

Winter flowers

Any garden planted for winter interest will almost certainly include *Jasminum nudiflorum* (winter jasmine); its bright yellow flowers start to appear in

Getting scent

Many of the flowers that are borne in winter are strongly fragrant so that they will attract the few insects that are active, and among the most popular shrubs are *Viburnum × bodnantense* and *V. farreri*, which produce rather insignificant but scented pink or white flowers on bare stems.

Chimonanthus praecox (wintersweet) makes a large shrub, to 4 × 3m (12 × 10ft). The waxy-looking, yellow flowers with purple centres are not particularly attractive from a distance, but they are deliciously fragrant. Look out for the cultivar 'Grandiflorus', which has larger yellow flowers with dark red stripes inside.

Sarcococca spp. (Christmas box, sweet box) are useful, not too large evergreen shrubs that do well in shade. The small white flowers are borne in winter and are followed by blue-black fruit. *Sarcococca hookeriana* var. *digyna* and *S. hookeriana* var. *humilis* are the most widely available forms.

top Plant *Cornus alba* 'Sibirica', preferably a group of them, where the winter sun can set the scarlet stems alight.

right *Viburnum tinus* is an immensely useful shrub, an unnoticed backdrop in summer that flowers profusely in winter.

Rhododendrons

At the height of their flowering season, from spring to early summer, rhododendrons and azaleas are among the most spectacular of all flowering shrubs.

Making a choice

There are about 900 species of rhododendrons and a huge number of cultivars has been developed: choosing is not a simple task. Most are evergreen, but some are deciduous. The flowers, which are sometimes delightfully scented, exhibit a wide range of shapes and colours, and although the spring- and early summer-flowering plants are well known, some rhododendrons flower late in the year. There is also a wide difference in size, with *Rhododendron sutchuenense* growing, in the right conditons, to 8m (25ft) or more high and across, while *R. pemakoense* is a dwarf, compact shrub, rarely exceeding 60cm (2ft) in height and spread.

The one thing to remember about the rhododendron family is that all prefer acid (lime-free) soil, so if you are gardening on strongly alkaline soil you will need to choose one of the smaller forms and grow it in a container or construct a raised bed, which you can fill with ericaceous compost. If the underlying soil is strongly alkaline, plants will benefit from an annual spring feeding with iron and manganese sequestrols.

Hardy hybrids

For a mass of blooms, there are no rhododendrons that surpass the group known as hardy hybrids. These are also the easiest to grow – they are sometimes known as iron-clad rhododendrons because, once established, they are almost indestructible. The hardy hybrids will survive in exposed sites, and will thrive in either sun or shade and in almost any soil that is not excessively chalky or limy.

All hardy hybrid rhododendrons are evergreen and make broad, dome-shaped shrubs, usually about 2–3m (6–10ft) high and as much across, although some are larger. Pruning is not usually necessary, although overgrown bushes can be cut back in spring; they will reshoot but you will lose that year's flowers.

left The tall *Rhododendron* 'Loderi King George' prefers a slightly sheltered spot, and shade suits its huge pale blooms.

Azaleas

Azaleas are deciduous rhododendrons and their hybrids, but also covers a range of compact evergreen shrubs. They are prized for their vibrant flower colours and fine foliage. Several are also scented.

Deciduous azaleas flower in early and midsummer. They are showy plants, with good-sized flowers in a wonderful colour range, including yellow, orange, pink, scarlet, crimson and many intermediate shades. Many form in clusters (though not as dense or large as a typical rhododendron) but some are scattered singly and liberally all over the plant. The leaves of some forms turn copper and crimson before falling in autumn. Mollis hybrids have large, late, unscented flowers, while Ghent hybrids usually have scented flowers in the early part of summer.

The evergreen azaleas are low, densely branched spreading shrubs with neat leaves and small to medium-sized flowers, freely produced in early and midsummer. Flowers range in colour from white to crimson, with many pink, carmine and scarlet blooms, but there are none of the yellow shades that characterize the taller, more open-branched deciduous azaleas. They are among the most showy of all shrubs when in flower and, being evergreen, give the garden a well-furnished appearance even in winter.

Some of the best evergreen azaleas are 'Addy Wery' (vermilion flowers in late spring); 'Elsie Lee' (red-purple flowers in late spring); 'Hinode-giri' (crimson flowers in spring); 'Hinomayo' (pink flowers mid- to late spring); 'Ima-shojo' (white-pink flowers late winter to early spring); 'Palestrina' (white flowers in late spring).

top left *R. suaveolens* is a rhododendron for the greenhouse or conservatory, a tender species with a sweet fragrance.

Top ten hardy hybrid rhododendrons

'Betty Wormald'
A large plant, to 3m (10ft) high and across, bearing deep rose-pink flowers in late spring to early summer.

'Britannia'
A spreading form, to 2.1m (7ft) high and 1.5m across, with light green leaves and scarlet flowers in early summer.

'Cynthia'
A large plant, to 6m (20ft) high and across, with rose-red flowers in late spring.

'Fastuosum Flore Pleno'
Growing to 4m (12ft) high and acorss, this has large, double, mauve flowers in late spring to early summer.

'Gomer Waterer'
A medium-sized shrub, to 2m (6ft) high and across, with blush-white and gold flowers in late spring and early summer.

'Loder's White'
A popular and reliable cultivar, to 3m (10ft) high and across, with pure white, scented flowers in midsummer.

'Mrs Furnival'
A rounded, fairly compact plant, to 2.1m (7ft) high and across, with rose and maroon flowers in late spring.

'Pink Pearl'
A strongly growing plant, to 4m (12ft) high and across, bearing rose-pink flowers in mid- to late spring.

'Purple Splendour'
A large plant, to 3m (10ft) high and across, and one that will grow in full sun, this has deep purple flowers in late spring to early summer.

'Sappho'
Another plant for full sun, this gets to 3m (10ft) high and across and bears white and maroon flowers in early summer.

Recommended rhododendrons

If you have space for more than one rhododendron in your garden, consider including one or more of the following to increase the range of flower colour and extend the flowering period.

R. augustinii
An evergreen, to 3m (10ft) high and across, with blue flowers, ranging from light to dark, in mid-spring. It will tolerate full sun.

'Blue Diamond'
A compact evergreen plant, to 1.5m (5ft) high and across, bearing violet-blue flowers in mid- to late spring.

R. cinnabarinum
A strongly growing evergreen, to 6m (20ft) tall and 2m (6ft) across, with tubular, orange-red, pendent flowers in mid-spring to early summer.

'Elizabeth'
A neat evergreen form, to 90cm (3ft) high and across, with a mass of bright red flowers in spring.

R. impeditum
A compact evergreen plant, to about 60cm (2ft) high and across, with deep purple-blue flowers in mid- to late spring.

'May Day'
A spreading, rangy evergreen plant, to 1.5m (5ft) high and across, with vivid red flowers in mid-spring. This will grow in full sun.

'Naomi'
A tall evergreen, to 5m (15ft) high and across, with scented flowers in various shades of lilac pink and greenish-yellow in mid-spring.

R. racemosum
A neat evergreen, to 2m (6ft) high and across, bearing plenty of small, rose-pink to white flowers in early to mid-spring.

'Temple Belle'
A tidy everygreen, to 2m (6ft) high and across, with bell-shaped, pink flowers in early to mid-spring.

R. williamsianum
A compact evergreen, to 1.5m (5ft) high and 1.2m (4ft) across, with masses of pale pink to white, bell-shaped flowers in mid- to late spring.

Groundcover shrubs

Include low-growing groundcover shrubs in your garden to enhance the appearance of an otherwise bare area of ground and to help suppress weeds. Evergreens are ideal because the ground is permanently covered, but even deciduous shrubs are useful because the soil is exposed only during the period when weeds are least likely to germinate. Weed seedlings that do germinate usually perish because they are deprived of light when the groundcover comes into leaf in spring. Groundcover shrubs are especially useful for clothing banks and other areas that are not easily planted with grass and mown or that are not cultivated as beds or borders.

Flowering plants for sunny sites

Cultivars of *Erica* and *Calluna* (heaths and heathers) make perhaps the finest flowering groundcover. Those with coloured foliage tend to lack the quality and quantity of flowers of the best of the ordinary forms, but they do make a more interesting groundcover taking the year as a whole. They do best in full sun but will tolerate partial shade.

Helianthemum nummularium spp. (rock rose, sun rose) is ideal for carpeting a sunny bank and just as happy growing in chalky ground. You will find rock roses with flowers in shades of pink, red and yellow, as well as white, with the main flush of flowers in late spring and early summer. They are semi-evergreen, and the winter cover can be rather sparse. Shearing them over immediately after flowering will help keep them bushy.

A good choice for an inaccessible bank, but not a plant for a site where its invasive growth might be a problem, is *Hypericum calycinum* (rose of Sharon). It grows to about 60cm (2ft) high and spreads freely by underground runners (shoots). It is evergreen except in severe winters, but shear it down to just above ground level in spring before growth starts to stimulate fresh shoots. It's a tolerant plant that will do well in shade, where the bright yellow flowers will shine like giant buttercups from midsummer to autumn.

Vinca minor and *V. major* (periwinkle) will grow almost anywhere, but choose a variegated variety because the long stems can look drab in those months of the year when the blue, purple or white flowers are absent.

Bright berries

There are several excellent ground-hugging evergreen cotoneasters, such as *Cotoneaster dammeri*, *C. conspicuus* 'Decorus' and *C. microphyllus*. The deciduous *C. horizontalis* (herringbone cotoneaster) is also sometimes used for groundcover, and this has the bonus of bright autumn tints before the leaves fall. Expect bright red autumn berries from all of them. They are tolerant plants, equally happy in full sun or partial shade.

A dwarf form of the rowan family, *Sorbus reducta*, spreads into a thicket 30cm (12in) high of grey-green leaves and, in autumn, a mass of pinkish-red berries in large clusters.

left The ground-hugging *Cotoneaster dammeri* provides good cover all year, brightened in autumn with scarlet berries.

If you can offer a position with acid soil in partial shade, you will find that *Gaultheria procumbens* (checkerberry, wintergreen) makes a pretty carpet of small evergreen leaves, studded with red berries in autumn and into winter.

Foliage effect

The popular cultivars of *Euonymus fortunei* make attractive evergreen groundcover, and there are plants with gold or white variegation (the leaves may also be tinged pink or red in winter). They all grow well in either sun or shade.

Some of the dwarf hebes will grow in sun or partial shade, and one of the best for carpeting is the silvery *Hebe pinguifolia* 'Pagei'. The small white flowers in late spring and early summer are a bonus, because this neat little plant looks good for most of the year.

Arctostaphylos 'Emerald Carpet' is a low, dense shrub with neat leaves that shine bright green all year. It prefers an acid soil.

Some people think that *Pachysandra terminalis* is a dull, rather uninspiring plant, but it's excellent as a groundcover for shady spots where many plants would not thrive. The glossy leaves reflect back light, and it's tolerant of all but the driest soil. The form 'Variegata' has white-edged leaves, which will help to brighten a dull spot. Make sure the ground does not dry out.

You can create an interesting tapestry of contrasting leaf shape and colour from a variety of groundcover shrubs, as long as you watch that the more vigorous do not overshadow their neighbours.

Creeping climbers

Don't forget that climbing plants do not always have to grow upwards. Forms of *Hedera* (ivy) will grow just as well along the ground as up a support, and in time they will make a dense groundcover in shady places where few other plants thrive. The smaller-leaved forms of *H. helix* are worth considering for a small area, but if you have a larger piece of ground to cover try *Hedera colchica* 'Dentata Variegata', with creamy variegated leaves that show up well in a dark corner. Don't bother pegging down the stems, which will root as they grow, and if an ivy grows beyond its allotted space simply pull up individual stems and cut them off.

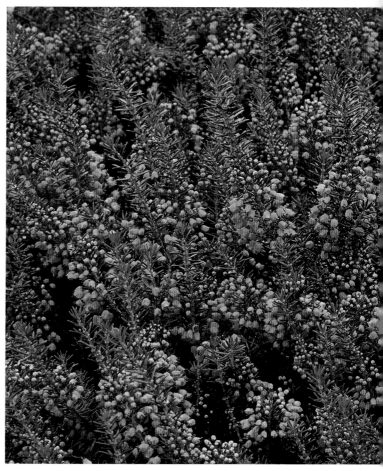

top The glossy gold-edged leaves of *Euonymus fortunei* 'Emerald Gaiety' are equally bright in sun or shade.

right Grow heathers in groups to form a thick, low mass of green. *Erica vagans* 'Birch Glow', a Cornish heath, will tolerate lime.

Hedging plants

Hedges play both a decorative and a utilitarian role in the garden. They can be used to provide privacy and to keep out intruders, to separate one part of the garden from another or to act as a fine background for a border of flowers. They can be clipped in simple or elaborate shapes or left to grow freely – an informal treatment that suits flowering shrubs and roses. If your garden is small, choose a shrub that can be clipped back neatly or you will find that the hedge is taking up valuable space that you want to devote to more ornamental plants.

Conifer hedges

The principal kinds of conifer used for hedging are *Chamaecyparis* and *Cupressus* (cypress), *Thuja* (arborvitae) and *Taxus* (yew). All are evergreens that will withstand frequent clipping, and yew, like *Buxus* (box), is much used for topiary. The most popular hedging cypress, *Chamaecyparis lawsoniana* (Lawson cypress), has rather ferny, green foliage and will make good hedges up to 3m (10ft) high. It's quick-growing, hardy and tolerates most soils. There are numerous cultivars of this cypress, some with lighter green foliage, some blue-green and some golden, all suitable for hedges either by themselves or in mixtures.

Thuja plicata (western red cedar) and *T. occidentalis* (white cedar) grow well in heavy soils, and will need clipping twice a year, in spring and late summer, to keep them neat. Take care with the clippings because they can cause allergies if you have sensitive skin.

Yew is one of the best of all evergreen hedging plants. There are dark green and gold-leaved forms, which can be planted separately or in combination. They are slow-growing and do not need frequent clipping. They are also easy-going and will grow in most conditions, including both chalky and limy soils. They also have the great advantage that, unlike most conifers, they will regenerate from old wood, so even if you cut a yew hard back it will reshoot. Don't forget, though, that all parts of yew are poisonous, but that is the only disadvantage of this wonderful plant.

The hybrid × *Cupressocyparis leylandii* (Leyland cypress) resembles Lawson cypress in many respects but grows almost twice as fast. It cannot be recommended as a hedging plant if you have a small garden – it takes all the nutrients and moisture from the ground around it – nor if you cannot spare the time to clip it back twice or even three or four times a year. Left untrimmed, these thuggish plants are the cause of more disagreements with neighbours than almost anything else.

Deciduous hedges

If you plant a hedge of shrubs that do not retain their leaves all the year, its appearance will change with the seasons, and this can add interest to the garden.

Fagus sylvatica (common beech) is the most popular deciduous garden hedge. It grows rapidly, has such strong stems that it can be used to make a tall yet narrow hedge, and, when trimmed, retains its reddish-brown, dead leaves throughout winter. Beech grows in all well-drained soils, but does especially well in chalky and limy soils. For a tapestry effect, copper and purple beech can be mixed with green-leaved beech, although there are few more attractive sights than a well-maintained hedge of copper beech.

top *Taxus baccata* (yew) clips well, to form a dense, tight hedge. It is always a favourite choice for a formal garden.

Carpinus betulus (common hornbeam) closely resembles beech and does better in clay and other wet soils. Plant and maintain as you would a beech hedge.

Prunus × cistena is a purple-leaved shrub, which makes an excellent small hedge up to about 1.2m (4ft) high. *Crataegus monogyna* (common hawthorn) makes a strong outer barrier and is inexpensive. It is also thorny and so good for deterring intruders and pets.

Small-leaved evergreens

Although the name *Lonicera* is usually associated with honeysuckles, the genus contains some of the most popular small-leaved, fully evergreen hedge shrubs. Two forms are commonly used: *Lonicera nitida*, which has slender stems and little round leaves, and *L. nitida* 'Yunnan', which has stiffer stems and slightly larger leaves. Both thrive in most soils and situations and will make good hedges up to 1.5m (5ft) high.

Buxus sempervirens (box) also has small, round, fully evergreen leaves. It is much favoured for topiary specimens. The cultivar 'Handsworthiensis' is best for hedges to 2.4m (8ft) high and for topiary, while 'Suffruticosa' is more suitable for low box edgings to beds and is often used in knot gardens and to edge herb beds.

Ligustrum ovalifolium (privet) is only fully evergreen in mild winters. The best cultivars are 'Argenteum', which has leaves edged with creamy-white, and 'Aureum', which has bright yellow leaves and is slow-growing. Both will grow practically anywhere and are excellent for hedges 1.2–2.4m (4–8ft) high.

Large-leaved evergreens

The popular *Prunus laurocerasus* (cherry laurel) has large, glossy, dark green leaves. It will grow well in most soils in full sun or dense shade and is an excellent choice for large, broad hedges. *P. lusitanica* (Portugal laurel) has smaller, darker green leaves and is also excellent for a big, thick hedge. Neither can be recommended for small gardens, however, since they are rather sprawling in habit.

Aucuba japonica (spotted laurel) has large, glossy, light-green leaves. It will grow almost anywhere, succeeding especially well in shade even in grimy industrial surroundings, and is excellent for large hedges. There are several good cultivars with variegated foliage: 'Crotonifolia' has yellow speckles on the leaves, and the leaves of 'Sulphurea Marginata' are edged with golden-yellow. This, too, makes a good hedge in a large garden.

Ilex spp. (holly) will make a dense, impenetrable hedge. There are dark green-leaved, golden-variegated and silver-variegated forms, which can be planted separately or in combination. *I. opaca* (American holly) is often used for hedging and comes in many variegated forms. Holly will make good hedges about 1.5–3m (5–10ft) high. Plants are hardy and long-lived, but rather slow-growing.

Ornamental hedges

Many flowering or fruiting shrubs make excellent informal hedges for larger gardens.

Berberis darwinii is neat, evergreen and prickly and has orange flowers in late spring.

B. stenophylla is yellow-flowered and less tidy.

Cotoneaster simonsii is deciduous and has scarlet berries in both autumn and winter.

C. henryanus is evergreen, scarlet-berried and looser in habit.

***Rosa rugosa* (hedgehog rose, ramanas rose)** grows quickly to make a dense, prickly hedge. Bright red hips follow the fragrant flowers.

***Viburnum tinus* (laurustinus)** is evergreen, with pink and white flowers.

below Berberis darwinii
bottom Rosa rugosa

Roses

Roses are probably the best known and most widely grown flowers in the world. They are enormously popular, with many thousand cultivars having been bred from about 150 species. There are numerous societies devoted to them, where enthusiasts can exchange views and information with like-minded gardeners, but even people who have no interest in gardening would recognize a rose and are familiar with them through references in literature and art.

Types of roses

Roses are more versatile plants than many people realize, and breeders are constantly striving to give us an even greater array to choose from. Modern groundcover roses really do cover the ground with a mass of flowers for months; dwarf floribundas are ideal for containers and beds on patios (the term patio rose is often used to described this group), and there are even roses that you can use in hanging baskets. Breeders have improved the disease resistance of many modern roses, and they have also worked hard to achieve a long flowering season. Despite all the exciting developments with modern roses, however,

the old-fashioned shrub roses still take pride of place in many gardens. The flowering season may be shorter than those of their newer cousins, but they often have big, showy blooms and an exquisite scent. With climbers and ramblers, standards and miniatures, there are roses to be used all around the garden.

Bush roses

A rose garden is almost certain to contain several bush roses, a term that is applied to both large-flowered roses (hybrid teas) and cluster-flowered roses (floribundas).

As the name suggests, large-flowered roses produce the largest and most beautifully formed blooms of all, and they have a colour range that lacks only blue and deep black. They are also often highly scented, but their greatest glory comes from their ability to produce continuous crops of flowers from early summer to midwinter. They can be grown in groups or on their own or in a mixed border.

Cluster-flowered roses (floribundas) bear clusters of flowers which look much more informal than large-flowered roses. For greatest impact, they are best grown in beds of one type, although they can, of course, also be placed in mixed borders.

top 'Fritz Nobis' is a rose with old-fashioned appeal. Its scented blooms are followed by a profusion of small red hips.

left Early-flowering and very fragrant, 'Frühlingsgold' is a beautiful rose that grows into a substantial shrub.

right above 'Parkdirektor Riggers' is a glossy-leaved climber with profuse clusters of slightly fragrant blooms.

Climbers and ramblers

A climbing rose can transform even the smallest of gardens with flourishes of colour. These are superb plants for covering house walls, framing windows and doors, climbing up pillars, arches and pergolas, and scrambling into trees. Climbers have a more permanent framework than ramblers, and their flowers range from small to the size of those of a large-flowered bush rose. Rambling roses bear huge trusses carrying hundreds of generally fairly small blooms. If you have room, allow a rambler to grow into a tall tree.

Shrub roses

The term 'shrub rose' is an all-embracing classification that covers a huge range of roses, including species and old-fashioned roses, such as Bourbon, China, Damask, Moss and Tea types. The flowers of shrub roses are mostly well perfumed and many-petalled – including the delightful 'quartered' roses beloved of Old Masters – and are now available in a range of wonderful colours.

Miniature and patio roses

These fascinating roses have small flowers and are compact enough to use for edging borders, planting in rock gardens and growing in containers. There are also dwarf polyantha roses, which are characterized by their bushy, compact habit.

Where to plant roses

If you are planning a bed or border that is dedicated to roses, plant the taller cultivars in the centre of the border and the smaller ones at the outsides. If the border is only seen from one side, plant the tallest roses – 'Queen Elizabeth' and 'Alexander', for example, which can get to over 2m (6ft) – at the back, with medium-sized growers in the centre and low-growing forms in the front row.

Try to plant roses in batches of three to five to form a group of one colour, and stagger the planting within a bed, so that you can always see one rose behind two others.

Do not make the bed any deeper than 1.5m (5ft), otherwise you will have difficulty reaching plants for pruning and deadheading, and keep the roses at least 45cm (18in) from the outside edges of the beds to avoid problems when you are cutting the lawn.

Some roses make good hedges, but do check the height and colour before you place your order. There are also many different roses, such as the patio types 'Sweet Dreams', 'Sweet Magic' and 'Cider Cup' and the older 'Ballerina', with its five-petalled blooms of light pink and white eye, which are ideal for planting in tubs and urns but which may become rather lost in the open garden.

Flower colours

Not only is the classification of rose plants complex, but the flower colours are also described in a particular way, and when you are buying you will often find the following terms used:

Single colour: one colour

Bicolour: the colours on the inside and outside of each petal are different

Blend: two or more colours on each petal

Multicoloured: colours change with age

Hand-painted: the centre is light-coloured and delicately feathered, merging with other colours towards the outside of the bloom

Striped: two or more colours positioned in bands or stripes

Pruning roses

To be maintained at their best, all roses need pruning, but each type of rose is pruned in a slightly different way (see page 170). However, every rosarian has a particular view about the best time to prune, and the only thing that can be said with certainty is that there are no certain rules.

An easy method to follow is to prune established bushes and autumn- and winter-planted roses in early spring, just when growth is beginning but before the leaves appear. Prune bushes that were planted in spring immediately after planting.

It helps to bear in mind the reasons for pruning. These are to remove dead, damaged, diseased and misplaced shoots and to encourage the plant to produce new, strong growths on which the flowers are borne. You should cut back long stems in winter to prevent bushes from being buffeted by the wind during winter storms, which could loosen their roots in the ground.

Flowering times

Roses flower over a surprisingly long period, some just once, others repeatedly. The term single flush, also known as once-flowering, refers to roses that generally have only one flowering period, usually in the latter part of early summer and into midsummer and lasting for several weeks. Occasionally a few flowers appear later, but there are rarely sufficient to create a

How roses grow

1 **Prostrate rose**
   30–38cm (12–15in) or less

2 **Miniature bush**
   38cm (15in) or less

3 **Miniature standard**
   20–30cm (8–12in) stem

4 **Patio rose**
   38cm (15in)

5 **Dwarf bush**
   45–60cm (18–24in)

6 **Bush rose**
   60cm (24in) or more

7 **Half-standard**
   75cm (30in) stem

8 **Full standard**
   90cm (3ft) stem

9 **Weeping standard**
   1.3m (50in) stem

10 **Pillar rose**
   2.1–2.4m (7–8ft)

11 **Miniature climber**
   1.2–2m (4–6ft)

12 **Climber**
   2.1–9m (7–30ft) or more

13 **Rambler**
   2.1–9m (7–30ft) or more

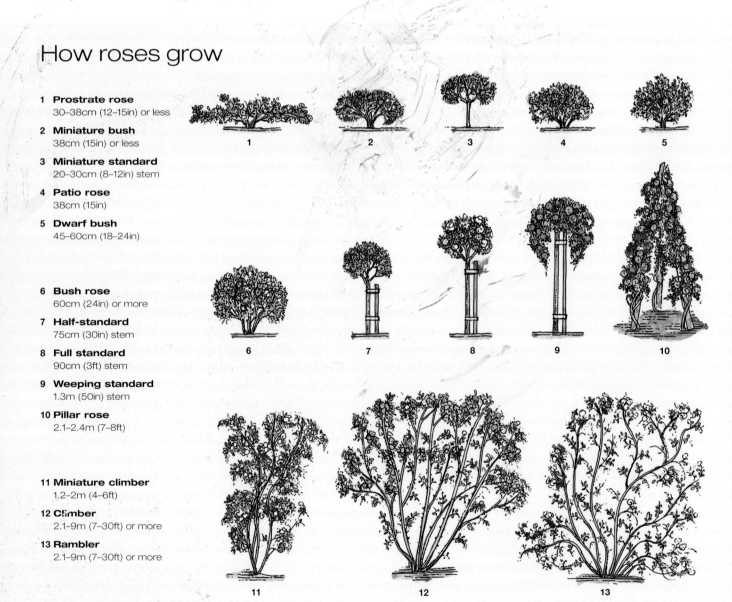

spectacular display. Some ramblers and shrub roses flower in late spring, early summer or late summer.

Repeat-flowering roses, also known as recurrent and remontant roses, have two or more flushes of flowers a year. If a rose produces flowers between the main flushes, it is known as perpetual or continuous flowering, but these terms can create a false impression about the flowering period, which is neither perpetual nor continuous. This repeating habit still gives good value, especially when flowers appear very late in the year.

Patio roses

The types referred to as patio roses are generally compact cluster-flowered (floribunda) roses that are suitable for growing in containers or in patio beds. Although small in stature, most of them create just as much colour as their larger cousins, and most bear a profusion of flowers for many months. Because most are really dwarf forms of ordinary cluster-flowered roses, some catalogues simply describe them as dwarf cultivars.

The boundary line between roses of different types can be blurred, however. Some patio roses are also sold as groundcover roses, and the largest of the miniatures can be almost as tall as the smallest of the patio roses. Most patio roses grow to about 45cm (18in) tall, but some may be 15cm (6in) shorter or taller.

Bedding and edging

Plant patio roses in a single row about 45cm (18in) apart to produce a ribbon of colour. Alternatively, plant in rectangular blocks of colour, using the same spacing between plants. Used like this they have a similar formal effect to traditional summer bedding but without the need for annual replanting.

Favourite roses

There are so many types of rose and so many roses within each group that it is impossible to nominate a 'top ten'. Everyone has a favourite rose. The following are recommendable and a good starting point.

Shrub roses

'Blanc Double de Coubert' (pure white, semi-double, scented flowers); 'Fritz Nobis' (pale salmon pink flowers); 'Frühlingsgold' (creamy-yellow, semi-double, fragrant flowers); 'Graham Thomas' (yellow, double, fragrant flowers); 'Nymphenburg' (salmon pink, semi-double, fragrant flowers).

Climbers and ramblers

'Albertine' (vigorous rambler with pink, double, scented flowers); 'Mme Alfred Carrière' (climber with creamy-white, very fragrant, double flowers); 'Mme Grégoire Staechelin' (vigorous climber with clear pink shaded to carmine, double flowers); 'New Dawn' (vigorous climber with pearly pink, double, fragrant flowers); 'Parkdirektor Riggers' (vigorous climber with deep crimson, semi-double flowers).

Large-flowered (hybrid tea) roses

'Grandpa Dickson' (light yellow, double flowers); 'Peace' (pinkish-yellow, double, fragrant flowers); 'Ruby Wedding' (crimson, double, scented flowers); 'Silver Jubilee' (soft salmon pink, double flowers); 'Whisky Mac' (amber-coloured, double, fragrant flowers).

Scented roses

'Fantin-Latour' (Centifolia rose with pale pink, double flowers); 'Gloire de Dijon' (vigorous climber with dark cream, double flowers); 'Mme Hardy' (Damask climber or shrub with beautfiul white, double flowers); 'Mme Isaac Pereire' (Bourbon climber or shrub with double, dark pink flowers); 'Zéphirine Drouhin' (thornless Bourbon climber or shrub with double, dark pink flowers).

Old-fashioned roses

'Charles de Mills' (Gallica rose with crimson-maroon, double, fragrant flowers); 'Ispahan' (Damask rose with clear pink, double, fragrant flowers); 'Mousseline' (Moss rose with blush-pink, semi-double, fragrant flowers); R. moschata (musk rose; clear pink, single to semi-double, scented flowers); R. gallica 'Versicolor' (rosa mundi rose; semi-double, pale pink flowers with crimson stripes).

above 'Whisky Mac'

below 'Mme Hardy'

Climbers

Climbers fulfil an essential part in the furnishing of a well-organized garden and can even play a dominant role in determining its character. Including the vertical, not just the horizontal, space in your garden can hugely increase its interest and the variety of plants that you grow. It is quite possible, even in the limited space of a small town garden, to create an air of jungle-like profusion by the generous use of some vigorous climbing plants.

Types of climber

Climbers may be shrubby, with more or less permanent woody stems, as is the case with *Lonicera* spp. (honeysuckle), roses and wisteria; they may be herbaceous perennials, with soft stems dying back to ground level each winter, as happens to *Lathyrus grandiflorus* (everlasting pea); or they may be annuals, completing their growth in one season and then dying, as happens with *Tropaeolum majus* (nasturtium) and *Lathyrus odoratus* (sweet pea). Some kinds, such as honeysuckle, twine themselves around any available support, even quite large objects such as the trunks of

trees. Others, such as clematis and sweet pea, climb by means of tendrils, which cling most readily to string, wire or trellis. Yet other types of climber, including *Hedera* (ivy) and ampelopsis, will attach themselves securely to walls and other smooth surfaces by means of aerial roots or adhesive discs. Roses and various forms of *Rubus* (bramble) do not actively climb, but rather sprawl through other plants and gain some support from their thorns.

top Gardeners are often concerned about the damage that ivy can cause to the structure on which it is growing, but on sound brick or stonework and mortar, no harm will ensue.

How climbers climb

1 **Twining climbers**
   Some, such as ***Lonicera*** **spp. (honeysuckle)**, twine themselves around a frame or wires by their growing tips.

2 **Tendril climbers**
   Others, such as ***Lathyrus odoratus*** **(sweet pea)**, use tendrils to hold them up.

3 **Aerial roots**
   Some, including ***Hedera*** **spp. (ivy)**, use aerial roots to climb and do not need any other support.

4 **Adhesive pads**
   Parthenocissus **spp. (Virginia creeper)** uses adhesive pads to attach itself to rough surfaces.

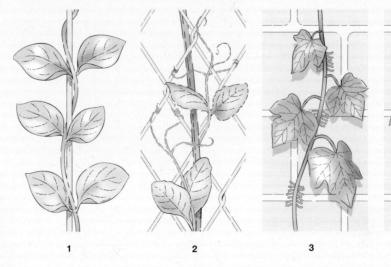

1   2   3   4

Top 20 climbers

Akebia quinata (chocolate vine)
A semi-evergreen, hardy climber, with pale purple, vanilla-scented flowers in spring followed by sausage-shaped fruit, each to 10cm (4in) long.

Aristolochia macrophylla (Dutchman's pipe)
Vigorous and easy to grow, with heart-shaped deciduous leaves and inconspicuous flowers whose odd, curling shape nevertheless make them a talking point.

Clematis
Different members of this huge and very popular genus flower in every month of the year – see page 86.

Hedera canariensis 'Gloire de Marengo'
A very handsome ivy with cream, grey and green variegated evergreen foliage.

Humulus lupulus 'Aureus' (golden hop)
A perennial, twining climber, with bright golden-yellow foliage.

Hydrangea anomala subsp. petiolaris (climbing hydrangea)
A deciduous plant, climbing by means of aerial roots, with clusters of white flowers in summer.

Itea ilicifolia
A lax wall shrub, rather than a true climber, but invaluable on a shady, sheltered wall. It has glossy foliage, like soft holly leaves, and, in late summer, long cream catkins.

Jasminum officinale (common jasmine)
A vigorous, deciduous, twining climber with beautifully scented white flowers in summer to early autumn.

Lathyrus grandiflorus (everlasting pea)
A tough perennial relation of the sweet pea, which climbs to about 2m (6ft) with pinkish-purple pea-like flowers.

Lonicera periclymenum 'Belgica' (early Dutch honeysuckle)
A very vigorous, deciduous, twining climber, with fragrant, red-streaked, white flowers that turn yellow and are borne in mid- to late summer.

Parthenocissus quinquefolia (Virginia creeper)
A strong, woody, deciduous climber, with outstanding red autumn colours.

Passiflora caerulea (passion flower)
Sadly not reliably hardy, this tendril climber has wonderfully exotic summer blooms.

Pileostegia viburnoides
Useful large evergreen with big heads of creamy flowers that make it look rather like a climbing viburnum.

Roses
See page 81.

Schisandra rubriflora
A medium-sized deciduous climber with bright, fresh foliage hung with broad bells of tomato-coloured flowers in mid-spring.

above Vitis 'Brandt'

Solanum crispum 'Glasnevin' (Chilean potato vine)
Large, long-stemmed shrub usually grown like a climber, covered in showy clusters of little lilac flowers over a very long season.

Trachelospermum jasminoides
A most beautiful twining evergreen climber for a warm wall. Highly fragrant white flowers have crimped, propellor-shaped petals.

Vitis 'Brant'
A woody, deciduous climber, related to the grape vine, with purple foliage and black, edible fruit in autumn.

Vitis cognetiae (glory vine)
A substantial vine with large round downy leaves that fulfils its common name in autumn with a glorious show of scarlet, claret and maroon.

Wisteria floribunda 'Alba'
A strongly growing, deciduous, twining climber that bears elegant, pendent racemes, to 60cm (2ft) long, of white flowers in early summer.

below Clematis armandii

Choosing and using climbers

Climbing foliage is particularly useful for clothing unsightly buildings and blending them into the garden scene. Types of *Hedera* (ivy), *Vitis* spp. (vine) and species of *Parthenocissus* (Virginia creeper) will all quickly grow and cover the building or wall against which they are grown. *Parthenocissus quinquefolia* (Virginia creeper) and *P. tricuspidata* (Boston ivy) have the added advantage of stunning crimson autumn foliage, as does *Vitis coignetiae*, the aptly named crimson glory vine.

Other recommended foliage climbers include *Actinidia kolomikta*, which has startling pink- and white-tipped leaves. It also produces cup-shaped, white flowers in summer, which are eye-catching against dark walls and fences.

For a spectacular show *Passiflora caerulea* (passion flower) has few peers. This climber produces truly exotic-looking flowers consisting of white, sometimes pink-flushed, outer petals and a circle of fringed inner petals, which are white, darkening to pale blue or purple at the tips. The centre of each flower is surrounded by a band of dark blue or purple.

Fremontodendron californicum (flannel bush) is another spectacular climber, bearing bright yellow, saucer-shaped flowers from late spring to mid-autumn. It is also evergreen, making it doubly useful. It is not reliably hardy, but brings an exotic look to a warm, sheltered wall.

Laburnum × *watereri* 'Vossii' produces long, drooping panicles of deep yellow, pea-like flowers in early summer. Although this is really classified as a tree, young stems can be trained over an arch or pergola to create a dense tunnel of shimmering colour. Remember that all parts of laburnums are poisonous, and if you have young children you may want to delay planting it until they have grown out of the habit of putting interesting-looking things in their mouths.

Climbers for fragrance

There are many scented climbers to choose from, perfect for warm alfresco evenings. Wisterias have beautiful, delicately perfumed pale mauve or white flowers in long, hanging panicles in early summer. *Jasminum officinale* (common jasmine) produces clusters of very fragrant, pink-tinged white flowers from summer to autumn. Another favourite, *Lonicera*

left Wisteria's graceful racemes are all too short-lived, although there is sometimes a smaller autumn flowering.

top The unmistakable form of the passion flower was used to relate the story of Christ's Passion.

(honeysuckle), produces delicately scented clusters of flowers ranging in colour from yellow and orange through to white and pink. All are beautiful, but not all the newer ones are scented. Cultivars of *Lonicera periclymenum* have a strong classic honeysuckle fragrance, and *L. japonica* 'Halliana' is a highly fragrant, pale-flowered evergreen.

Aspect

When you are choosing climbers for planting against houses or high walls, the direction that they will face will be a crucial factor because climbers on shaded walls will get little direct sunshine; those on some sunny walls may get too much; and those on walls with sun for part of the day may be exposed to cold winds. The problem hardly arises with fences, since plants quickly rise above them. In addition, the soil close to house walls can be dry, and until climbers become established they may need regular watering.

Training wall plants

Shrubs such as *Pyracantha* spp. (firethorn), *Hydrangea anomala* subsp. *petiolaris* (climbing hydrangea), ceanothus, *Chaenomeles japonica* (Japanese quince) and *Cotoneaster horizontalis* (herringbone cotoneaster) can readily be trained against walls and, because they have stiff stems, are almost self-supporting. All the same, trellis or wires will greatly facilitate the training of such plants, since young growths have a natural tendency to grow forwards, away from the wall or fence, and they can be drawn back towards the support and tied in. All supports should be fixed at least 5cm (2in) from the wall so that the growth, tendrils and ties can go round them.

Climbers for special locations

When choosing a climber to grow against a house or wall, always consider how much sunlight it will receive.

For shady walls

- *Akebia quinata* (chocolate vine)
- *Celastrus* spp. (bittersweet, staff vine)
- *Hedera* spp. (ivy)
- *Humulus lupulus* (hop)
- *Hydrangea anomala* subsp. *petiolaris* (climbing hydrangea)
- *Jasminum* spp. (jasmine)
- *Lonicera* spp. (honeysuckle)
- *Parthenocissus* spp. (Virginia creeper)
- *Schizophragma hydrangeoides*
- *Tropaeolum speciosum* (flame creeper)

above *Parthenocissus* spp. (Virginia creeper)

For sunny walls

- *Actinidia kolomikta*
- *Campsis* spp. (trumpet vine, trumpet creeper)
- *Clematis* (some spp. and cultivars)
- *Eccremocarpus scaber* (Chilean glory flower)
- *Ipomoea* spp. (morning glory)
- *Lathyrus* spp.
- *Passiflora* spp. (passion flower, granadilla)
- *Solanum crispum* (Chilean potato tree)
- *Tropaeolum tuberosum*
- *Wisteria* spp.

below *Clematis texensis* 'Gravetye Beauty'

Clematis

Clematis are among the most valuable of all garden climbers. There are many species and hundreds of cultivars, differing in vigour, time of flowering and the size and colour of their blooms, and it is possible to have a clematis in flower from spring to autumn, and some may even flower in winter if the climate is not too harsh.

Thanks to the enormous choice, something can be selected for almost every possible purpose, and there are also several herbaceous clematis, which die back in winter like other herbaceous plants. Climbing clematis may be broadly divided into small- and large-flowering kinds, and understanding the different types of clematis will help you to appreciate the different pruning requirements (see page 166) and provide inspiration for a collection of clematis that will provide interest for most of the year.

Early-flowering species

The plants in this group flower on shoots produced the previous season, so pruning is always modest and never done before they flower in spring. Both *Clematis alpina* and *C. macropetala* have little, nodding, bell-shaped blue or soft mauve-pink flowers in mid- and late spring. *C. montana*, which has masses of small white or pink flowers in early summer, is one of the most vigorous of all clematis, but can be kept in check by shortening side growths in early autumn.

Don't grow these clematis through shrubs that require regular pruning, or you will find there will be a conflict of requirements.

top The many-petalled flowers of *Clematis macropetala* 'Blue Bird' form a mass of frilly tutus in mid-spring.

left *Clematis* 'Nelly Moser' is an old favourite. It prefers to be out of full sun, which fades its two-tone colouring.

Early, large-flowered varieties

Large-flowered hybrid clematis are grown for the size and beauty of the flowers, which appear mainly in early and midsummer. 'Nelly Moser', 'The President' and 'Lasurstern' are examples. They flower on shoots produced the previous year, so are pruned only when necessary and not severely in spring.

Late-flowering species and cultivars

Late-flowering clematis, such as *C. viticella* and related cultivars and *C.* 'Jackmanii' and related cultivars, bloom in late summer and into autumn on shoots produced in the current year. These are pruned to within about 30cm (12in) of the ground in spring to encourage flowers on new stems that are not too tall.

Evergreen clematis

Clematis cirrhosa has evergreen, fern-like leaves and white, bell-shaped flowers between midwinter and early spring. Plant *C. armandii*, which has clusters of fragrant white flowers, to follow in early and mid-spring. These species are not as hardy as the other types of clematis and will do best if they are grown by a sheltered wall.

Herbaceous clematis

Less well known than the climbing clematis are the herbaceous and semi-herbaceous forms. *C. heracleifolia* is a woody plant, which does not die back completely in winter. It has purplish-blue flowers in late summer to early autumn; the form 'Wyevale' has fragrant, mid-blue flowers. The herbaceous *C. integrifolia* has violet-blue flowers from early summer through to early autumn.

Favourite clematis

Florida group

'Belle of Woking' (double, mauve flowers from spring to late summer); **'Duchess of Edinburgh'** (double, white flowers in early sussmmer, semi-double flowers later).

Jackmanii group

'Comtesse de Bouchaud' (single, soft pink flowers in summer); **'Gipsy Queen'** (single, violet-purple flowers from midsummer to early autumn); **'Jackmanii Superba'** (deep violet-purple flowers from midsummer to early autumn); **'Perle d'Azur'** (pale blue flowers from midsummer to autumn); **'Star of India'** (violet and red flowers in midsummer).

Lanuginosa group

'Beauty of Worcester' (violet-blue double flowers in late spring and single flowers in late summer); **'Henryi'** (white flowers in summer); **'Lady Northcliffe'** (lavender flowers from early to late summer; **'Mrs Cholmondeley'** (pale blue flowers from spring to early summer); **'William Kennett'** (deep lavender and red flowers in early summer).

below Clematis 'Duchess of Edinburgh'

Patens group

'Barbara Jackman' (blue-purple and magenta flowers in summer); **'Lasurstern'** (purple-blue flowers in early summer); **'Nelly Moser'** (mauve and carmine flowers in early summer).

Texensis group

'Étoile Rose' (violet flowers from midsummer to late autumn); **'Gravetye Beauty'** (red flowers from midsummer to autumn).

above Clematis 'Ernest Markham'

Viticella group

'Ernest Markham' (petunia red flowers in summer; **'Huldine'** (pearly white and mauve-pink flowers in summer); **'Lady Betty Balfour'** (violet-blue flowers in late summer and early autumn); **'Ville de Lyon'** (carmine flowers in midsummer).

Perennials

Large borders devoted solely to herbaceous perennials may be old-fashioned, but perennial plants are as desirable as ever in the modern garden, as mixed borders, as groundcover, as focal points and planted in containers.

If your garden is small you may prefer to use hardy perennials in a mixed border containing some shrubby plants and annuals, but if you have space for an island bed or a border of herbaceous plants you will be able to grow some of the most striking of all cultivated plants.

Not all hardy perennials are truly herbaceous in the sense that they die back to the ground for winter. Some non-woody evergreens, such as bergenias (elephant's ears), hellebores, some irises and the delightful sedge *Carex oshimensis* 'Evergold', are perennials. Indeed, it is a positive advantage to include a sprinkling of these plants to provide some winter interest in the garden.

Some border plants can even be used in containers; others make pleasing groundcover in front of shrubs; a few – such as the more stately cultivars of *Kniphofia* (red-hot poker) or *Acanthus* spp. (bear's breeches) – can be used as isolated specimens to form focal points. You'll find there's always space somewhere for a few choice perennials.

Using perennials

An open, sunny position is best for beds or borders devoted exclusively to herbaceous perennials, because these conditions will suit the majority of species, but there is no shortage of kinds that will grow in shade, as long as it is not too dense.

Most herbaceous plants flower for three or four weeks each year, so, if a bed or border devoted exclusively to them is to remain interesting, you must choose plants with different flowering times and place them so that so that they can be seen and admired as they come into bloom and are not hidden by other, taller plants that are beginning to go over. Herbaceous borders are usually planted with irregular groups of a

species or cultivar, with the taller plants at the back or in the centre of the border, and the shorter ones in front or around the edge. To avoid a too-regulated, tiered effect, add a few 'see-through' tall plants, such as feathery grasses, and *Verbena bonariensis* near the front. It is better to make individual groups long and narrow rather than broad since they will be less conspicuous when they are not in bloom.

Some perennials add interest to a border even when not in flower – the purple-stained leaf clumps of heuchera, for example, or the silvery spikes of ornamental thistles – while others such as *Papaver* (poppies) die away messily leaving an ugly gap. Anticipate this by planting a late developer in front to mask the hole, or by using plants in pots to fill the space. Lilies can make a great contribution to the late-summer border in this way.

top Golden rudbeckias and an airy perennial grass rise over pink spires of persicaria to create a colourful late-summer scene.

Top 20 best perennials

Acanthus spinosus
This is a tall, stately perennial, as popular for its foliage as for its summer flowers. The arching leaves are deeply cut with pointed ends, while the flowers above the leaves are pale mauve and white.

Achillea filipendulina 'Gold Plate'
For a splash of summer colour, include a clump of this cheerful plant in your border. It has bright golden-yellow flowers above fern-like leaves.

Anemone x hybrida 'Honorine Jobert'
A good choice for early autumn interest, this anemone produces simple, single white flowers with yellow centres from summer until autumn. The dark green leaves are deeply divided.

Aster x frikartii 'Mönch'
This is one of the most popular of the autumn-flowering perennials, and the daisy-like mauve-blue flowers last well into late autumn.

Astilbe x arendsii 'Brautschleier'
The feathery plumes of delicate white flowers are borne in summer above finely cut, fern-like, bright green leaves.

Campanula persicifolia (peach-leaved bellflower)
Lovely, cup-shaped flowers, in shades from white to lilac blue, are borne on erect stems from early summer onwards.

below Achillea filipendulina 'Gold Plate'

Delphinium Black Knight Group
This excellent form of these favourite plants of the summer borders has majestic spires of deep purple flowers with black eyes.

Euphorbia polychroma
Good for spring interest, this plant has bright acid-green flowers produced above bright green leaves in spring. The whole plant forms pleasing cushions of bright colour.

Hosta sieboldiana var. elegans
An excellent foliage plant, this hosta has huge, puckered, blue-grey leaves and pale lilac flowers in early summer.

Kirengeshoma palmata
Dainty, nodding, pale yellow flowers are borne on erect stems in late summer and early autumn. This does well in moist, acid soil in a shady spot.

Kniphofia 'Little Maid' (red-hot poker)
The subtly coloured pale yellow flowers are borne in spires up to 60cm (2ft) tall in late summer to early autumn.

Leucanthemum x superbum (Shasta daisy)
This reliable perennial has daisy-like, white flowers from summer into autumn. It will grow in any position in moist but well-drained soil.

Liatris spicata 'Kobold' (gayfeather)
The leafy stems are topped with bottlebrush, deep rosy-mauve flowers in summer.

Nepeta x faassenii (catmint)
A good, scented choice for the border. The foliage is a soft, greyish-green and the flower spikes are covered with purple-blue flowers from late spring through to early summer.

Paeonia 'Sarah Bernhardt'
The fragrant flowers of this herbaceous peony are fully double and a most beautiful shade of pale pink, lightly touched with silvery white. They are borne in summer, above the mid-green leaves.

Papaver orientale 'Black and White'
Creating a truly spectacular display in early summer, this poppy has large flowers of white, papery petals, each with a deep crimson-black splodge at the centre.

above Liatris spicata 'Kobold' (gayfeather)

Penstemon 'White Bedder'
Large, funnel-shaped, white flowers are carried on erect stems from midsummer to mid-autumn. This cultivar is sometimes available under the evocative name 'Snow Storm'.

Phlox paniculata 'White Admiral'
A reliable plant, producing dense clusters of white flowers on top of erect stems from summer through to early autumn.

Salvia x superba (sage)
This ornamental sage has deep violet and crimson flowers in summer, which are held on spikes above oval, dull green leaves.

Sedum 'Herbstfreude'
This delightful perennial is a must for any planting scheme. The attractive fleshy leaves are greyish-green in colour and provide spring interest, while the flat, saucer-shaped flowerheads or unopened green flowers provide summer interest. Towards late summer, these open out into bright pink flowers to create an eye-catching patch of colour in the garden. By autumn, they have turned a deep coppery-red.

Mixed borders

If space in your garden is limited, it makes good sense to have a mixed border that includes both shrubs and perennials. You can choose the best of both to create a border with a long period of interest and use the opportunity to introduce some unusual and eye-catching plant combinations.

A mixed border always has a structure, even in winter, and even if most of the shrubs are deciduous. Woody plants provide height and shape, and there may even be small patches of colour from those that flower in winter. With early bulbs and perhaps winter-flowering hellebores, and the brave *Iris unguicularis*, the border should not look totally bleak through the coldest months.

Designing a border

The best mixed borders appear well integrated, with plants of different kinds blending together. Try to avoid positioning a row of shrubs at the back with the perennials in front: that's just what it will look like. Use some tall perennials towards the back, such as some of the taller cultivars of *Kniphofia* (red-hot poker), with their stiff orange, yellow and red flower spikes, and *Crambe cordifolia*), which will create a cloud of little white flowers above the other plants. Use a few small shrubs – *Caryopteris × clandonensis*, *Ceratostigma plumbaginoides* (hardy plumbago), *Potentilla fruticosa* cultivars (shrubby cinquefoil) and *Perovskia atriplicifolia* (Russian sage), for example – towards the front of the border. A few plants of *Helianthemum* spp. (rock rose, sun rose) can be placed along the front edge of the border.

If the border is a large one, almost any shrub or perennial can be included in the scheme, but where space is at a premium it's important to choose plants that integrate well. Place the emphasis on shrubs that look as if they could almost be herbaceous plants – such as perovskias (Russian sage) and shrubby peonies – and use perennials that will stand their ground against the woody and usually more dominant shrubs.

Don't overlook the importance of foliage. Choose shrubs with bright or interesting foliage rather than those with dull leaves. The golden form of mock orange, *Philadelphus coronarius* 'Aureus', will make a bright background early in the year, although the colour deteriorates as the season progresses, and by cutting out one-third of the oldest stems each year after flowering you can restrain its height. *Ligustrum vulgare* 'Aureum' (golden privet) serves a similar purpose and can be kept compact by regular pruning.

Grey-leaved *Brachyglottis compacta* and *B.* Dunedin Group 'Sunshine' will blend in with most mixed borders, their yellow daisies not looking out of place. Low-growing *Pachysandra terminalis* 'Variegata' will relieve a dull, not too dry, spot beneath a taller shrub.

left A mixed planting of shrubs, biennials and perennials means that this border will have a long sucession of colour and interest.

top This planting, featuring alstroemeria, achillea, heuchera and stachys, is especially suited to a free-draining site.

Creating a mixed border

This planting will suit any sunny border with a sheltered yet fairly open aspect and with light, well-drained, slightly alkaline soil. The herbaceous plants may die down in winter, but the evergreens will provide much-needed winter interest.

1 **Phlox paniculata 'Sandringham'**
A perennial with cyclamen-pink flowers from mid- to late summer.

2 **Foeniculum vulgare 'Purpureum' (purple fennel)**
A perennial, this has feathery, dark purple-bronze fronds and clusters of little yellow flowers in summer.

3 **Alcea rosea (hollyhock)**
An upright perennial with spikes of single or double, funnel-shaped, cream, pink, apricot or red flowers in summer.

4 **Sidalcea 'Rose Queen'**
A perennial, producing silky-pink, mallow-shaped flowers from midsummer on.

5 **Cimicifuga simplex 'Brunette' (bugbane)**
This perennial has deep purple leaves with erect, white cats'-tail-like flowerheads in late summer.

6 **Prunus sargentii (sargent cherry)**
A deciduous tree, to about 20m (70ft) tall, with coppery-red leaves that fade to green for summer and then colour well for autumn. The single, pink flowers are borne in spring.

7 **Elaeagnus x ebbingei**
An evergreen shrub with grey-green foliage.

8 **Abelia x grandiflora**
An evergreen or semi-evergreen shrub. The leaves are green, tinged red, and the white, pink-tinged flowers are borne from late summer to early autumn.

9 **Helichrysum italicum subsp. serotinum (curry plant)**
A semi-evergreen shrub, this has silvery, aromatic foliage and produces yellow flowers in summer.

10 **Achillea ptarmica 'The Pearl'**
A perennial with bright green leaves and small white buttons of flowers in early to late summer.

11 **Campanula lactiflora (milky bellflower)**
An upright perennial, to 1.2m (4ft) tall, with lavender-blue flowers from summer to early autumn.

12 **Anaphalis triplinervis (pearl everlasting)**
This clump-forming perennial has greyish-white leaves and white, papery flowers in mid- to late summer.

13 **Physostegia virginiana 'Bouquet Rose' (obedient plant)**
A spreading perennial with bright green foliage. The pale pink, tubular flowers appear in late summer and last into autumn.

14 **Aster thomsonii 'Nanus'**
A reliable perennial with grey-green foliage. The lavender-blue, yellow-centred, daisy-like flowers appear from summer to autumn.

15 **Artemisia pontica (Roman wormwood)**
This attractive perennial has feathery, silver-grey, highly aromatic foliage.

16 **Armeria maritima 'Ruby Glow' (sea thrift)**
An evergreen perennial with clump-forming foliage and small, deep pink, pompom flowers, borne from midsummer to autumn.

17 **Dianthus 'Doris'**
This modern garden pink is a semi-evergreen perennial; the grass-like, grey leaves and sweetly scented, pink flowers are borne from midsummer on.

18 **Platycodon grandiflorus 'Mariesii'**
A compact perennial with deep-blue, cup-shaped flowers in late summer.

19 **Solidago 'Queenie' (dwarf golden rod)**
A perennial with plumes of yellow flowers that are borne in late summer.

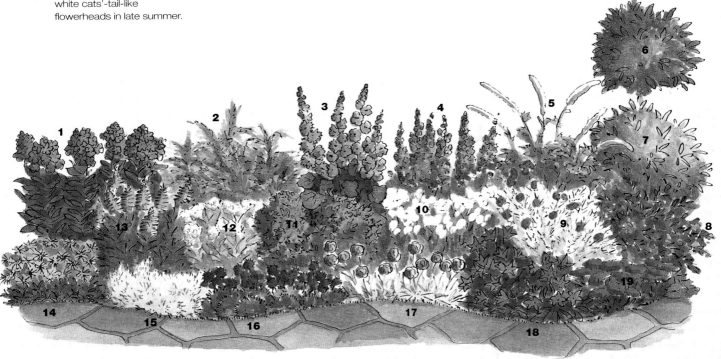

Carnations and pinks

Carnations and pinks are famed for the scent as well as the beauty of their flowers, and no traditional herbaceous border is complete without at least one. There are many kinds, however, and it's important to know that some are much more suitable for the border than others are.

Although most carnations and pinks can be grown in most gardens, they do particularly well in alkaline (chalky) soils. If the ground in your garden is on the acid side of neutral – that is, if the pH is below 6.5 – it's worth adding some limestone chippings in the planting area to make it more alkaline.

Border carnations

These plants are derived from *Dianthus caryophyllus* (wild carnation) and generally have a relatively short flowering peak in midsummer, although in good years a few blooms will continue to be produced until the end of summer. The flowers are usually heavily scented and normally self-coloured although some are picotees (with petals outlined in a second, darker colour). Unfortunately, they require staking to keep the flowering stems upright.

What colour is it?

The terminology that has developed to describe the coloration of pinks and carnations can be mystifying.

Self: the flower is all one colour

Fancy: the flower has stripes, streaks, flecks and spots in a second colour

Picotee: the edge of each petal is finely margined in a second colour

Bicolour: each flower has a central splodge or eye of a second colour

Laced: it has a zone of a second colour around the centre and the second colour extends to edge each petal

Old-fashioned (Old World) pinks

These pinks are believed to be descended, at least in part, from *Dianthus plumarius*. There are many flower colours and forms, ranging from selfs (single colours), bicolours (outer zone one colour, the eye or central zone a different one), laced (central zone extended to form a loop around the edge of each petal) to fancies (irregular markings).

Old-fashioned pinks flower in early summer, so the season is shorter than that of modern pinks, but the scent is usually more intense.

Modern pinks

This group of pinks originated when plant breeders crossed the old-fashioned pink and perpetual-flowering carnations (which flower over a long period but are generally regarded as greenhouse plants). In flowering terms these are an improvement on the old-fashioned pinks, because as well as blooming during early and midsummer they often flower again in early autumn. They come in all the same forms as old-fashioned pinks but not all are as sweetly scented. The magenta 'Denis', frilly white 'Haytor' and 'Alice', white with a dark eye, all have a good fragrance.

above left *Dianthus* x *allwoodii* 'Fair Folly' (also known as 'Constance Finnis') is a pretty modern pink.

top 'Alyson' is not a common dianthus, but is well worth seeking out from a specialist nursery.

Evergreen perennials

Your borders will look attractive and interesting all winter long if you include a few evergreen border plants. Next time you're shopping for perennials, look out for plants that retain their foliage through winter. The reliable bergenias (elephant's ears) remain bright and glossy all year, some taking on brilliant red tints when they're frosted. Evergreen ferns such as *Phyllitis scolopendrium* (hart's tongue fern) and hellebores will also add winter greenery but quite different shapes and textures. Many grasses (see page 100) keep a presence all winter, some softening to a russet brown, while the blue-tinted *Festuca glauca* becomes more intensely blue.

When you're planting, don't space out the evergreens around the border so that they remain as isolated plants when the other perennials die down in autumn. Arrange them in several groups to create pockets of winter interest and link them with drifts of winter bulbs such as snowdrops and winter aconites.

top The thick, serrated leaves of *Helleborus argutifolius* make it an interesting plant even when it is not in flower.

Best evergreen foliage

Green

- *Bergenia* **spp. (elephant's ears)**;
- *Dryopteris affinis* **(golden male fern)**
- *Epimedium* **spp. (barrenwort, bishop's mitre)**
- *Helleborus* **spp.**
- *Iris unguicularis* **(winter-flowering iris)**
- *Liriope muscari* **(lilyturf)**
- *Persicaria affinis*
- *Phyllostachys bambusoides* **(giant timber bamboo)**
- *Sisyrinchium striatum*

Gold

- *Acorus gramineus* **'Ogon'**
- *Carex hachijoensis* **'Evergold'**

Silver and grey

- *Dianthus* **spp. (carnation and pink)**
- *Festuca amethystina* **(large blue fescue)**

Red, purple and black

- *Ajuga* **spp. (bugle)**
- *Bergenia* **spp. (elephant's ears)**
- *Euphorbia amygdaloides* **'Purpurea'**
- *Heuchera micrantha* var. *diversifolia* **'Palace Purple'**
- *Ophiopogon planiscapus* **'Nigrescens'**

below Bergenia 'Abendglut'

Bold perennials

Every garden needs at least a couple of large or bold plants to act as focal points or as 'statements' within a border. These plants sometimes act as punctuation points, arresting the eye and preventing the border from being taken for granted. In a large garden they help to tie the garden together visually.

Feathers and plumes

A focal point plant does not have to be bright and colourful. Sometimes sheer size is enough, and in a shaded area a white plant can be more conspicuous than a coloured one. Among the best of these is *Aruncus dioicus* (goatsbeard), which looks like a large white spiraea. The individual flowers are tiny, but the plumes are big and bold, to 50cm (20in) long, and are borne on stems to 2m (6ft) long. They stand out well against dark trees or shrubs in the background. This is a plant for a big garden, where its midsummer flowers and large leaves help to fill up a space.

The plumes of *Macleaya microcarpa* and *M. cordata*, also rising to 2m (6ft) or more, are pinkish-buff, so they need a lighter background as a backdrop. The visual effect of *Crambe cordifolia* is more cloud-like but no less imposing. The small, white flowers are fragrant, but the first thing you notice is the hazy mound of white, about 2m (6ft) tall and almost as much across.

Eye-catching grasses

The various forms of *Cortaderia* (pampas grass) are among the best known of the large grasses. The species *Cortaderia selloana* will send its silvery-white plumes up to 2.4m (8ft) or more, and as the evergreen clump gradually expands in girth this is not a plant to go unnoticed. It is often planted in isolation – as a feature in the centre of a lawn, for example – but it can look rather stark. If you place it in a border, you will be able to mask the base with more interesting plants. If the species is too tall, try 'Pumila', which grows to about 1.2m (4ft) high; if it is not tall enough, look out for 'Sunningdale Silver', which will get to 3m (10ft).

Arundo donax (giant reed) is suitable only for the back of a large border, where it can be grown for its attractive foliage. If conditions suit it – moist soil and a position in full sun – it will grow to 5m (15ft) tall.

A more realistic choice for most gardens will be some of the cultivars of *Miscanthus sinensis*. 'Zebrinus' (zebra grass) has horizontal creamy stripes on the leaves – the variegation becomes more noticeable as the season progresses – and attractive, fan-shaped flowerheads in autumn. At only 1.2m (4ft), this is a more modest plant but will still make a large clump. Other forms of miscanthus are of similar stature and are grown mainly for their flowers. 'Silberfeder', a taller cultivar, growing to about 2m (6ft), has plumes of pale pink-brown flowers that last throughout autumn and into winter.

Two grasses that are undistinguished out of flower but stunning once the long-lasting flower spikes appear are *Deschampsia caespitosa* (tufted hair grass) and *Stipa gigantea* (golden oats, Spanish oats). The deschampsia grows to about 2m (6ft), while the stipa will reach 2.4m (8ft). Both look like stunning fireworks as the autumn sun catches the flowerheads.

right *Aruncus dioicus* thrives in well-drained soil. It is grown for its hummocks of broad, fern-like leaves and plumes of white flowers.

Conversation piece

Eye-catching perennials will create a focal point in your garden and provide visitors with something to talk about.

The stunning **Rheum palmatum 'Atrosanguineum'** is a kind of ornamental rhubarb that always attracts attention. The leaves resemble those of a large rhubarb, and the tall, crimson flower spikes are borne on stems to 2m (6ft) or more.

Even bigger is the giant of perennials, **Gunnera manicata**. It needs damp ground to grow but will throw up enormous leaves in spring, each one to 2m (6ft) across on stems of a similar height. It is an awe-inspiring sight.

In a sun-drenched spot there are few more dramatic perennials than the cannas. These will need winter protection, but in a single season can shoot up to 2m (6ft) or more, topped by exotically brilliant flowers. Most have bright green leaves, but there are also some eye-catchers with variegated foliage.

above Gunnera manicata
above right Rheum palmatum 'Astrosanguineum'
right Canna 'Rosemond Coles'

Launching rockets

Some big or bold plants have tall flower spikes that seem to demand attention. The popular red and orange *Kniphofia* cultivars (red-hot poker) simply shout out to be noticed, but even these are outdone by *Eremurus robustus* (foxtail lily, desert candle), which pushes its rocket spikes to over 2.1m (7ft). *Ligularia przewalskii* and *L.* 'The Rocket' have long, yellow-flowered spikes, about 2m (6ft) tall.

Unusual plants

It can be fun to grow a few weird and wonderful perennials, and they can make a conversation piece when you show visitors your garden.

Try growing plants that are not especially beautiful, that may even smell unpleasant or that don't have long-lasting and beautiful flowers as they might bring some other quality to the garden. Most visitors love to be surprised or amazed, and a few plants with interesting features or peculiarities make for a more interesting garden.

The family Araceae provides some of the most unusual plants for a perennial border, and the frost-hardy *Dracunculus vulgaris* (dragon

arum) is one of the boldest. It grows to about 1.2m (4ft) or more tall and has mottled stalks and white-streaked leaves. In late spring or early summer it produces a blackish-maroon spike from the centre of a deep maroon-purple spathe. The whole flower is more than 30cm (12in) long. It doesn't stop there, however: the putrid smell of rotting flesh attracts beetles and flies from far around.

Sauromatum venosum (voodoo lily, monarch of the east) is widely sold as a novelty plant to grow indoors without soil or water, but it can also be used in the garden, where you can enjoy the foliage that follows the flowers. The spathe emerges and grows at an amazing rate, to a height of 30cm (12in) or more, then peels back to reveal a skin of brownish-purple and yellow, with a spike in the middle sticking up like a poker. Take care if you plan to examine it closely – the smell is truly nauseating. Grow a clump for real impact and be grateful that it will not survive over winter.

Not all interesting arums are large. *Arisarum proboscideum* (mouse plant) produces a carpet of arrow-shaped leaves about 10cm (4in) high, among which you will find the flowers in spring. They have a spathe that is drawn out into a tail up to 15cm (6in) long. The flower really does resemble a mouse's tail sticking out from the clump of foliage.

left No one who has ever seen *Dracunculus vulgaris* will forget it – or its smell.

top *Kniphofia rooperi* is one of the latest in the year to send up its red-hot pokers.

Scented perennials

Scent will enhance the appeal of your borders, but you will have to position fragrant plants carefully to make the best of them. The very nature of a herbaceous or mixed border makes it difficult to appreciate scented plants. The fragrance has to be very powerful to carry from the back of a border, for example, and plants with aromatic foliage have to be positioned at the front to be appreciated. If you can, grow scented perennials along paths or in containers on the patio, close to an open window or in a windowbox, so that you can really appreciate the scent on a warm summer evening.

If we exclude bulbs, there are relatively few strongly scented border plants that are truly herbaceous in the sense that they die back to the ground for winter, but that doesn't mean you can't introduce scent from other sources. Use bulbs such as lilies and *Galtonia candicans* (summer hyacinth) and clumps of scented annuals, such as *Lathyrus odoratus* (sweet pea) and *Matthiola longipetala* subsp. *bicornis* (night-scented stock).

Beware of books and catalogues that describe scented plants in a loose way. Alliums (ornamental onions) and calendulas (pot marigolds) do have a smell, but few of us would compare those 'scents' with the sweet fragrance of sweet peas or lilies.

top The bells of *Galtonia candicans* are sweetly fragrant and rise on elegant flower stems about 1m (3ft) tall.

Best scented perennials

Convallaria majalis (lily-of-the-valley)
A much-loved little spring flower whose spikes of delicate creamy bells exude sweetness.

Crambe cordifolia
A haze of flowers in summer to provide a lightly scented cloud at the back of the border.

Dianthus 'Mrs Sinkins'
One of the reliably scented old-fashioned pinks.

Filipendula kamtschatica
The aptly named meadowsweet, which creates a froth of starry little flowers in summer.

Matthiola incana (stock, gillyflower)
A warm-scented cottage-garden flower that should be grown more often.

Nicotiana sylvestris (tobacco plant)
A more elegant plant than *N. alata*, with a more powerful fragrance from its narrow, trumpet-shaped white flowers.

Paeonia lactiflora 'Sarah Bernhardt'
A full-petalled rose-pink peony, one of the few with a scent.

Phlox paniculata (perennial phlox)
Tall late-flowering stalwart of the traditional herbaceous border, with a strong peppery fragrance not to everyone's taste.

Oenothera speciosa (evening primrose)
A beautiful showy yellow flower at its best in the evening.

Viola odorata (sweet violet)
A sweet old-fashioned scent that you need to bend low to catch.

below *Crambe cordifolia*

Foliage perennials

A foliage plant will be attractive for at least six months of the year, a claim that can be made for few flowering plants. Bold foliage plants will also bring a different kind of visual 'texture' to your borders and can act as a visual link to hold together the design as the more transient flowers come and go. The beauty and seemingly endless variation of leaf shapes, patterns, textures and colours make them vitally important as garden features.

Colour

In horticultural terms, grey is not a drab colour. Grey and silvery foliage helps to break up bright colours and is often a refreshing change from the multitude of greens. *Verbascum* spp. (mullein) can be dramatic in leaf and flower. Many forms, such as *V. bombyciferum*, are biennial or short-lived perennials, and in the first year grow a handsome rosette of large grey, evergreen leaves, the spike of yellow flowers being produced in the second season.

There are many silver-leaved border plants among the artemisias (mugworts), and they grow in an attractive and symmetrical way that always makes a neat-looking plant. Among the popular forms are *A. ludoviciana* (western mugwort) and *A.* 'Powis Castle'.

Black leaves sound particularly unattractive, yet the dark, grassy leaves of *Ophiopogon planiscapus* 'Nigrescens' obviously hold a fascination, judging by the number of them planted. This will do best in slightly acid soil, but doesn't mind sun or partial shade. It looks particularly effective in a modern planting with strong contrasts.

Dark purple and red foliage can also be attractive. *Euphorbia amygdaloides* 'Purpurea' makes a vivid show with its maroon stems and dark evergreen foliage. *Heuchera micrantha* var. *diversifolia* 'Palace Purple' is another evergreen (semi-evergreen in cold areas) with very dark leaves. The large leaves of *Rheum palmatum* 'Atropurpureum' have rich purple undersides.

top The grass-like *Ophiopogon planiscapus* 'Nigrescens' makes an unusual fringe to a border.

left *Dicentra spectabilis* is a delightful spring flower which also has delicate foliage that continues to contribute to a planting once the flowers have faded.

right The leaves of *Rodgersia podophylla* are often likened to those of a horse chestnut, and they make a bold impact in a shady spot.

Texture

The popular *Alchemilla mollis* (lady's mantle) always delights with its ability to hold rain or dew in drops on the surface of its hairy, pale-green leaves. The woolly silvery leaves of *Stachys byzantina* (lamb's ears) have a felted texture and a special fascination. Trimming the mats from time to time will encourage new, more softly furry leaves to appear.

Feathery and fern-like leaves contribute their own sense of texture to the border, especially if there's a mass of the foliage. *Dicentra* spp. are particularly attractive in late spring and early summer when the pink, red or white, locket-shaped flowers dance above the soft, divided foliage, but long after the flowers have died the mat of frond-like foliage will continue to please.

Size and shape

Rodgersias need a damp position out of full sun to do really well, but you can grow them in the herbaceous or mixed border if you keep the roots moist. They are worth the effort. The palmate (hand-shaped) leaves are big and well displayed. Two imposing species are *Rodgersia aesculifolia*, to 2m (6ft) tall, and *R. podophylla*, to 1.5m (5ft) tall. The sprays of white or pinkish flowers are a bonus too.

Even bigger and bolder, but again demanding moist shade to do well, is

Astilboides tabularis, which has circular leaves almost 90cm (3ft) across and apparently perching on their stalks like plates balancing on sticks in a circus act.

Acanthus leaves were depicted in classical architecture, which gives an indication of their worth. The heavily indented leaves of *Acanthus mollis* are up to 60cm (2ft) long; those of *A. spinosus* have wickedly sharp spines. The leaves are almost evergreen, which are a useful bonus in the winter months.

Bergenias (elephant's ears) have thick leathery evergreen leaves that make an impenetrable groundcover. They are grown as much for their pink, red or white spring flowers as for their foliage, but the leaves of many cultivars turn reddish or purple in winter – they look superb in winter sunshine or in juxtaposition with plants such as green-flowered hellebores, *Helleborus viridis* (green hellebore) and *H. foetidus* (stinking hellebore).

If you have a shady position where you can grow a trillium (trinity flower, wood lily) or two, you'll not only have striking white or purple three-petalled flowers in spring, but a plant with leaves distinctively arranged in threes.

Interesting patterns

Leaves that are attractively marbled are usually eye-catching, and if they also have the distinctive arrow-head shape like *Arum italicum* they make even more desirable border plants. The white-veined leaves are followed by green or creamy-white flower spathes, then in autumn by a spike of red berries.

Variegated perennials

Attractive variegated plants are much rarer in herbaceous perennials than among shrubs, so you may have to search hard to find some suitable plants. They are best used sparingly to break up what might otherwise be dull areas of the border.

When the flowers have finished, too many variegated plants too close to each other will look odd and contrived. It's better to have a bold splash of one variegated plant, with perhaps three or more specimens planted together, than three different kinds in close proximity.

The plants suggested here will act as punctuation points in the border, but keep your eyes open for others. Remember that you can use plants such as variegated phormiums to great effect, even if they are not herbaceous plants.

Don't forget that grasses, bamboos and sedges look pleasing in any herbaceous or mixed border, retaining their shape and structure during the cold months.

top Cut back the spotted leaves of pulmonarias (lungworts) when they begin to look dry and new leaves will shoot up almost immediately.

Top ten variegated perennials

Ajuga reptans 'Multicolor'
This form of bugle has dark bronze and green leaves and blue flowers in summer. It makes excellent groundcover.

Convallaria majalis 'Albostriata'
Grow this lily-of-the-valley as a carpet at the front of the border. The fragrant flowers appear in mid- and late spring and the leaves have fine longitudinal white stripes.

Erysimum linifolium 'Variegatum'
A variegated form of perennial wallflower, this has cream-variegated leaves that are topped by lilac flowers.

Houttuynia cordata 'Chameleon'
This versatile plant will grow in water or boggy ground, yet still perform well in a border or container. The green, cream and red variegation makes it one of the best variegated plants for the front of a border.

Iris pallida 'Variegata'
The sword-shaped, upright, evergreen leaves are edged with white. There are blue flowers in summer.

Lamium galeobdolon 'Hermann's Pride'
A non-invasive deadnettle, with silver-and-green finely patterned leaves. This is a useful plant for growing in shade.

Liriope muscari 'Variegata'
One of several variegated forms of this useful evergreen. It has blue flowers in autumn.

Phlox paniculata 'Norah Leigh'
Unlike most border phlox, this is grown for its variegated foliage rather than its pink flowers. **'Harlequin'** is another variegated variety, this time with bolder purple flowers.

Polemonium caeruleum 'Brise d'Anjou'
An outstanding form of the popular Jacob's ladder, this has yellow-edged leaves, topped by violet-blue flowers in summer. It does best in shade or partial shade.

Pulmonaria 'Sissinghurst White'
In spring the leaves of this lungwort are covered with white dots. The white flowers open from pink buds.

Striped grasses

Variegated grasses are especially useful because they bring a different kind of texture to the border, often being tall and spiky.

Acorus gramineus 'Variegatus'
The variegated Japanese rush, which should be grown as a pool marginal, has green and gold bands along the length of the evergreen leaves.

Carex hachijoensis 'Evergold'
This sedge has evergreen. grass-like foliage longitudinally striped yellow and green.

Cortaderia selloana 'Aureolineata'
A tall pampas grass with yellow-margined leaves and large silvery flower plumes in autumn.

Hakonechloa macra 'Alboaurea'
A low-growing grass with a mound of green-striped yellow leaves.

above Carex hachijoensis 'Evergold'

Miscanthus sinensis 'Zebrinus' (zebra grass)
A tall grass, to 1.2m (4ft), this has distinctive horizontal, yellowish-white bands and striking, fan-shaped flowerheads in autumn.

Ferns

Ferns rather fell from favour against the competition for brighter and bolder plants, but now they are returning to our gardens. It can come as something of a surprise to many novice gardeners that there are so many kinds of hardy ferns. A further surprise is how easy and undemanding they are to cultivate. In addition, many of them will thrive in places where other plants struggle, and many are evergreen.

Most ferns will thrive in shade, and some will even do well in dry shade beneath trees, although others are moisture-lovers. One of the grandest of all, the 2m (6ft) tall *Osmunda regalis* (royal fern, flowering fern), is to be seen at its best when it is grown in either boggy or waterside conditions.

There are ferns that grow in dry walls and others that require high humidity around their flimsy fronds. Yet the majority of readily available hardy ferns are undemanding and easy to grow, and many can be included in the herbaceous border if you find a suitable spot for them. Better still, create a special fern bed or border.

The show-offs

A number of ferns are particularly showy, especially where they are planted in a drift for a more spectacular display. One of the most attractive is *Matteuccia struthiopteris* (ostrich fern, shuttlecock fern), which looks like a giant shuttlecock when its fronds have unfurled. It does best in moist shade.

If you live in a mild, sheltered area, where winter frosts are rare or not severe, it may be possible to grow a stunning tree fern, such as *Dicksonia antarctica*. This evergreen, tree-like fern has a stout trunk with palm-like fronds, and will eventually grow to 5m (15ft) or more. At this size, it is clearly not suitable for the middle of your border, and for such a special plant you should find a spot in the garden where it can become a focal point.

Easy and reliable

Start with easy ferns, *Dryopteris filix-mas* (male fern), a semi-evergreen, for example, or polystichums, such as the semi-evergreen *Polystichum setiferum* (soft shield fern) or the evergreen *Polypodium vulgare* (common polypody), or *Onoclea sensibilis* (sensitive fern). Some of these have been bred to exhibit variations in leaf shape, such as a border frill of fancy curling frondlets, so there are plenty to choose from.

Best ferns

- *Asplenium scolopendrium* (hart's tongue fern)
- *Athyrium filix-femina* (lady fern)
- *Blechnum gibbum*
- *Dryopteris affinis* (golden male fern)
- *Matteuccia struthiopteris* (ostrich fern, shuttlecock fern)
- *Osmunda regalis* (royal fern, flowering fern)
- *Onoclea sensibilis* (sensitive fern)
- *Polypodium cambricum* 'Cristatum'
- *Polystichum setiferum* (soft shield fern)

below *Onoclea sensibilis* (sensitive fern)
bottom *Matteuccia struthiopteris*

Hostas

Most gardeners recognize these popular plants simply as some of the best foliage plants for the border. It is the sheer versatility of this group of plants that fascinates many gardeners, as well as their handsome foliage. They will grow in shade (even under trees) or in full sun. They thrive in moist ground but will tolerate dry conditions. They make ideal border plants, but small ones are suitable for the rock garden and they make impressive container plants. Flower arrangers love the foliage and the Japanese even eat the leaf stalks! There are many hundreds of cultivars, and only a small selection can be described here.

Big leaves

There are some very large hostas, which are best planted where there is space to show them off. *Hosta sieboldiana* grows to about 90cm (3ft), and has an even wider spread. The heart-shaped leaves, which are puckered and deeply ribbed, are bluish-grey but tend to turn a dull green in full sun. *H. sieboldiana* var. *elegans* has even larger leaves, usually bluer in colour. 'Krossa Regal' is smaller but still stately in stature, growing to about 75cm (30in). The slightly wavy-edged leaves form a dense, arching clump.

The cultivars 'Royal Standard', rich green leaves, and 'Bressingham Blue', blue-green leaves, both grow to about 90cm (3ft) and make a bold statement in the border, while 'Big Daddy' grows to about 75cm (30in).

Small leaves

The popular 'Ginko Craig' has small, lance-shaped leaves, edged white, and grows to about 25cm (10in). Its strong horizontal growth and low height make it an effective plant for groundcover. *H. tardiflora* is smaller and has lance-shaped, leathery leaves about 15cm (6in) long. It makes a plant about 25cm (10in) tall. Even tinier, for the rock garden rather than the herbaceous border, is *H. venusta*, which has leaves only about 2.5cm (1in) long.

left *Hosta sieboldiana* var. *elegans* is one of the most robust hostas, with deep corrugation adding texture to the glaucous leaves.

top A truly lovely hosta, but *H. crispula* needs moist shade – also the favourite habitat of slugs and snails – to grow to its full potential.

Fragrant hostas

Usually flowers are a secondary feature of hostas, but some, such as 'Honeybells', are worth growing for their flowers alone. Many hostas are pleasantly fragrant, including *H. plantaginea* and cultivars such as 'Honeybells', 'Royal Standard', 'Sugar and Cream' and 'Summer Fragrance'.

Blue leaves

You have to use a little imagination here, but, in comparison with the green varieties, these hostas definitely do look blue. Cultivars to look for include 'Big Daddy', 'Blue Moon', 'Bressingham Blue' and 'Hadspen Blue'.

Golden leaves

There are fewer cultivars with all-gold leaves than with gold variegation, and they can be more difficult to place. Impressive plants include 'Sun Power', 'Midas Touch' and 'Zounds' (the puckered foliage of the last two tolerates sun better than most yellows).

Some reliable variegated forms are almost all gold, so should also be considered here. 'Gold Standard' is delicately edged dark green, but the dominant impression is of a golden variety, and it's first-rate.

Variegated leaves

There's a huge range of hostas with variegated foliage and they come in all sizes – you could fill a garden with them. Some of the popular varieties that have stood the test of time are *H. undulata* var. *univittata* with a white central splash; 'Shade Fanfare' with a broad creamy-yellow edge; and *H. undulata* var. *albomarginata*, which has a broad cream edge.

above right *Hosta fortunei* 'Albo-picta' is at its best in early summer, before the fresh creamy yellow in the centre of its leaves dulls to pale green.

below right The aptly named *Hosta* 'Midas Touch' has thick, leathery leaves, which means it can stand a good deal of sun; in shade it will be less golden.

Bedding plants

Bedding plants are the budget way to a bright and ever-changing display, where each year you can change the appearance of your garden so that it never becomes dull or predictable. Although cheap and cheerful, there's nothing second-rate about these plants, and they are at the heart of some of the best and brightest gardens.

Annuals

Annuals are plants with a short but busy life. In the space of a few months they grow, flower and die, leaving the ground free for further cultivation, if necessary, and for other plants. These plants are among the cheapest flowers to grow and the quickest to give a return. They are invaluable for furnishing new gardens before more permanent plants have been put in or have become sufficiently established to require all the space. They are also excellent for filling any vacant spaces that may occur in the flower beds.

There are many different kinds of annuals and innumerable cultivars of some of the most popular ones, such as marigolds and petunias. They vary greatly in height and habit as well as in the colour and form of their flowers. Some sprawl over the ground and make colourful flower carpets beneath taller plants. Some are bushy, some erect, and a few, such as *Lathyrus odoratus* (sweet pea), *Tropaeolum peregrinum* (canary creeper), *Tropaeolum majus* (nasturtium) and *Ipomoea hederacea* (morning glory), are climbers. There are also annuals, such as *Reseda* (mignonette), *Matthiola* (stocks) and *Nicotiana* (tobacco plant), with sweetly scented flowers. Annuals can be divided into hardy annuals and half-hardy annuals (see page 18).

Biennials

Biennials are plants that must be renewed annually from seed, because they die after they have flowered and set seed. In this they resemble annuals, but biennials take over a year to complete their cycle of growth. Seed sown one year will produce plants that will flower the next year, ripen their seed and die before the second winter. However, to be sure of a regular succession of biennials it is necessary to sow seed every year at the correct season.

Many biennials flower in early and midsummer, thus usefully filling an awkward gap that can occur between spring and summer flowers. Like annuals, they are temporary plants, which should be pulled up and put on the compost heap when they have finished flowering. Although it's easy enough to save seed of most kinds it is usually impossible to prevent cross-fertilization of different types, and as a result home-saved seed produces only a mongrel population.

The distinction between annuals, biennials and perennials is not always clear-cut, because some plants can be treated in several ways: *Alcea* (hollyhock), for example, can be grown as an annual, biennial or short-lived perennial.

Tender perennials

Tender perennials are plants which cannot be left outside over winter. Examples include the always popular pelargoniums and fuchsias, which should be planted out in borders and containers only when all risk of frost has passed. They will then flower throughout the summer months, usually with a stunning and long-lasting display of blooms, but would probably die from cold over winter if you left them outside. However, you can take cuttings in autumn and keep them in a cold greenhouse if you want to have them again next year or simply buy new plants in spring.

top Zinnias are due for a resurgence in popularity. They come in a range of bold colours, are easy to grow and last well as cut flowers.

Top 20 bedding plants

Antirrhinum majus (snapdragon)
This short-lived perennial, grown as an annual, has spikes of tubular or trumpet-shaped flowers in many colours, including white, yellow, orange, red, pink and purple, from spring through to summer.

Brachyscome iberidifolia (Swan River daisy)
The small, daisy-like flowers of this annual are fragrant and come in colours ranging from blue, mauve and purple to pink and white. They appear in summer and early autumn.

Chrysanthemum carinatum (painted daisy)
In summer this annual chrysanthemum produces daisy-like flowers in many colour combinations, including red with yellow centres or white with red centres.

below Chrysanthemum carinatum (painted daisy)

Coreopsis 'Sunray'
Although a perennial, this is grown as an annual, producing double, bright yellow, daisy-like flowers in summer.

Cosmos Sensation Series
This group of annuals has large, bowl-shaped, pink or white flowers in summer and early autumn.

Gypsophila elegans
An annual plant, producing a mound of grey-green leaves surmounted by a mass of small white, pink or purplish flowers in summer.

Helianthus annuus (sunflower)
In summer the annual sunflower produces very large, daisy-like flowers with bright yellow petals and brownish-purple centres.

Impatiens walleriana Accent Series (busy lizzie)
Another perennial that is grown as an annual. From spring to autumn these compact plants produce a succession of flowers in white and shades of violet, red, pink and orange.

Lathyrus odoratus (sweet pea)
A climbing plant, the annual sweet pea has delicate, scented flowers in many colours, from white to mauve, purple, pink and red.

Lavatera trimestris
In summer and early autumn this annual bears shallow, trumpet-shaped flowers in shades of pink or in white.

Limnanthes douglasii (poached-egg plant)
Bright yellow and white, fragrant flowers are borne from summer to autumn. This annual makes excellent groundcover and can also be used as a green manure.

Limonium sinuatum
This perennial, usually treated as an annual for summer bedding, has clusters of purple flowers on erect stems. This is popular with flower arrangers.

Nicotiana x sanderae Merlin Series
This annual form of the tobacco plant is a dwarf form, ideal for containers and edging, with flowers in shades of purple, crimson and green.

Nigella damascena (love-in-a-mist)
The many-petalled flowers of this hardy annual are either blue or white, and are produced in summer amid feathery, bright green leaves. The seedcases are also attractive.

Petunia Surfinia Series
These large-flowered petunias are in white and shades of pink, dark red, pinkish-blue and blue. They are more weather-resistant than some petunias, and the trailing habit makes them perfect for hanging baskets and windowboxes.

Salvia splendens (scarlet sage)
This is a perennial but is usually grown as an annual. It has bright flowers, ranging in colour from scarlet and salmon-pink to white, which are produced in summer and early autumn.

Sanvitalia procumbens (creeping zinnia)
A carpet-forming annual producing eye-catching, bright yellow, daisy-like flowers with black centres from early summer to early autumn.

Tagetes Hero Series
These French marigolds (derived from *T. patula*) have large, double flowers in shades of yellow, orange, red and mahogany from late spring to early autumn. They get to about 25cm (10in) tall and do best in full sun in well-drained soil.

Tropaeolum majus (nasturtium)
This trailing plant has trumpet-shaped flowers in shades of bright yellow, orange and red in summer through to autumn.

Zinnia elegans Thumbelina Series
These colourful annuals have single and double flowers in yellow, red, magenta or orange in summer and early autumn.

Best biennials

Dianthus barbatus (sweet william)
In early summer, these plants produce flat heads of brightly coloured, bi-coloured flowers in shades of pink, red or white, each with a different-coloured central zone.

Digitalis purpurea (common foxglove)
The tubular flowers in shades of pink, red, purple and white are produced on tall spikes in summer.

below Digitalis purpurea

Erysimum cheiri (wallflower)
From spring to early summer this biennial produces heads of fragrant, four-petalled flowers in colours ranging from deep red, yellow, bronze and orange to white.

Myosotis sylvatica (forget-me-not)
From spring to early summer little blue flowers, with yellow centres, are borne in dense clusters.

Viola cultivars (pansy)
The velvety blooms come in many colours, from creamy white and yellow to pink and purple, each with a black eye in the centre.

Bedding displays

Bedding displays can be simple or elaborate according to taste, and the patterns may be given permanent form by being edged with small shrubs, such as box or lavender. Bedding out simply means putting plants in the garden for a limited period, while they are able to contribute most to the display, and then replacing them with other plants. Spring bedding plants are those that make their display from early to late spring; summer bedding plants are those that are at their peak from early summer to early autumn.

Beds can be filled with a number of plants of differing habits and, usually, mixed colours. Carpeting plants are used as a base planting, with taller plants employed to produce a second or third tier of flowers.

Any annuals, biennials and tender perennials can be used for bedding and the plants you choose will have a big impact on the style of the display. Gone are the days when bedding consisted of nothing but blue lobelia and red salvias arranged in rows. Nowadays people are much more imaginative and combine all sorts of colours and styles. Try lime green and orange, lilac and silver, or red and black – there are so many different bedding plants available now that you can find them in just about any colour you want.

A bedding display doesn't have to follow a formal pattern. Try a cottage-garden style by mixing softer plants in a random profusion, such as *Cosmos*, with its feathery foliage, cheerful antirrhinums, single poppies and *Nigella* (love-in-a-mist).

Foliage

Plants with silver or grey leaves are useful in summer bedding schemes as a foil to the colours of the flowers. *Leucophyta brownii* (cushion bush) is silvery, with wiry stems and narrow leaves. It can be grown as a small column and as a dot plant, or the growing tips can be pinched out frequently, making it into a dwarf, spreading plant suitable for carpet bedding. Although a perennial in its native Australia, it is treated as an annual in temperate areas. *Senecio cineraria* is a bushy, fairly hardy perennial with deeply divided silvery-white leaves. *Centaurea cineraria* and *C. rutifolia* are similar in appearance. *Senecio serpens* is a creeping plant only a few centimetres high, with blue-grey leaves, which is useful for outlining carpet bedding. *Tanacetum ptarmiciflorum*, a tender perennial often grown as an annual, has deeply divided, ferny leaves, which are covered with silver hairs. Dense clusters of white, daisy-like flowers are borne in spring.

Coloured foliage can be as useful as silver and grey foliage in diversifying the effects in summer bedding displays. *Bassia scoparia* f. *trichophylla* (summer cypress, burning bush), is an annual that makes a 60cm (2ft) column of fine leaves and looks rather like a miniature conifer; the leaves are green at first, turning to

left *Nigella damascena* (love-in-a-mist) brings a fairy lightness to a planting and will seed itself around freely.

top Smaller-flowered varieties of pansy, such as 'Jolly Joker', look best planted *en masse* or in 'rivers' among other plants.

purplish-red in late summer. *Abutilon pictum* 'Thompsonii' is a shrubby plant with light-green leaves heavily mottled with yellow, and with orange, dropping, trumpet-shaped flowers. Particularly useful as a dot plant, it will quickly grow to a height of up to 90cm (3ft) and can be used as a background or a centrepiece. A form of feverfew, *Tanacetum parthenium* 'Aureum', is also known as golden feather because it has bright yellow, feathery leaves.

Fuchsias

Many fuchsias make excellent summer bedding plants. They can be grown as bushes or trained as standards, and they can be raised from cuttings or bought in late spring or early summer, ready for planting out. They are beautiful and decorative flowering shrubs, which are particularly valuable in pots and hanging baskets. Their natural colours are purple and carmine-red, although there are also variants of white, all shades of pink, lilac, red and crimson. Some are even orange.

Pelargoniums

The geraniums used for summer bedding are correctly known as pelargoniums. There are two main types:
- zonal pelargoniums, which have round, downy leaves and strong, upright stems;
- ivy-leaved pelargoniums, which have smooth, angular leaves and trailing, weaker stems.

There are many, many cultivars, all indispensable summer bedding plants, which flower prolifically from early summer until the first frosts, even with minimal attention. Use them in formal bedding displays, containers, hanging baskets and windowboxes, using trailing varieties to cascade over the edges of containers.

Top ten fuchsias

The following are some of the hardiest and best fuchsia species and cultivars. All flower from summer well into autumn.

'Alice Hoffman'
A compact shrub with bronze-green foliage and small, semi-double flowers, with pinkish-red tubes and sepals and milky-white, red-veined petals.

'Brutus'
The single or semi-double flowers of this vigorous, freely branching plant are either crimson-red or deep purple.

'Corallina'
The scarlet and purple flowers are medium-sized and freely produced. The foliage has a bronze tint. Growth is arching and spreading.

'Golden Marinka'
The single flowers of this trailing form are rich dark red. The leaves are variegated with yellow and green. Grow it in a hanging basket.

'Lady Thumb'
A dwarf, upright, free-flowering shrub, this fuchsia is very bushy and can be used as an edging plant, in a hanging basket or trained against a support. It has small, semi-double flowers: the white petals are pink-veined and the sepals and tubes are reddish-pink.

'Lena'
This vigorous fuchsia makes a good standard. It has double, pale-pink flowers with pink-flushed, purple outer petals.

'Madame Cornélissen'
This fuchsia has large scarlet flowers, with scarlet-veined, white inner petals. The flowers are small and the growth is strong and upright.

***F. magellanica* var. *gracilis* 'Versicolor'**
This upright shrub has small flowers. The leaves are grey-green, tinted pink when young and variegated creamy-white. This is not as hardy as its green-leaved parent. Both have long, slender, red and violet flowers.

'Mrs Popple'
In sheltered areas, this upright, bushy fuchsia may be grown as a hedge. Large scarlet and violet flowers are profusely produced.

'Riccartonii'
The small red and purple flowers of this fuchsia are very striking and are produced from midsummer to mid-autumn.

below Fuchsia 'Tango Queen'

Climbers and trailers

Don't forget the vertical accent when you plan bedding displays. Annual climbers can provide effective screens or clothe walls and fences with seasonal colour. Trailing plants make effective use of container space by continuing the display ever further downwards.

Annual climbers

Annual climbers are unsuitable as screens where you want to mask something all year round, such as an ugly wall or fence, but many are ideal for a summer screen on the patio or other part of the garden where you might need the extra light after the plant dies in autumn. They are also great for adding colour and interest to bare walls and fences or growing through evergreen shrubs to give them a visual boost.

Climbers to start under glass

Tender climbers have to be started off in warm conditions and the young plants can be planted outdoors only when there is minimal risk of frost and after gradual acclimatization. Most of them are fast growers, however, and well worth the effort, for the particularly beautiful effect they create.

- *Cobaea scandens* (cathedral bells, cup-and-saucer vine) is a vigorous plant with large leaves, giving dense foliage cover. From summer through to autumn it bears large blue or white flowers.
- *Eccremocarpus scaber* (Chilean glory flower) offers less dense foliage cover but has vivid bright red, orange or yellow flowers from late spring to autumn.
- *Ipomoea lobata* (Spanish flag) will give reasonable foliage cover. The conspicuous flowers shade from yellow to red, changing colour as they mature.
- *Senecio scandens* is very different from its low-growing cousins, its pale green leaves forming a column of foliage that late in the season is studded with delicate-rayed yellow daisy flowers.

left *Tropaeolum peregrinum* (canary creeper) is a tender climber but will quickly grow to 2m (6ft) in a season.

top As well as the well-loved annual sweet pea, the *Lathyrus* genus includes a number of perennial species.

Climbers to sow *in situ*

These no-fuss plants can be sown where they are to flower, but check the seed package for detailed instructions. Some are hardier than others and can be sown sooner.

- *Humulus japonicus* 'Variegatus' is a twining perennial, although usually treated as a half-hardy annual, with dark green leaves, boldly splashed and streaked with white.
- *Ipomoea tricolor* (morning glory) is a fast-growing, twining annual that has glorious blue flowers in summer.
- *Lathyrus odoratus* (sweet pea) has modest foliage cover, but superb flowers. It is popular for both colours and scent.
- *Tropaeolum majus* (nasturtium) provides dense foliage cover. It has bright flowers, in shades of red, yellow and orange.
- *Tropaeolum peregrinum* (canary creeper) provides good foliage cover and, as the name suggests, bears bright yellow flowers.

Trailing plants

Trailing plants are invaluable for hanging baskets and windowboxes, but use them freely to soften the walls of raised beds and to mask the edge of tubs. Many excellent trailers can be raised from seed, but some of the best have to be propagated from cuttings. Some of these, such as ivy-leaved and cascade pelargoniums, are easy to propagate and overwinter at home. Others, such as Surfinia Series petunias and *Scaevola aemula* (fairy fan flower), are more difficult to maintain through winter without a suitably heated greenhouse, but they are readily available as young plants in spring. Remember to harden them off (acclimatize) slowly, and don't be too impatient to move them outside.

Cascades of colour

Any of these will add a pretty trailing softness to containers, especially hanging baskets.

Trailers from seed

- *Fuchsia* 'Florabelle'
- *Hedera helix* (common ivy)
- *Lobelia erinus* Cascade Series
- *Pelargonium* ivy-leaved cultivars
- *Petunia* Wave Series
- *Silene pendula* (nodding catchfly)

Trailing plants from cuttings

- *Fuchsia* cascading cultivars
- *Glechoma hederacea* 'Variegata' (variegated ground ivy)
- *Helichrysum petiolare*
- *Lobelia lutea*
- *Lotus berthelotii* (coral gem, parrot's beak)
- *Lysimachia nummularia* 'Aurea' (golden creeping jenny)
- *Pelargonium* ivy-leaved cultivars
- *Petunia* Surfinia Series and Million Bells Series
- *Plectranthus* spp.
- *Scaevola aemula* (fairy fan flower)
- *Verbena* 'Peaches and Cream'

below *Helichrysum petiolare*

Bedding for shade

Most of the bedding plants we grow originate in sunny climates, but most small gardens have gloomy areas in shade cast by buildings, fences or hedges. These plants will put on a respectable show in shade, though they may grow taller and flower less than those growing in a sunny position.

Shady areas are often dry, because the obstruction that blocks the sun may just as easily cause a rain shadow. Avoid handicapping your plants further by incorporating plenty of moisture-retaining material, such as well-rotted garden compost and manure, into the soil and be prepared to water thoroughly in periods of dry weather.

The biennial *Lunaria annua* (honesty) will tolerate full shade and do even better in partial shade. The flowers of the regular form are quite a bright purple, but there is a good white variety whose pale flowers seem to glow in the half-gloom. Also lovely for shade is *L. annua* 'Variegata', with pretty marbled foliage. Honesty flowers in late spring and then develops its distinctive 'silver penny' seedheads, from which it multiplies profusely.

Foliage plants for shade

Don't overlook foliage plants for shade – they often look more appropriate than masses of flowers. One plant whose leaves are as bright as any flowers, however, is the multicoloured *Solenostemon scutellarioides* (coleus), with its prettily patterned leaves in shades of red, yellow, pink and green. Coleus is usually regarded as an indoor plant, but it is a perennial grown as an annual and there is no reason why it cannot be used for seasonal bedding if acclimatized carefully first and planted in a sheltered position. It will do surprisingly well in the shade beneath trees and large shrubs if kept well watered, and the exotically marked leaves will create an interesting and different effect.

top In the wild *Digitalis purpurea* (foxgloves) grow best in the dappled shade beneath deciduous trees.

left *Myosotis sylvatica* (forget-me-nots) are undemanding plants that happily self-seed in sun or shade.

Top 20 bedding plants for shade

Ageratum houstonianum (floss flower)
Small blue flowers are borne in clusters on strong erect stems. Although these half-hardy annuals like sun, they will grow in light shade.

Anchusa capensis
A biennial, usually grown as a hardy annual, bearing blue, forget-me-not-like flowers and growing to 18cm (7in). It will tolerate partial shade.

Asperula orientalis (woodruff)
A hardy annual with fragrant, lavender-blue flowers and growing to 30cm (12in). It will tolerate full shade.

Begonia Semperflorens Cultorum Group (fibrous-rooted begonia)
Half-hardy annuals with masses of small red, pink or white flowers and green or bronze foliage. Heights range from 15 to 23cm (6–9in). This will tolerate full shade but does better in partial shade.

Bellis perennis (double daisy)
This biennial has double daisy-type flowers in shades of red, pink and white in spring on stems to 10–15cm (4–6in). It will tolerate partial shade.

Bidens ferulifolia
A short-lived perennial, this has pretty golden-yellow flowers above dark green, ferny foliage. It will grow in light shade.

Digitalis purpurea (common foxglove)
This popular biennial bears spikes of purple, pink or white flowers to 1.2–2m (4–6ft) high. It does best in partial shade but tolerates full shade.

Hesperis matronalis (sweet rocket)
A biennial producing large spikes, to 60–90cm (24–36in), of single lilac or purple flowers, which are fragrant in the evening. It tolerates full shade but is better in partial shade.

Impatiens balsamina (balsam)
This half-hardy annual has spikes of double flowers in a range of colours, including white and shades of pink, red and purple, which are not at all like the more popular busy lizzies. Plants grow to 75cm (30in) tall. Although they will tolerate full shade, they will do better in partial shade.

Impatiens walleriana cultivars (busy lizzie)
Although strictly perennials, these variable little plants are usually treated as half-hardy annuals. There are many named cultivars, with flowers in a wide range of colours. Plants are usually 15–30cm (6–12in), although some forms are taller and some smaller. They will grow in full shade but do better in partial shade.

Lobelia erinus cultivars
The popular half-hardy annual is widely used for both bedding and in containers. Although most cultivars are shades of blue, forms with pink flowers are also available. Plants get to about 15cm (6in), although trailing forms have longer stems. They will grow in full sun or partial shade.

Lunaria annua (honesty, satin flower)
A biennial, this bears purple or white flowers in late spring, followed by decorative seedheads. The plants tolerate full shade but will do better in partial shade.

Mimulus x hybridus Magic Series
The small flowers are in shades of red, yellow and orange on plants that are no more than 20cm (8in) high. Grow in moist soil in light dappled shade.

Myosotis sylvatica (forget-me-not)
A popular biennial with blue flowers (sometimes pink) in spring. Growing to 15–30cm (6–12in), forget-me-nots tolerate partial shade.

Nemesia strumosa
This annual has clusters of white, red, yellow, pink, blue or purple flowers in mid- to late summer. Plants grow to about 30cm (12in) high and need neutral to acid soil in sun or light shade.

Nemophila menziesii (baby blue eyes)
A hardy annual, this grows to no more than 15cm (6in) tall and has small blue flowers with white centres. Grow it in partial shade.

above Nemophila menziesii (baby blue eyes)

Nicotiana x sanderae (tobacco plant)
There are many cultivars of this half-hardy annual, ranging from compact plants with flowers that open during the day to taller ones with evening-opening flowers. Plant in moist soil and in sun or partial shade.

Petunia cultivars
One of the most frequently grown bedding plants, petunias are available in a wide range of colours. These half-hardy annuals get to about 30cm (1ft) tall. Grow in partial shade.

Reseda odorata (common mignonette)
This annual bears pretty heads of yellowish-green or white, fragrant flowers from summer to early autumn. Grow in well-drained soil in sun or partial shade.

Viola cultivars (pansy)
These popular hardy annuals or biennials are grown everywhere. There are many cultivars and colours, most with a height of 10–15cm (4–6in). They tolerate partial shade.

below Lobelia erinus

Bulbs

Bulbs bring us so many of our most beautiful and common flowers that it's hard to imagine our gardens without them. As well as the familiar tulips, crocuses, snowdrops and daffodils, there are gems for the rock garden, plenty to grow in pots and choice specialities for the enthusiast to discover. Bulbs are not reserved just for spring; many flower in summer and autumn too.

The word 'bulb' is here used as a general word to cover true bulbs and also corms, tubers and rhizomes. No matter what form the plant's underground storage organ takes, these are exceedingly easy plants to grow. With few exceptions, if you plant a flowering-size bulb you can be sure of flowers. Most of the hardy bulbs, corms and tubers are particularly tough, although you might have to lift frost-sensitive ones, such as dahlias and gladioli, and protect them from frost in winter. Even some of these can be left in the ground if deeply penetrating frosts are rare where you live and you don't mind taking a risk.

Losses are usually due to pests or diseases – mice and other vermin find bulbs an attractive meal – but you can usually leave the hardy kinds undisturbed to grow into bigger and better clumps for many years. Eventually they will become so congested that they have to be lifted, divided and replanted.

Using bulbs

Tulips and hyacinths are particularly useful for spring bedding displays and for cultivation in pots, windowboxes and other containers. Daffodils, crocuses and snowdrops are usually planted more informally and may be naturalized in grass, provided it is not mown until their leaves are beginning to ripen and to turn yellow in early summer. Small bulbs, such as *Muscari* (grape hyacinth) and scillas, are often grown in rock gardens or used to make carpets of spring colour beneath taller plants. Because spring-flowering bulbs die down in summer they are especially effective with deciduous shrubs, which are bare of leaves when the bulbs are flowering, or with herbaceous plants, most of which will hardly have started to grow so early in the year. *Eranthis* spp. (winter aconite), snowdrops, crocuses, scillas, chinodoxas, *Muscari* (grape hyacinth) and daffodils are all good for this kind of two-tier planting, as they do not have to be lifted every year but can be left undisturbed for several years until they become overcrowded.

top The giant of the flowering onion family, *Allium giganteum* can grow to 2m (6ft) with heads over 10cm (4in) across.

above These tulips would look equally elegant alone in a pot, beneath a tree in blossom or rising from a froth of forget-me-nots.

Be odd

If you are planting a small number of bulbs, plant them in a group rather than a row and plant an odd number. Six bulbs will generally look less natural and less pleasing than five or seven.

Be bold

Large drifts are more effective than a number of small clumps. If you can't afford many bulbs, buy the usually cheaper mixtures or a larger quantity of one kind, rather than a half-a-dozen bulbs of a dozen different kinds – which will usually be more expensive. Twenty small clumps dotted around the garden will have less impact than the same number of bulbs in a single bed or border.

Naturalizing bulbs

One of the most popular ways of growing bulbs – snowdrops, daffodils and crocuses, in particular – is to naturalize them in drifts so that they spread at will. This is usually done in grass, but those bulbs preferring shady woodland conditions can be naturalized in soil under trees and shrubs. It is also possible to establish bulbs beneath a planting of groundcover, such as scrambling ivies. See page 40 to see how to plant bulbs in grass.

When you are choosing a grassy site, remember that the grass cannot be cut for up to six weeks after the bulbs have flowered. If you are planting in established grass, choose your bulbs carefully because not all types can compete with turf, especially the more vigorous grasses already growing. Aim to create an area that looks as natural as possible, so plant the bulbs at random, scattering them on the ground and planting them where they fall. Either grow a single type or plant a mixture of bulbs in order to create the effect of an alpine meadow.

Top ten bulbs

Chionodoxa luciliae (beauty of the snow)
Star-shaped, white-centred, blue flowers are borne on short stems, to 15cm (6in) high, in early spring.

Crocus chrysanthus 'Snow Bunting'
There are many spring-flowering crocuses to choose, all with funnel-shaped, long-tubed flowers, both plain and striped, in colours including white, yellow and purple. This cultivar, to 5cm (2in) tall, has lovely white flowers, delicately marked with silvery grey.

Cyclamen hederifolium
Pale to deep-pink flowers are produced among ivy-shaped, silvery-green leaves in autumn.

Fritillaria meleagris (snake's head fritillary)
Bell-shaped, chequered flowers appear in spring. These range in colour from pinkish-purple to white.

Galanthus nivalis (snowdrop)
The small white flowers, to 10cm (4in) tall, have delicate green markings and appear in early spring.

Gladiolus 'Cherry Pie'
There are dozens of cultivars with spikes of funnel-shaped flowers in summer in a wide range of colours, including white, yellow, red and pink. This cultivar has ruffled bright flowers, finely lined with white.

Lilium candidum (Madonna lily)
Among a genus of beautiful plants, this is a lovely species, with large, white, sweetly fragrant flowers on erect stems in late summer.

above Cyclamen hederifolium

Narcissus 'February Silver'
Everyone has a favourite daffodil, but this vigorous and early-flowering cultivar is exceptionally attractive. Pale yellow petals surround a slightly darker yellow trumpet, borne on sturdy stems about 30cm (12in) tall.

Scilla siberica 'Alba'
White flowers, on stems to about 20cm (8in) tall, are borne in clusters in spring.

Tulipa 'Queen of Night'
Extremely dark maroon, silky-looking flowers are carried on erect stems, to 60cm (2ft) tall, in late spring. A beautiful tulip.

below Galanthus nivalis (snowdrop)

Bulbs for spring

For many gardeners, bulbs are synonymous with spring. The leaves often emerge by midwinter, and the first flowers from autumn-planted bulbs can be expected by late winter. The daffodil comes into its own in early spring and, from then on, there is a succession of spring-flowering bulbs that will bloom through until late spring. Despite the vast number of bulbs planted each autumn, however, the results seldom look quite as breathtaking as the pictures in the catalogue would suggest, unless you plant for a spring spectacular the way the professionals do.

Bulbs can be expensive, especially new cultivars or those that are difficult or slow to propagate. Many individual cultivars are bought by amateurs perhaps half-a-dozen at a time (in the case of very expensive bulbs, often single specimens are bought). If you plant these in a border and leave them to multiply, they will make very impressive clumps after a couple of seasons. However, because most of us space the new bulbs out to make our money appear to stretch further, the impact is usually lost.

If you look at photographs in catalogues or observe the displays in show gardens, you will find that they are crammed in so that the bulbs are almost touching. That's the way to achieve the effect of an established clump, even though the planting is new. The way to have a spectacular spring display of bulbs is to plan carefully and plant for a bold effect.

Cover the ground

If you can afford to, you can plant a whole bed or border densely with bulbs. If you are gardening on a budget, make the most of spring-flowering biennials, such as double daisies, *Myosotis sylvatica* (forget-me-not) or pansies, to increase the display. You can buy these as inexpensive plants in autumn or raise them yourself from seeds for minimal cost. Use spring bedding plants like these to cover the bare ground. If the bulbs are planted sparsely, they will show up better against a carpet of foliage, with the flowers looking far more attractive than they would against a background of soil. You will also be able to stretch the weeks of colour beyond the short time that bulbs are at their best.

left The tulip 'Couleur Cardinal' is in flower by mid-spring. Its rich scarlet petals are lightly flamed with purple.

top A lovely species of daffodil, *Narcissus obvallaris* flowers early in the season and will naturalize well.

Plan for succession

The best way to overcome the drawback of a short flowering season is to plant different cultivars of the same kind of plant, so that as one fades another is coming to its peak. If you buy bulbs in a garden centre, information about flowering times may not be displayed, but if you buy from a bulb specialist you will usually find information about which ones are early, which mid-season, which late. Athough you can't predict precise dates, they will remain constant in the order in which they flower.

The problem with planting for succession is that the garden never looks as spectacular as it would if all the bulbs were in bloom together. Interplanting with spring bedding plants helps to overcome this, especially if their flowering period spans from early to late, to provide continuity.

Short-term and long-term planting

Avoid short-term planting. This may be inevitable with bulbs that have to be lifted because they are not frost-hardy, but most hardy bulbs can be planted and left undisturbed to multiply on their own. If you try to plant one bulb that you can leave to grow in a permanent position for every one that has to be short-term (perhaps because they must be lifted for summer bedding or are in containers), your garden will look more impressive every year.

Try planting large drifts in the herbaceous or mixed border. Don't worry too much about bare patches in summer. It may be possible to plant shallow-rooting annuals over the top – but don't cut the foliage off the bulbs prematurely.

The areas under deciduous trees are ideal for planting bulbs. They bring a carpet of colour in spring when the light is good, and the ground probably remains unplanted anyway because the canopy of leaves in summer makes the area dry and shady. Species crocus such as *C. tommasianus*, which bloom even earlier than the larger-flowered hybrids, will happily naturalize in a situation like this, to give an ever-increasing pool of early colour. Winter aconites and spring-flowering hardy cyclamens are similarly suited to growing beneath trees, although they will be slower to establish and spread.

left *Leucojum vernum* is the earliest of the snowflakes to appear. This beautiful variety is 'Carpathicum'.

top Primroses and forget-me-nots provide long-lasting groundcover support around a succession of spring bulbs.

Summer bulbs

Summer-flowering bulbs are less widely planted than spring bulbs, probably because there are so many other plants to grow for summer colour. Yet, if you don't plant some of these bulbs, you'll be missing out on some of the most spectacular flowers in the border.

There are some wonderful bulbs that can be used for summer bedding, for containers, and in flower borders, and there are many imaginative ways in which summer-flowering bulbs can be used. Many are exceptionally useful for providing highlights among the other herbaceous plants, and you can use them to fill in those inevitable gaps that occur from time to time.

Some border bulbs, such as crocosmias (corms), *Zantedeschia aethiopica* (rhizomes), and *Hemerocallis* cultivars (daylily) (fleshy rhizomes), are sometimes sold growing in pots, along with the normal herbaceous plants, but all the plants mentioned here can be obtained from bulb suppliers.

The lily is sometimes said to be the queen of the bulbs, and you will find a large selection of species and hybrids in garden centres as well as in bulb catalogues. There are many different types, but whatever type you choose to grow should do well in a border or among shrubs. They prefer light or partial shade, though most of them will put in an admirable effort even in full sun. Plant in a group of at least five bulbs if you want them to make a statement among the other border perennials, but don't hesitate to pop in an isolated bulb or two wherever there is space between other plants. As lily stems and foliage are hardly attractive, it doesn't matter if these are hidden by lower-growing plants and only the flowers are visible.

Drumsticks and balls

Allium spp. (ornamental onion) include some stunning border plants. The 15cm (6in) rosy-purple balls of *Allium giganteum*, on stems up to 1.5m (5ft) tall, are an arresting sight. Many other species have imposing drumstick flowerheads, including *A. rosenbachianum*, at 90cm (3ft), and *A. sphaerocephalon*, at 60–90cm (2–3ft), both an attractive purple.

A. cristophii never fails to attract interested comment. It only grows to about 30–45cm (12–18in) high, but its spherical heads are enormous: 15–20cm (6–8in) across, studded with well-spaced, star-shaped purple flowers. This is popular with flower arrangers because the flowerheads dry well to make an unusual winter decoration.

Tall spikes

Try to find space for a clump of *Galtonia candicans* (summer hyacinth). The 1.2m (4ft) stems have hanging bells along their length. It is best to lift the bulbs in autumn if the soil is liable to freeze deeply.

Gladioli are often appreciated more as a cut flower than as a garden plant, because they do not blend easily with the other border plants. Grow them in a large clump, and think about growing the miniature forms, butterfly hybrids, or primulinus types for a garden display. The species *Gladiolus × colvilei* and *G. communis* var. *byzantinus* grow to 60–90cm (2–3ft) and have smaller and looser flowers. The colours are less varied, but they look more at ease among border plants. The corms of all of them will have to be lifted in cold regions, but the two species mentioned can be left in the ground where severe penetrating frosts are unlikely.

top *Lilium pyrenaicum* is an early-flowering lily. Its spotted yellow turkscap blooms are attractively showy, but this is not one to plant for its fragrance.

right above After decades of being ignored, the bold and beautiful canna is once again being recognized as a star, especially if you are looking for something with an exotic air.

right below Dahlias come in an enormous range of sizes, shapes and colours, from the neat single flowers to huge heads 20cm (8in) or more across.

Bright and beautiful

Canna spp. (Indian shot plant) are tall, beautiful plants and have what it takes to impart a sense of the exotic. At 1.2–2m (4–6ft), even a single clump in the border will not go unnoticed. Most have bright red, orange or yellow flowers, and the foliage is bronze or almost brown, sometimes variegated. Cannas have to be lifted for winter and stored in a frost-free place in areas where frosts occur.

Crocosmia masoniorum and its associated hybrids are first-rate border plants, forming large clumps of sword-shaped leaves from which arch long sprays of orange or yellow, funnel-shaped flowers. Smaller cultivars stand about 60cm (2ft) tall but dramatic 'Lucifer' can reach three times that. They may need a winter mulch of straw or other protective material in cold areas.

Dahlias are likely to be the brightest plants in the border in late summer and into autumn, but they come in many guises, from Lilliputs of about 30cm (12in) to giants with flowers the size of dinner plates. These tubers must be lifted for winter and stored in a frost-free place.

Cool and classy

Zantedeschia spp. (arum lily) have big white, pink or yellow spathes set among large green leaves. What they lack in colour they make up for in their cool, aristocratic appearance. Unfortunately, they prefer a winter temperature of at least 50°F (10°C), although *Z. aethiopica* is tougher and will survive winter outside where frosts do not penetrate to root level. The form 'Crowborough' is considered to be a fairly hardy plant, but it is still not suitable for really cold areas.

Weird and wonderful

Arisaemas are arums with hooded spathes and often highly exotic markings. *Arisaema candidissimum* has pale pink, cowl-like spathes about 15cm (6in) long and delicately striped white. *A. consanguineum*, a taller plant to 90cm (3ft), has a whip-like end to the spathe, which is striped maroon-purple and white. Just a single plant of either, placed where it can be discovered almost accidentally, will create that useful element of surprise and arouse curiosity.

Dierama pulcherrimum (angel's fishing rod) needs a moist but not waterlogged position to do well. It will reward with sprays of pendulous pink bells delicately poised on stems that reach about 1.5m (5ft) and arch elegantly just like miniature fishing rods.

Bulbs for autumn

Autumn-flowering plants help to make winter seem a little bit shorter. They put on a colourful display towards the end of the season, just as everything else seems to be dying down. You don't need many autumn-flowering bulbs to transform the garden as the nights draw in and flowers in the garden become fewer. The fact that they are scarce makes the impact greater. A single clump of colchicums (autumn crocus, naked ladies) in front of an otherwise gloomy shrub, a drift of miniature *Cyclamen hederifolium* beneath a tree or a patch of bright yellow sternbergias (autumn daffodils) among the brown autumn leaves scattered by the wind over a border – all these are sufficient to lift the spirits as the gardening year comes to a low ebb.

Most autumn-flowering bulbs are easy-going and should multiply and give you a better show from year to year, so they make a worthwhile investment.

Crocuses, true and false

There are more than a dozen true crocuses that you could plant to recreate memories of spring, but only a couple of them are likely to be readily available unless you go to a specialist supplier. *Crocus kotschyanus* subsp. *kotschyanus* is one of the first to flower in autumn and rapidly increases into clumps. The flowers are pale lilac with a yellow zone or blotch in the throat. Also easy to grow, and widely available, is the delightful lilac or violet *C. speciosus*; *C. speciosus* 'Albus' has white flowers. The species has an intensity of colour that makes it especially attractive against the autumn leaves through which it often flowers.

C. nudiflorus is a good choice if you want a crocus to naturalize in grass. The orange stigma and rich purple petals make it surprisingly striking. If you see what looks like a yellow spring crocus from a distance, it will almost certainly be *Sternbergia*. These are not crocuses at all, but members of the Amaryllidaceae family. They look superb against a background of gravel or autumn leaves, but they are not as easy to grow as proper crocuses. They require a hot, sunny position and well-drained neutral or alkaline soil.

The colchicums are sometimes called autumn crocuses, but they are more closely allied to lilies. They are also much larger than crocuses. Try them in clumps between other plants near the front of a border, or beneath trees and shrubs or naturalize them in rough grass. Plant them in the rock garden with caution, because the leaves – which don't appear until spring – grow much taller than the flowers and may swamp small plants nearby. They come in shades of pink, lilac and white, and there are also some with double flowers. Colchicums will flower within weeks of planting, so the results can be almost instant.

Amaryllis and crinums

One of the most impressive autumn bulbs, sure to bring your herbaceous border back to life, is the exotic-looking *Amaryllis belladonna*. It needs a sunny spot, and if you don't live in a warm part of the world it's best to plant it at the base of a sunny wall. It will bring new interest where wall shrubs and climbers are nearing the end of their season. The leafless stems grow to 60–90cm (2–3ft), topped with up to six large, bright pink, fragrant flowers. The leaves appear after the flowers and remain until the following summer. Winter protection will be needed in cold areas. Don't confuse this plant with the tender hippeastrum, popularly called amaryllis and sold as a houseplant.

Crinums are also very showy, with large, funnel-shaped flowers in early autumn on stems to 90cm (3ft) tall. They are generally tougher than the amaryllis, but choose *Crinum × powellii*, hardier than most, unless you live in a mild area. It has up to ten large pink or white blooms on each stem. Grow it in a herbaceous or mixed border, but if you live in a cold area it will be best in front of a sunny wall.

left The flowers of *Colchicum autumnale* (naked ladies) look like extra-large crocuses standing high on bare stems.

right above *Cyclamen coum* has pink, white or red flowers with dark red mouths, and rounded dark green leaves.

Snowdrops and snowflakes

These autumn-flowering versions of the popular spring plants are not particularly showy, but they are worth planting for a little extra autumn interest. The autumn-flowering snowflake, *Leucojum autumnale*, carries tiny, white, pendent, bell-shaped flowers on plants 10–15cm (4–6in) high. It is best in a warm position in the rock garden. *Galanthus reginae-olgae* looks like a normal spring snowdrop but blooms at the opposite end of the year. It prefers more sun than its spring-blooming cousins.

A final fling

Schizostylis coccinea (kaffir lily) is a rhizomatous plant that deserves to be better known. It's easy to grow, and the red or pink flowers on 45–60cm (18–24in) spikes rising above the grassy foliage stand out from across the garden from early to late autumn. It needs a moisture-retentive soil if possible, and may need winter protection in cold areas, but it's worth a little care. *Schizostylis coccinea* 'Major' is the most widely grown.

Nerines often provide the last fling of really showy colour at the tail-end of the autumn and may still be colourful in early winter. *Nerine bowdenii* is the hardiest species, with 45–60cm (18–24in) stems topped with bright pink flowerheads, the undulating petals giving them a spidery appearance from a distance.

There are other nerines, including *N. sarniensis* (Guernsey lily), but they require more warmth. Even *N. bowdenii* is not the easiest plant to grow if you live in a cold area. Plant the bulbs in front of a sunny wall if possible, and leave undisturbed to form large clumps. In cold regions a thick winter mulch over the surface may help, but remember to remove it in spring.

Winter wonders

Winter is always a difficult period in the garden, and the few hardy bulbs that flower at this time help to bring a little relief to those drab days. The hardy bulbs that are tough enough to put in an appearance at this time tend to be small and best appreciated when seen close to, so it makes sense to plant them near winter-flowering shrubs and other winter-interest plants. Focusing the eye like this makes the most of them.

Although only a couple of flowers are suggested here, many spring-flowering bulbs, including *Galanthus nivalis* (snowdrop), *Eranthis hyemalis* (winter aconite) and *Crocus tommasinianus*, often start to flower in late winter, although this will depend on where you live and the severity of the winter in a particular year. Plant plenty of these early bloomers because they will still bring early colour before the main flush of spring flowers.

Crocus laevigatus flowers in mild spells from late autumn to late winter. The flowers are fragrant and white or in shades of lilac. This is good for naturalizing in grass. *Cyclamen coum* starts to flower in mid- or late winter in mild areas, slightly later elsewhere.

below Eranthis hyemalis (winter aconite)

Rock plants

Whether you call them alpines or rock plants doesn't matter, and you don't even need a rock garden to grow them. Their diminutive size appeals to many gardeners, and, of course, they allow you to grow a large number of plants in a small area.

Rock-garden plants are immensely varied in character, some being tiny shrubs, some herbaceous plants, others bulbs, corms or tubers. Although most of them enjoy open, sunny sites and well-drained soils, suitable rock plants can be found for almost any situation in the garden, including those that are moist and shady. The fact that rock plants have developed from wild plants brought from many different mountainous areas accounts for their fascination with collectors, who can grow a wide variety of plants with different origins in a small area.

Where to grow them

A true rock garden is the ideal home for many of the plants described here, and it could be one of the garden's strongest focal points if it is well constructed. However, it is not essential to have a rock garden to grow rock plants. Many will grow just as well in ordinary beds, provided the soil is suitable and they are not overpowered by larger plants. Dry walls and raised beds are also good locations for rock-garden plants and these may fit more appropriately into the design of a small garden, including those with a formal layout.

Think of your back

Rocks are heavy and you could injure your back if you are not accustomed to lifting weights or do not use the right techniques. Whenever possible, move rocks on rollers and lever them into position with a pole or iron bar. If you do have to lift a heavy rock, enlist help and let your legs and knees do the lifting, not your back.

Another possibility is to grow rock-garden plants in pots, pans or other containers. Old stone troughs and sinks are excellent for this purpose as long as they can be provided with adequate drainage holes through which surplus water can escape. An attractive trough or sink garden can make a beautiful and interesting ornament for a terrace or patio, and a group of them would allow you to specialize, restricting each container to plants with similar requirements, so that exactly the right kind of soil can be supplied and the best aspect chosen.

Some rock plants prefer acid soil and can be grown most successfully in special peat beds that have been built in shallow terraces and retained by low walls of peat blocks. A cool, partially shaded position is best and it is usually necessary to mix some coarse sand with the peat filling in order to improve its porosity. Provided the peat beds are built above the surrounding level, lime-hating plants can be grown even in limestone districts.

top *Gentiana sino-ornata* is not the easiest alpine to grow, but given a moist, acid soil will become covered in autumn with gorgeous deep blue trumpets.

How to make a rock garden

If you garden on a sloping site, build your rock garden into the hillside. You will have less soil-moving to do, and it will look more convincing. If your garden is flat, however, try building it by the method described here, in a sunny position where there is a natural backdrop at the back – don't make a mini-mountain in the middle of your lawn.

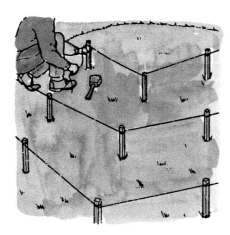

1 Mark out the shape of your rock garden with string. Dig out the topsoil within the area and mix your soil (equal parts soil, coarse sand, and peat or peat substitute will suit the majority of alpines); then make a mound in your marked area.

2 Remove the string and begin positioning the rocks, starting at the lowest level. Pack more soil behind the rocks and around the sides to make sure they are stable. Check that the rock strata lines run in the same direction.

3 Build up the rock garden a layer at a time, always keeping an eye on the strata so that they look as if they are part of the same larger underlying rock. Use a crowbar or pole to lever heavy rocks into position. Set each layer further back so that the sides slope, but leave a reasonably flat top – don't build it too high or into a peak. Pack the soil firmly to remove large air pockets, then finish off with a layer of coarse sand.

4 Arrange the plants on the rock garden while they are still in their pots, moving them around until you are happy with the arrangement. Don't forget to leave the plants space to grow. When you have decided on their positions, start planting. Scrape back some of the sand and make a hole a little larger than the rootball. You will find a narrow-bladed trowel useful. Sit the plant in the hole, then trickle more of the soil mix around the rootball and tamp it well. Finish off by covering the exposed soil with sand.

Plants for paving

Despite their small size, some rock plants are remarkably resilient and will even tolerate being trodden on occasionally. Plant them in the gaps between paving slabs to make the most of planting spaces that would otherwise go unused and unadorned. No plant will tolerate being pounded by feet several times a day, however, so plant in little-used crazy-paving paths or towards the side of a path where only straying shoots are likely to be stepped on.

If you are planting in an area that has been paved for sitting, choose a position to one side where the expanse of paving can be relieved with minimal risk to the plants. In such a situation, many of the more succulent types of plants, such as fleshy sedums, can be used very effectively.

Planting in crevices

Although many alpines are naturally adapted to growing in crevices with minimal soil or nutrients, you want your plants to get off to a good start. Whenever possible, scrape out the existing soil from between the paving slabs and expand the planting space as much as possible. Insert the plant roots, then pack in a good potting compost with the addition of a slow-release fertilizer. Water well after planting and until established. Losses are most likely in the weeks immediately after planting.

If you are sowing seed, fill the excavated crevice with potting compost mixed with a generous amount of extra grit or sand and sow a small pinch of seeds directly into this. Water and protect until the seedlings emerge, then thin to one plant. Continue to protect from crushing, and water in dry weather until the plant is growing vigorously.

Creating a sink garden

Sink gardens make attractive features in their own right, and if you choose the plants carefully it's possible to find space for perhaps a dozen plants.

If you have an old glazed sink you can coat it with 'hypertufa', a mix of equal parts coir (peat substitute), coarse or fine sand and cement. Clean the sink

left A dry-stone wall may seem an inhospitable home, but many small rock plants will flourish in the tiniest crevices.

top Creeping plants such as campanulas and thymes will soon spread themselves between paving slabs.

The best rock plants

Aubrieta is a trailing and mound-forming plant with blue, mauve or purple flowers, which appear in spring. Also spring-flowering, **Aurinia saxatilis (gold dust)** has large spikes of bright yellow flowers. **Viola cornuta (horned violet)** is a delicate-looking plant with pale to deep bluish-purple flowers and **Primula 'Wanda'** is a neat, clump-forming plant with crimson-purple flowers.

Cerastium tomentosum (snow-in-summer) is a groundcovering rock plant, which can be invasive, with silver foliage and star-shaped, white flowers in late spring and early summer. Once this is over, there are many choices for summer flowers, including **Campanula cochlearifolia (fairies' thimbles)**. This mat-forming plant has tiny white or pale blue bells, while **Dianthus 'Pike's Pink'**, an alpine pink, has fragrant, double pink flowers.

Phlox douglasii produces masses of saucer-shaped, white flowers in summer and is as popular for its leaves as for its flowers. **Sempervivum giuseppii (houseleek)** is good for carpeting. The leaves of this plant form mats made of rosettes of leaves and clusters of star-shaped flowers.

thoroughly first. Use hot water and a detergent to remove any traces of grease, then leave to dry. When the sink is clean and dry, brush a PVA adhesive onto the outside, top rim and about 5cm (2in) down the inside. Wearing gloves to protect your hands, slap on the hypertufa while the adhesive is still tacky. Press to create a seamless finish, but don't worry about a smooth surface. Mould the mixture over the rim and extend it down the inside of the sink to below the final soil level. When the mixture has dried, brush it with a liquid fertilizer or rice water to encourage algae to grow.

To plant your sink garden, begin by covering the drainage hole with broken pots or fine-mesh netting, and then add 8–10cm (3–4in) of coarse sand. Partly fill the trough with a gritty potting compost, then position any rocks that you plan to use. Top up with more gritty compost, then position the plants to make sure they are suitably arranged before planting. Firm all the plants in carefully, then cover the surface with coarse sand or stone chips to improve the appearance.

top An alpine trough makes an excellent home for a small rock-plant collection. This one includes miniature dianthus, a creeping thyme and a sempervivum.

Plants for paving

- **Acaena microphylla**
- **Arenaria balearica (Corsican sandwort)**
- **Armeria maritima (sea thrift)**
- **Aurinia saxatilis (gold dust)**
- **Erinus alpinus (fairy foxglove)**
- **Mentha requienii (Corsican mint)**
- **Saxifraga,** mossy kinds
- **Sempervivum spp. (houseleek)**, not to be walked on
- **Thymus serpyllum**
- **Veronica prostrata (prostrate speedwell)**

below Sempervivum

Vegetables

As gardens have got smaller in recent years, the vegetable plot has all but disappeared. Now, however, increasing numbers of people are beginning to realize what they are missing: taste. Home-grown vegetables may not look as perfect as those produced under the sanitized eye of the supermarket, but they undoubtedly taste better and are much fresher.

The problem with most gardens is that there is never enough space to do half the things you want to. Areas such as lawns and patios are multipurpose because they can be used for relaxation, entertainment, play and other activities, such as hanging out the washing. Vegetable plots can only be used for growing vegetables, and so they are given a low priority when it comes to the allocation of space. It is, however, possible to grow quite a lot of vegetables in a small space as long as they are tended regularly and as long as you do not grow things like rows of potatoes, which take up a lot of space – if you want some new potatoes, grow a few in tubs for that unique taste. Use raised beds where the soil can be kept fertile and where you can plant close together. Blocks are better space-savers than rows. As soon as one crop comes off, replace it with another.

Mixing it

Many vegetable plants are decorative and can happily mix with flower borders. The red stems of ruby chard, the frilly leaves of carrots and the colourful flowers of runner beans would all be worthy as ornamental plants, irrespective of their culinary qualities. The only problem with this type of approach is that you get gaps in the border when you harvest the vegetables, although, of course, flowering plants do not last for ever either.

Taking short cuts

Many garden centres and nurseries sell young vegetable plants, such as tomatoes, runner beans, sweetcorn and cabbages, ready for planting out. Although more expensive and available in only a rather limited choice of varieties, buying these plants offers a quick and easy way in which to raise your own vegetables.

top Home-grown tomatoes are much more flavoursome and can be easily grown from seed or bought as young plants for growing on.

left and right A traditional vegetable plot in full growth is very satisfying and straight rows make it easy to manage. However, many vegetables are highly ornamental and could be incorporated into a mixed border.

Growing in containers

A surprising number of vegetables can be grown in containers of one sort or another. The most elegant type of container is the terracotta pot, but for convenience and to cut down on watering, many vegetables, especially tomatoes and runner beans, are grown in plastic pots or bags containing specially formulated compost. Containers can be placed anywhere in the garden as long as they are not in shade – tomatoes, for example, can be grown against a warm wall. Plants in containers need to be watered at least once a day, and in hot, dry weather they will require it more often.

Beans, tomatoes and peppers are particularly suited to growing bags – that is, plastic bags filled with a special compost mix. Lay the bag down, cut up to three squares out of the top and plant the plants through these. For other vegetables choose a large container, preferably one that is 45cm (18in) or more across. Place this in a sunny position. Make sure there are drainage holes in the bottom and place a layer of small stones over these to aid drainage. Fill the container with multipurpose compost (you could even buy growing bags and empty the compost into the container). Plant or sow the vegetables. Water daily and give a liquid feed once a week as soon as the vegetables start to swell.

How to grow vegetables

With few exceptions, good vegetables can be produced only under good conditions. They need to be grown in an open position with plenty of light and sunshine; they will never flourish if they are tucked away in dark corners, under the shadow of buildings or in the shade of trees. Nor will they do well if grown in an exposed or drafty position.

By far the most important factor, however, is the soil. Vegetables must have fertile soil, and the key to successful vegetable growing lies in building up soil fertility, and there are many ways in which poor soil can be improved (see page 27). Most vegetables do best on slightly acid soils, with a pH of around 6.5.

Rotation

It is a good idea to avoid growing the same type of vegetable in the same piece of ground several years running. This is because soil pests and diseases, which attack members of the same botanical family, will build up if they have constant access to their favourite plants. In practice, rotation is a problem in small gardens, but it is easier when vegetables are grown in several small or narrow beds rather than a few large ones; there are more permutations to allow greater flexibility. Wherever possible, try to rotate over at least a three-year cycle. The main family groups that should be grown together in one area and then moved on another year are: legumes (all the peas and beans); brassicas (all the cabbage family, including swedes, radishes and turnips); and onions and leeks. Important crops – lettuces, potatoes and carrots – should also be rotated.

Preparing the ground

Vegetable seeds can be sown indoors in pots or outdoors in the soil, depending on the variety. The ground outside has to be right for sowing; it should be neither so wet that the soil sticks to your feet nor so dry that it is unworkable. In spring, especially on heavy soil, it is often a question of waiting until it dries out sufficiently. In very dry conditions the soil may need to be watered before you can sow.

The aim is to create a surface tilth where the soil is fine enough for seeds to germinate. The underlying soil needs to be firm, but not so consolidated that roots cannot penetrate. Some soils can simply be raked in spring and a fine tilth is created with no difficulty. More compacted soils may need to be forked over first, then raked, breaking down large clods with the back of the rake and raking off large stones and earth lumps. Tread the soil lightly so that it is reasonably firm, and continue raking backwards and forwards until a good tilth is formed.

Seeds are normally sown in a shallow furrow. Having prepared the soil, mark the position of a row with a garden line and make the furrow, which is really just a slit in the soil, with the point of a trowel or corner of a hoe. The depth of the furrow varies with the seed: most

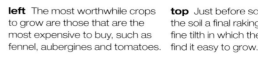

left The most worthwhile crops to grow are those that are the most expensive to buy, such as fennel, aubergines and tomatoes.

top Just before sowing, give the soil a final raking to provide a fine tilth in which the seeds will find it easy to grow.

seeds are sown at a depth roughly two or three times their width, but check with the directions on the packet. The packet will also give guidance on the space that should be left between rows.

Sowing vegetable seeds

The golden rule is to sow seeds as thinly as possible. There is always a temptation to sow thickly in case germination is poor, but in practice either soil conditions and seeds are right and there will be a very high germination (and the resulting seedlings may be of poor quality because they are so crowded) or virtually none will germinate and you will have to sow again anyway.

Either space the seeds evenly along the furrow or, to save on thinning, sow two or three seeds together at 'stations' a few centimetres (inches) apart. Thin to one seedling at each station after germination. If your plants will eventually be grown, say, 15cm (6in) apart, station sow about 8cm (3in) apart.

Large seeds, such as beans, peas, sweetcorn, cucumbers and marrows, can be sown by making individual holes with a pointed trowel.

Don't forget to label the rows to remind you of what you have planted where.

top Recycle plastic drinks bottles as mini-cloches. They will protect individual seedlings until the plants are strong enough to thrive on their own.

Choosing seeds

Most vegetables are raised from seeds, either bought over the counter or from mail-order seed producers, whose catalogues are a mine of information. Several developments in seed technology have been of particular help to gardeners, and these include:

F1 hybrids: These are specially bred varieties that produce exceptionally vigorous and uniform crops. The seeds are more expensive than ordinary 'open pollinated' varieties, but are usually worth the extra cost.

Disease resistance: Several varieties of vegetables have been bred with resistance to, or at least tolerance of, serious disease. These can be very useful.

Treated and dressed seeds: Seeds can be treated by the seedman to kill diseases that are normally carried on the seed – celery, for instance, can be treated against celery leaf spot. Seeds can also be dressed with chemicals to combat soil diseases likely to attack after sowing. Sweetcorn and pea seeds are often dressed in order to increase the chances of success with early outdoor sowings.

Pelleted seeds: The seeds are made into tiny balls with a protective coating of clay, which breaks down in the soil. The individual seeds can be handled easily and spaced out accurately, so that thinning is not required. The ground must be kept moist until the seeds have germinated.

Foil packaging: Seeds packed in airsealed foil packs keep fresh much longer than seeds in ordinary packets. Once the packets are opened, however, the seeds deteriorate normally.

Thinning

Seedlings grow rapidly and must never be allowed to become overcrowded. Thin them in stages, so that each stands just clear of its neighbour, until they are the required final distance apart. To avoid disturbing the remaining plants in the row, seedlings can be nipped off at ground level, although in some cases – lettuce, for example – they can be eased out carefully and replanted elsewhere.

Sowing indoors

Half-hardy vegetables – tomatoes, cucumbers and peppers – should be started indoors in cold areas, otherwise they would never mature in short summers. With other vegetables, such as celery and lettuces, early crops or larger specimens can be obtained by sowing indoors. 'Indoors' implies sowing in a protected environment, such as a greenhouse or cold-frame or even on a windowsill. These early sowings are often made in an electric propagator, which provides gentle heat from beneath.

For details on sowing and caring for seeds in pots and hardening them off see page 44.

Watering

Vegetables need moisture throughout their growth, but certain times are more important than others. Soils must be moist for seeds to germinate, for planting and when fertilizers are being applied.

For different groups of vegetables there are also critical periods, when shortage of water is very damaging. Leafy vegetables – spinach, lettuces, brassicas, celery and so on – are thirsty plants and will benefit from heavy watering throughout their growing season. Their critical period is 10–20 days before maturity. If regular watering is impossible, concentrate on giving one very heavy watering during this period.

'Fruiting' vegetables such as peas, beans, tomatoes, courgettes and sweetcorn are less demanding in the early stages, but, once the flowers appear and the fruit start to form, they need heavy watering.

Root vegetables have a shorter critical period, but if the soil dries out root quality will be poor. Light watering may be needed in dry weather when the plants are small, with heavier watering later in the season, when the roots are swelling.

It is much more useful to water occasionally, but heavily, than frequently but lightly. Surface watering simply evaporates before it reaches the plant's roots. Large droplets damage the soil surface and young plants, and splash mud up onto the leaves. Use a watering can with a fine rose when watering seedlings and young plants.

left Grown in individual pots, these cabbage seedlings will transfer to their final site with minimum root disturbance.

top A traditional wooden cold-frame is useful for starting off vegetables earlier than would be possible in the open ground.

Favourite vegetables

Carrots

There's nothing so crunchy and sweet as a freshly pulled carrot and they are simple to grow. If you sow a few seeds at fortnightly intervals from spring, you will get a succession of sweet young carrots throughout summer. You need a light, fertile soil. Sow the seeds thinly in a shallow drill, water evenly and regularly and thin out seedlings are soon as they are large enough. Pull the carrots when they are large enough to eat – small ones are often especially delicious.

Courgettes

Courgettes are reliable plants and usually produce plenty of fruit throughout summer. They are available in green or yellow varieties and are perfect for growing in containers. Because they are tender, it is best to sow the seeds indoors in early spring so that the plants are already well established when it is warm enough to plant them out. Plant two seeds each in small plastic flower pots of multipurpose compost and water well. Stand the pots on a windowsill and keep the compost moist until the seedlings emerge. If both seeds in a pot germinate, simply pull out one of the seedlings and let the other develop. After all risk of frost is past, harden the seedlings off (see page 44) and plant the young plants in large containers in a sunny place. Keep well watered and feed regularly when they start to flower and fruit.

Runner beans

Runner beans are among the easiest vegetables to grow and also the most attractive. They are climbing plants and need some support, such as trellis, bean poles or strings, to grow up. Use them to create screens of foliage and flowers in summer and a bumper crop of beans into the bargain. Sow the seeds in the garden – in a border or in pots – in late spring when there is no longer a risk of frost. Make sure the soil is fertile and moist by incorporating plenty of organic matter. Sow the seeds 5cm (2in) deep and 15cm (6in) apart. As soon as the young plants emerge, start to wind them around the supports to encourage them in the right direction. Water well and often and pick the beans regularly when they form.

above Juicy fresh-pulled carrots

above A golden variety of courgette

above Runner bean 'Painted Lady'

Herbs

A herb can be defined as any type of plant that is grown for its culinary and medicinal qualities as well as for its aromatic and decorative contribution to the garden.

Most herbs thrive in the same type of conditions, despite their diversity in size, shape and habit, so it's easy to group together in a special herb garden, formal or informal, which will delight all year round.

Herbs with coloured and variegated foliage have been developed over the years, adding a further visual dimension to these invaluable plants. The golden-leaved form of marjoram, *Origanum vulgare* 'Aureum', for example, makes delightful little tussocks, although is apt to scorch in full sun, and there are forms of thyme with both silver- and golden-edged leaves. The bronze form of fennel is very striking and just as tasty. Don't overlook the flowering ability of many herbs: chives produce fluffy pink flowerheads, borage has deep blue flowers, nasturtiums and marigolds have flowers ranging in colour from golden-yellow to dark orange. Many herb flowers are highly attractive to butterflies and bees.

Growing herbs

For an impressive formal feature use symmetrical beds of herbs divided by paths, perhaps in gravel or brick, and edged with chives, *Buxus* (box), santolina or lavender. On a smaller scale, a selection of plants growing in a herb wheel can make a delightful feature in a sunny corner of the garden.

When space is really limited, lift three or four flagstones from a patio for an easy-maintenance herb bed, or use a windowbox in a sunny posiiton – you will be surprised at how many different herbs you can grow in a small area.

Some of the more decorative herbs are ideal among border plants in an ornamental flower bed, while those with an upright habit of growth, such as lavender and some thymes, can also be used to edge patios or paths or to enliven areas of paving by planting them in the cracks between the paving.

Ornamental herbs

Many herbs are grown as much for their decorative appeal as their culinary uses. *Lavandula angustifolia* (lavender) is a good example of a well-known herb used mostly in the flower garden. It has spikes of purple or pale blue flowers and small, grey-green leaves, and is highly fragrant.

For a splash of colour, the annual *Calendula officinalis* (pot marigold) is a good cottage-garden plant with vivid orange-yellow flowers, each with a dark eye. *Tanacetum vulgare* (common tansy) is another

top Most herbs flourish in a warm sheltered spot, and pots gathered into a sunny corner make an ideal location for a herb collection.

above Thyme, marjoram and chives are all easy to grow and favourite choices for a herb garden.

right above *Monarda didyma* is usually grown nowadays for its flowers (this is 'Cambridge 'Scarlet'), but it was used in North America as an infusion; its flowers taste slightly of orange.

favourite plant for cottage gardens. It has deeply cut leaves and small yellow flowers held on tall stems.

There are many other colourful ornamental herbs to brighten up the flower garden, including *Tropaeolum majus* (nasturtium), which is also an annual, with round leaves and bright red, orange and yellow, trumpet-shaped flowers. *Monarda didyma* (bergamot, bee balm) has spectacularly colourful flowers of red, pink, white or purple and the whole plant has a delightful fragrance.

Mostly grown for its foliage, *Ruta graveolens* (rue) has blue-green, deeply divided leaves and acid-yellow flowers. Take great care when you are handling rue; not only can all parts cause discomfort if eaten, but the foliage may cause photodermatitis. *Helichrysum italicum* subsp. *serotinum* (curry plant) is a bushy plant with attractive, narrow, silvery leaves and clusters of small dull yellow flowers.

Artemisia abrotanum (lad's love) is a shrubby plant, which bears spherical yellow flowers in panicles, but it is grown mainly for its silky, grey-green, fine foliage. *Levisticum officinale* (lovage) is another handsome choice with large but delicate light green leaves.

The annual *Carum carvi* (caraway) is a graceful plant with flat, lacy heads made up of many tiny white flowers. *Chamaemelum nobile* (camomile) has small, daisy-like flowers of white, cream, yellow or orange; this is a good border plant, flowering all summer. Attractive grey-green foliage makes it a popular plant for flower arrangements indoors. The form 'Treneague' is the best for a camomile lawn.

Making a herb wheel

An attractive and novel way of growing herbs is to construct a herb wheel. Traditionally, these were simply cartwheels laid on the ground, but now it is more usual to use brick, which tends to look rather formal, or stone, which is more natural in appearance. The individual compartments between the 'spokes' help to confine the more invasive herbs.

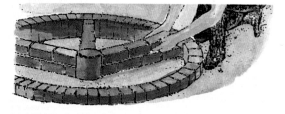

1 Begin by marking out a circle by hammering in a peg in the centre of the site and marking out the circumference with a stick and length of string.

2 Dig out the soil inside the circle to a depth of about 15cm (6in) and remove the earth. Tread the surface flat. Lay a row of bricks or stones on the outside of the circle, keeping the tops level. Use mortar to keep the bricks or stones in place.

3 Place a length of drainpipe or a chimneypot in the centre of the circle and mark out the spokes leading from this centre to the outside of the wheel. Lay bricks or stones along these lines and cement them in.

4 Fill the segments with potting compost and gently firm, bringing the level to the top of the brick edging. Plant the herbs and water them in thoroughly.

Culinary herbs

There is a vast range of culinary herbs, and some of the most popular ones are sold in supermarkets so that you can keep a small container near the kitchen door, making it easy to snip off leaves as you need them. If you have a warm, sunny spot, **Ocimum basilicum** (basil) can be grown as an annual, but it is tender and must be renewed each year. The purple-leaved form 'Dark Opal' is a striking plant, although few cultivars surpass the species for flavour.

Hardy herbs, such as those described here, will form the backbone of any herb garden. Plant them where you can get to them easily when you need them.

Allium schoenoprasum (chives)

Chives are one of the most important culinary herbs, with a mild onion flavour. The chopped leaves can be used to garnish soups, salads and cooked vegetables, in omelettes or mixed with cream cheese. The narrow, grass-like leaves grow in clumps up to 38cm (15in) high. Round, pink flowerheads appear in summer, pretty enough to qualify chives to be used as edging plants in a cottage garden. For the best flavour, however, flowers should not be allowed to form on the plant.

Chives can be raised from seeds sown in shallow drills in spring and transplanted in early summer, or you can start with young plants and set them out in light, moisture-retentive soil. Water well in dry periods. Every few years, in autumn, divide the clump into several sets and replant them in fresh soil. Chives do well in windowboxes or small pots, which can be kept indoors for a winter supply.

below chives in flower

Artemisia dracunculus (tarragon)

There are two species of tarragon for the kitchen garden: **A. dracunculus (French tarragon)** is far superior to **A. dracunculoides (Russian tarragon)**, which is somewhat lacking in aroma. The sharp pointed leaves can be used in egg and chicken dishes.

Set out groups of young plants in good, well-drained soil in spring or autumn. Full sun is essential, and it is advisable to feed the plants during the growing season to achieve a good flavour. Pinch out the growing tips to encourage leaves to develop. Tarragon is a perennial, so cut down the plants in late autumn and cover the crowns with straw to protect them from frost. Divide and replant every three years in fresh soil. Alternatively, treat plants as annuals.

Foeniculum vulgare (fennel)

Fennel is both highly decorative, with feathery bluish-green leaves, and very useful in the kitchen. The anise-like flavour is even stronger in the dried seeds than it is in the fresh leaves. The leaves are best used to accompany fish, vegetables and salads, while the seeds add flavour to bread or soups. At 2.1m (7ft) high, this herbaceous perennial makes a stately addition to the border.

Sow seeds in late spring in well-drained, rich soil. If seeds are not required, remove the flower stems as they appear. Self-sown seedlings will grow freely if the plants are allowed to flower; if not, propagate them by dividing the parent plants every three years or so. The seeds are ready to harvest when they have turned a grey-green colour and have hardened. Cut off the whole flowerhead and dry slowly indoors.

above Laurus nobilis (bay)

Laurus nobilis (bay)

Bay is an indispensable culinary herb, whether it is used in a bouquet garni, in the poaching liquid for fish, in stews and soups or even in rice pudding. An evergreen, the leathery leaves have as much flavour in winter as in summer, a rare quality among herbs.

Set out the plants in spring on any type of soil. A sunny, sheltered spot is preferable – the leaves are easily damaged by sharp winds. Most trees will reach about 3.6m (12ft) in maturity if left alone, while specimens grown in tubs of about 45cm (18in) in diameter should be pruned to shape in summer. Propagate from cuttings taken in late summer or by layering low-growing shoots.

Mentha (mint)

The popularity of mint is undeniable, but all the mints are to varying degrees invasive and will eventually take over the herb bed if left unchecked. Grow mint in tubs or large containers to keep the roots under control. If you want it in the garden, grow it in a submerged bucket with the bottom knocked out or restrict the roots with slates buried vertically around them. Mint is used with many vegetables, in yogurt as a dressing, with fish and salads and with fresh fruit.

There are many types of mint. **Mentha spicata (spearmint)** has pointed leaves; **M. suaveolens (apple mint)** is a round-leaved variety and the cook's favourite. Decorative mints include **M. x piperita f. citrata (eau-de-Cologne mint, lemon mint)**, which has almost heart-shaped lemony leaves, and **M. requienii (Corsican mint)**, a prostrate, spreading species with tiny, round, scented leaves.

Set out rooted runners of this hardy perennial in spring, in rich, moist soil. Water well during the growing season and pinch out the tips to encourage a bushy shape. Plants are easy to propagate by division in spring.

Origanum (marjoram)

Marjoram belongs to the mint family, and the small rounded leaves have an aroma like thyme, but sweeter. Primarily a culinary herb, **Origanum majorana (sweet marjoram)** is the best for flavour and is good with meat and stuffings for vegetables. **O. onites (pot marjoram)** is a hardy perennial with a strong aroma, **O. vulgare (common or wild marjoram or oregano)** is a hardy perennial, and the decorative **O. vulgare 'Aureum' (golden wild marjoram)** has leaves splashed with gold.

Treat sweet marjoram as a half-hardy annual. Sow seeds under protection in early spring and set out hardened-off plants in early summer in light but fertile soil in a sunny position. Sweet marjoram is useful for edging herb gardens or raised beds of aromatic plants. Perennial species can be increased by cuttings of basal shoots taken in spring.

below Origanum vulgare (oregano or wild marjoram)

Petroselinum crispum (parsley)

Parsley is one of the most popular herbs and one of the few that good cooks insist on using fresh. It is an essential component of a bouquet garni, and in traditional cottage gardens parsley was often used with alyssum as an edging plant. It attracts bees and is thought to repel greenfly, making it doubly useful.

Sow seeds outdoors in early spring in moist, rich soil. Parsley is notoriously slow to germinate, so if you delay sowing for a few weeks the warmer temperature will speed things along. Thin the seedlings to 20cm (8in). Water well in dry weather and cover with cloches if frost threatens. Later sowings, especially in pots that can be brought indoors, will provide leaves well into winter. Although biennial, parsley is best grown as an annual and raised from fresh seed each year.

Rosmarinus officinalis (rosemary)

Hardy almost everywhere, **Rosmarinus officinalis** reaches 1–2m (3–6ft) or more in height, making a dense, semi-erect bush of small, narrow, dark green leaves, which are intensely aromatic. Pretty pale-blue flowers appear in early summer; if you are prepared to forgo the flowers, rosemary can be clipped to make a hedge. Because of its powerful aroma, rosemary should be used sparingly when cooking.

Set young plants in a dry, sunny spot where they can be left to achieve full height. Cut back mature plants to half their height in autumn to keep the shape neat. Increase by tip cuttings taken in summer. No regular pruning is needed but the shrub should be kept under control.

Salvia (sage)

The green-leaved garden sage **Salvia officinalis** is grown primarily for its culinary uses, but there are several decorative forms equally useful in the kitchen and which often feature in scented gardens. All are hardy, evergreen subshrubs of attractively bushy habit, reaching about 60cm (2ft). The slightly bitter oval leaves can be used in any number of dishes. They retain their flavour well when dried and are often used in combination with onions as a stuffing for roast pork.

Sow seeds in the open in late spring in a sunny position in well-drained soil. Remove flowers as they appear. Trim plants two or three times during summer; they become leggy after a few years and should be replaced. Propagate from cuttings taken in early autumn.

Thymus (thyme)

After mint, thyme is one of the most widely used culinary herbs. It is included in bouquets garnis, in stuffings, with vegetables, in omelettes and on pizzas. Place a sprig underneath a roasting joint or fowl. Dried thyme keeps its flavour well. **Thymus vulgaris (common thyme)** has dark green narrow leaves and a good flavour. **T. pulegioides 'Goldentime'** is an ornamental golden-leaved form. **T. x citriodorus (lemon-scented thyme)** has broader leaves; silver and gold-leaved forms are available. **T. herba-barona (caraway thyme)** is a mat-forming species, but is not fully hardy.

Plant in spring in a sunny position in well-drained soil. Thyme is excellent in troughs, as an edging plant and for groundcover. Replace the plants when they become leggy. Propagate by division in spring.

below Salvia officinalis (sage)

Fruit

There is no reason why even the tiniest garden should not produce some sort of fruit. Most crops are adaptable in their demand on space and time. You can even find fruit for deep shade, peaty soils, cold gardens, containers, conservatories or even a moderately sunny windowsill.

Climate

All gardeners should remember that local climate is far more important than latitude. For example, there are gardens in coastal areas that will produce splendid crops of peaches, apricots and figs from wall-trained trees, yet a small distance inland even quince trees, reputed to be hardy, can be killed by the cold. One of the best ways of finding out what will grow well in your area is to look at neighbouring gardens, to contact – or, better still, join – a local gardening club or to ask at a local nursery. You will discover which varieties and which crops do especially well in your area.

Whatever your location and no matter how windy and cold it is, do not despair. There are excellent apple and pear varieties that will bear fruit in the coldest gardens; even wet mountain hillsides can provide strawberries and raspberries.

Your soil

Unless your soil is permanently waterlogged or completely dry, there will be some fruit that will grow for you. Having said this, most species will do best in deep loamy soil with a pH of about 6.5, that is, slightly on the acid side of neutral. Dampish soils will produce excellent pears, plums and raspberries. Dryish soils suit many apples, peaches, nectarines and figs. Strongly acid, peaty soils, with a pH of about 5, will produce blueberries and cranberries, but little else.

Fertilizers

Most soft fruit require a good diet. Apply garden compost, well-rotted manure or a slow-release fertilizer each winter. Cherries, strawberries, raspberries and currants need plenty of potash, so add extra at planting time and dress the soil again in winter.

If you cannot get hold of well-rotted manure and do not have room to make a compost heap, feed the plants in summer by watering them with suitable soluble fertilizers. Crops that need a diet rich in potash will like liquid ferilizers of the type used for tomatoes. A general fertilizer will suit the rest.

top Peaches fruit best when trained against a wall, to catch as much sun as possible and benefit from the warmth radiated by the bricks.

above Autumn-fruiting raspberries like 'Autumn Bliss' are even simpler to look after than summer varieties, and provide a welcome late crop.

Planting bare-rooted fruit trees

The trouble you take over planting, the first piece of work that you will have to do for your fruit, will affect most of your subsequent tasks. It is important that the plant gets the best possible start in life so that even if you eventually have no time to devote to it you will still have a tree that will try to go on being productive. Fruit that gets a bad start may take years to become established.

If you have ordered plants from a distant nursery, they will arrive some time in late autumn or in winter and will be bare-rooted – that is, most of the soil will have been shaken from the roots. Although most nurseries send out well-packed, healthy material, open the package as soon as it arrives to check that the roots have not begun to dry out. If they have, soak the roots in water for a couple of hours.

If you cannot plant immediately because the ground is frozen hard or sodden and too wet to work, the trees should be stored until the soil is workable. Keep them in a shed, garage or cellar with the roots surrounded by moist peat substitute, such as coir. If the soil is fine for planting, but you do not have time to get the plants in the ground properly, simply dig a rough trench, put the roots in and cover them with enough soil to keep them firm. This process is known as heeling in.

When weather conditions permit and you have enough time, dig a hole at the chosen site that will comfortably hold the roots when they are well spread out. If possible, fork a bucketful or two of compost or well-rotted manure into the soil at the bottom of the hole. Failing these, use a good handful of bonemeal and mix it into the soil.

Filling in

Stand the young plant in the hole to make sure that the size is right. Spread the roots out evenly. Neatly trim off any that are broken or damaged. Put a spadeful or two of excavated soil over the roots and shake the plant gently to settle the soil between the main roots. To get the planting level right, find the graft – the point at which the top growth has been attached to the rootstock and which is usually visible as an oblique swelling on the stem – and make sure that it is several centimetres (inches) above the soil level. It is sometimes possible to see where the old soil level was when the plant was in the nursery bed, in which case simply plant to the same depth.

Shovel in some more soil and shake again. Firm down with your feet. Continue until the hole is filled and the tree firmly planted.

Secure the tree to the stake. If you do not have any proprietary tree ties, use strips of cloth or stout twine threaded through a piece of hosepipe. Do not use nylon string or twine alone because it will cut into the bark. A buffer of some sort between the tree and stake is useful (see page 160).

Once planted, water the young tree or bush copiously over the whole root area. Keep a close watch on the plant in the following months, especially in hot weather. It will take at least a season before there are sufficient new roots to let the tree fend for itself.

Staking fruit trees and bushes

All fruit trees need support for the first year or two while the root system becomes strong enough to provide suffficient anchorage for the leafy top. Once you have excavated the planting hole and worked in some manure, place the stake in position. Square or round stakes are equally good, but they must be strong enough to do the job. The length of the support depends on the length of the plant's stem. The top of the stake, when driven into the base of the planting hole, should be just below the first branch of a standard-trained tree. Position the stake on the prevailing windward side of the tree, so that the tree generally pulls on the stake. With fruit bushes, the stake inevitably stands among the branches. Secure the base and a strong central branch firmly to the stake.

below Red-flushed gooseberry 'British Oak'

Container-grown plants

Fruit trees and shrubs bought as container-grown plants can be planted at any time of year, using exactly the same method as for bare-rooted trees. Open up the lowest part of the rootball as much as you can before planting, paying attention to the coil of roots that often forms at the bottom of the bag or pot.

Soft fruit

These popular fruit include blackberries, raspberries, currants of all colours and gooseberries. They are planted in the same way as fruit trees, but because the bushes are usually small when sold they do not need staking.

Pruning

Pruning helps to keep a tree or bush within bounds, produces a supply of fruiting wood and allows light and air to reach the ripening fruit. The method of pruning varies from species to species and depends also on the form of plant that is required.

Most fruit trees and bushes produce flowers and fruit along shoots that were formed the previous season. In some fruit, such as peaches and sour cherries, those shoots will not go on to produce flowers in the third year. In other cases, including apples, pears, plums and sweet cherries, flowerbuds continue to form in subsequent years, often on short sideshoots called 'spurs'. Most fruit fall into this group.

It is nevertheless also useful to think in terms of the spur when treating the first group of fruit types, where pruning has to provide a constant supply of new wood. In general, this replacement wood can be thought of as very long spurs. 'Long spur' fruit include raspberries and blackberries, vines, peaches and nectarines.

Most pruning is done in winter. Remember that fruit against a wall will start to grow as soon as the sunlight begins to gain strength. Get all pruning done before there is the slightest sign of the buds expanding. Do not prune plums or cherries in winter, because this can allow the entry of silverleaf disease (see page 209). Leave these until mid- to late summer.

left Pears are grown less often than apples, but they are very beautiful in blossom. This is the juicy 'Doyenne de Comice'.

top Growing strawberries in pots will prevent the berries from being spoilt from lying on the ground.

Pruning soft fruit

These are naturally small and seldom outgrow their allotted space. Gooseberries and currants, which can be made to spur, are best treated in the same way as bush apples. When the main branches and the spurs become too congested, cut one or two branches out each year. Of the new, replacement shoots select the strongest and remove the others.

Currants should be cut to within 2.5–5cm (1–2in) of the ground just after planting. The prunings can be used as cuttings to raise new plants. No further pruning should be necessary until the bush is several years old when, after harvesting, you should cut out between one-quarter and one-third of the branches at near ground level. This will encourage plenty of new growth, while keeping the bush open enough to ripen both fruit and new wood.

Pollination

Most fruit need pollination to take place before the crop can develop. The task is generally performed by bees.

Self-fertile plants can fertilize themselves and in the garden a single plant will produce a crop.

Self-sterile plants can only be pollinated by pollen from a plant of another variety. To get a crop, therefore, two trees of different varieties that flower at the same time must be grown. Apples, pears, plums and sweet cherries have varieties that flower at different times in spring. If you plant an early and a late sort, cross-pollination may not result because the flowers of one have faded before those of the other have opened. Varieties of these crops have been split into groups, all members of which flower at the same time. If possible, plant trees from the same group. The time of flowering is not related to ripening times, so you can still spread your crops over several weeks. There might be a compatible tree in a nearby garden or you might have to have two trees. When you are buying, ask the advice of the nurseryman.

Greenhouse crops will need pollinating by hand. You will also need to do it for certain fruit, such as apricots and some plums, planted against walls. The shelter and warmth of a wall or glass encourage fruit

trees to flower early, long before there are any bees around to pollinate them. To see if the time is right, have a look at the anthers of the open flowers. It is easy to see if they have split open, revealing white or yellowish pollen. Dab a small paintbrush into each open flower you can find, transferring the pollen as you go. On a dry sunny day the brush should show the colour of the pollen.

Harvesting

The time of ripening depends on the variety and season. If there is room for several varieties, choose some that ripen at different times to provide an even supply. Most fruit need to be picked as soon as they are ripe. Currants can be left on the bush for a week or two after they have reached their full colour, provided they are protected from the birds.

Test pears and apples for ripeness by lifting each fruit gently from the branch in the palm of your hand. If it separates easily, harvest time has arrived. Remove the fruit carefully, as bruised or damaged specimens cannot be stored. If possible, harvest them into shallow baskets or boxes.

right Apples are ready for harvesting from high summer right to the end of autumn, depending on variety. Late varieties keep better than early types.

Formative pruning for a bush

It will take about four years to train an apple or pear tree as a bush, beginning with a one-year-old tree with a single stem and no sideshoots (called a maiden).

1 Plant a bare-rooted maiden in winter, taking care not to knock or excessively stain the graft or the area around it. Begin pruning whenever the air temperature is above freezing by cutting the stem back to 75cm (30in), just above a healthy bud. For a dwarf bush, cut down to 60cm (2ft).

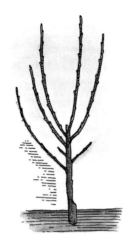

2 By the following winter, the plant will have developed several strong stems that grow upwards. The bush should have shoots that form wide angles with the main stem, and some shoots will be growing from lower down on the stem.

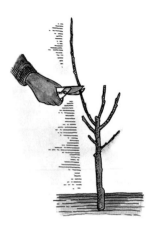

3 Select four strong, well-spaced shoots to form the main framework and cut them back by two-thirds. Prune each to just above a healthy, outward-facing bud. Cut out all unwanted shoots flush with the main stem.

4 In winter, cut back all leading shoots by about two-thirds of their length. Cut out damaged shoots, as well as those that cross the top of the bush. Small lateral shoots should be cut back to three buds to encourage the formation of fruiting spurs.

5 By the following winter, the four-year-old bush will have several leading shoots as well as younger, slender sideshoots. The severity of winter pruning influences the subsequent growth and development of fruit: the greater the proportion of wood removed, the more vigorous the following year's growth will be and the smaller the crop of fruit produced.

7 In winter, shorten the leading shoots by one-third to a half, depending on the bush's vigour. Cut back lateral shoots that are growing on the insides of the branches and towards the bush's centre to about 10cm (4in) long. Prune out dead and crossing shoots.

Forming an espalier

A well-trained espalier looks marvellous in flower and fruit. Espaliers are more useful than fans as they are easily trained to fill all the available space and each of the side branches can be extended as far as necessary.

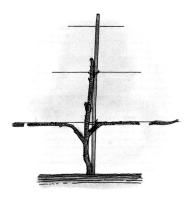

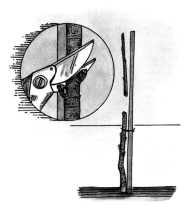

1 Begin in winter with a maiden apple or pear tree. Cut back the stem to a healthy bud just above the bottom wire. There should also be two other healthy buds positioned immediately below it.

2 The top three buds will grow from early to late summer. Loosely but firmly tie the leading shoot to a vertical cane, and the two sideshoots to two others at angles of 45 degrees. Tie the canes to the wires.

3 In the following winter, cut off the leading shoot just above the next wire. Shoots will develop to form the next tier. Lower the two side branches and shorten them by one-third to a healthy, strong, downward-pointing bud.

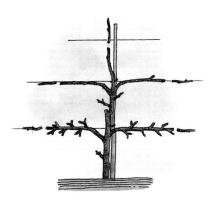

4 In summer, secure the leading and two top sideshoots to canes. Cut off any shoots growing between the first and second tier to three leaves long. Prune sideshoots on the bottom tier to three or four leaves long.

5 In subsequent winters, form further tiers in the same way as detailed earlier. Lower the tier created in summer and cut it back by one-third. Also, remove the tips of the shoots on the lower tier.

6 In early summer, when the top wire is reached, cut off the leading shoot. When the arms fill the wires, cut off their ends. Cut back sideshoots to three leaves and sublaterals to one leaf.

Water plants

Ponds, water features and bog gardens not only bring life and movement to a garden, but they also provide a habitat for growing some of the wonderful aquatic and moisture-loving plants on offer.

There are various types of water plant: waterlilies, deep-water aquatics, floating aquatics, submerged plants, marginal plants and bog plants. Waterlilies, deep-water aquatics and, to a lesser extent, floating aquatics all provide cover for fish and insects and shield the water from sunlight, so helping to keep algae under control. Submerged plants and floating aquatics also play an important role in a pond because they feed off the nutrients in the water that algae need in order to live, and in this way they help to reduce their proliferation.

Once you have your quota of functional plants, use marginal and bog plants as decoration. Choose those that suit the design of your pool. An informal pool should include a variety of plants that have been positioned at random. They should complement the surrounding area to make the feature look as natural as possible. Because a boggy area will help to merge the pool into the wider garden, the bog plants should match groups of nearby plants. For formal pools it is best to select three or five specimen plants and place them in a definite pattern rather than at random.

Keeping fish

As well as beautiful plants, ponds can be stocked with fish, which bring life and movement to the garden. Plants and fish combine well, as the latter benefit from the protection that floating and submerged leaves provide. Yet, if the fish are to be enjoyed to the full, planting must not be too dense or they will be screened almost completely from view. One advantage of having both fish and plants in a pool is that the plants will help keep the water fresh.

Year-round interest

When you are planting an ornamental pool it is important to take into account the flowering seasons of the ornamentals. Most waterlilies are at their peak in summer, so try to supplement these with marginal and bog plants that will provide spring and autumn interest. Because foliage plants have a longer period of interest than flowering plants, use them to form the backbone of your planting.

top The taller primulas, such as *P. florindae* and the many-coloured candelabra hybrids, do best in really damp soil at the water's edge.

right Waterlily breeders, in particular the French, have expanded the range of blooms to cover a wide range of subtle colours.

Controlling algae

Although a pond should receive plenty of light, direct sunlight will encourage the growth of algae which will turn the water to 'pea soup'. You can counteract this by adding submerged and floating aquatics, which consume the nutrients in the water on which the algae feed. You can also starve algae of sunlight by shading the water surface. About one-third of the surface should be covered by waterlilies and other deep-water aquatic plants.

Waterlilies

With their startling flowers and rounded, leafy pads, *Nymphaea* spp. (waterlilies) are a familiar sight in most garden pools. They come in a wide array of colours, including white, yellow, pink and red, and there are different types to choose from, including single and double; some have star-shaped flowers and some cup-shaped, while others have incurved petals or petals that are papery to touch.

Most waterlilies will provide colour from early summer until early autumn. They do not, however, tolerate moving water, so are not suitable for fast-flowing streams. If you have a fountain or cascade, posiiton the waterlilies where their foliage will not be constantly splashed and splattered. Use the special baskets to plant them at the correct depth, which will vary according to type.

Planting depths

It is important to grow each plant in the correct depth of water Grow waterlilies (a), deep-water aquatics (b) and submerged plants (c) in the deeper parts of the pool according to their depth requirements, leaving the shallow areas for marginals (d) and the marshy areas for bog plants (e).

a **waterlilies**

b **deep-water aquatics**

c **submerged plants**

d **marginals**

e **bog plants**

Other water plants

The largest and most colourful groups of plants for the water garden are those known as marginal plants and bog plants. Not all pools have a moist, marshy area for bog plants, but bog gardens contribute greatly to the overall look of the pool since they help merge it into the rest of the garden.

Marginals

Marginal plants grow around the edge of pools in shallow water up to about 15cm (6in) deep. They are decorative and adaptable plants and are useful for masking the edge of the pool where it meets the land. These plants also provide the main flowering interest around the pool. Grow them in planting baskets on the marginal shelves of the pool.

Bog plants

Although bog plants enjoy wet conditions, unlike marginals they do not actually like to stand in water. They must be planted directly into soil that is permanently moist but never actually waterlogged.

Deep-water aquatics

Plants that have their roots on the bottom of a pool and their leaves floating on the surface are known as deep-water aquatics. These plants are mostly of less ornamental value than waterlilies, with their large exotic blooms, but they help keep algae at bay. *Aponogeton distachyos* (water hawthorn) has long, oblong leaves and very distinctive, highly fragrant 'forked' white flowers in spring. *Hottonia palustris* (water violet) has white or lilac-tinted flowers and large whorls of bright green leaves.

There are several plants with yellow flowers, including *Nuphar lutea* (yellow pond lily), which has small, bottle-shaped yellow flowers and leathery, green leaves. *Nymphoides peltata* (water fringe) has delicately fringed, buttercup-yellow flowers and round, purple-mottled leaves.

Floating aquatics

Along with the leaves of waterlilies and deep-water plants, floating plants help to cover the water's surface to reduce the amount of sunlight that algae thrive on. These plants do not need planting as they float around the pool. They are prized primarily for their foliage. *Azolla mexicana* (water fern, fairy moss) has divided leaves varying in colour from red and purple to green. *Hydrocharis morsus-ranae* (frogbit) has kidney-shaped leaves and small, white flowers. The purple-splashed rosettes of *Pistia stratiotes* (water lettuce) are decorative but tender.

Submerged plants

For the most part, these plants have totally submerged foliage and emergent flowers. They play the vital role of maintaining water clarity by starving the algae of their life-giving food. *Eleocharis acicularis* (grass hair) has fine, grass-like leaves which form underwater colonies that cannot be seen from above. *Myriophyllum aquaticum* (parrot's feather) is a feathery plant with spreading, blue-green foliage; the foliage of *M. spicatum* (spiked milfoil) is much-divided and held on long, slender stems, coppery-green turning bronze. *Potamogeton crispus* (curled pondweed) has seaweed-like bronze and green shiny foliage.

left Whether formal or informal in style, all ponds need oxygenating plants that will help keep the water healthy and clear.

Favourite waterlilies

above Nymphaea 'Escarboucle'

Pink or red waterlilies

'American Star' (star-shaped, semi-double, deep pink flowers); **'Attraction'** (cup-shaped, semi-double, garnet-red flowers); **'Escarboucle'** (cup-shaped, semi-double, deep crimson flowers); **'Firecrest'** (star-shaped, semi-double, deep pink flowers): **'Froebelii'** (open tulip-shaped, deep blood-red flowers); **'James Brydon'** (peony-shaped, crimson flowers); **'Laydekeri Fulgens'** (miniature, star-shaped, semi-double, bright crimson flowers); **'Rose Arey'** (star-shaped, semi-double, deep pink flowers).

Yellow waterlilies

'Marliacea Chromatella' (cup-shaped, semi-double, canary-yellow flowers); **'Odorata Sulphurea Grandiflora'** (star-shaped, semi-double, fragrant flowers); **'Pygmaea Helvola'** (star-shaped, semi-double, canary-yellow flowers); **'Sunrise'** (star-shaped, semi-double flowers).

White waterlilies

N. alba (cup-shaped, pure white flowers); **'Caroliniana Nivea'** (star-shaped, semi-double flowers); **'Gladstoneana'** (semi-double, papery petals); **'Marliacea Albida'** (cup-shaped, semi-double, scented flowers); **N. tetragona** (miniature, single flowers); **'Virginia'** (star-shaped, semi-double, papery petals).

Top ten marginal plants

Acorus calamus (sweet flag)
This has greenish-yellow, horn-like flowers and fresh green iris-like leaves.

Butomus umbellatus (flowering rush)
Umbels of pink or red flowers grow among grass-like leaves.

Calla palustris (bog arum)
This delicate-looking plant has white spathes and heart-shaped, glossy green leaves.

Caltha palustris (kingcup, marsh marigold)
A popular sight in many informal-looking pools, this has cup-shaped, bright yellow flowers.

Iris laevigata
A lovely blue iris with many attractive hybrids including those with flowers in soft pink, white and violet and white, with fine variegated types.

Juncus effusus 'Spiralis' (corkscrew rush)
A curious-looking plant with twisted, curled stems.

Lysichiton camtschatcensis (white skunk cabbage)
Bold, eye-catching, white spathes rise amid glossy, dark green leaves.

Menyanthes trifoliata (bog bean)
An attractive marginal plant with fringed white flowers and mid-green leaves.

Pontederia cordata (pickerel weed)
Spikes of blue flowers rise above lance-shaped, glossy leaves.

Schoenoplectus lacustris subsp. tabernaemontani 'Zebrinus' (club rush)
This spectacular marginal perennial has green and white striped stems.

below Iris laevigata

Top ten bog plants

Ajuga reptans (bugle)
There are several fine cultivars of this creeping plant: 'Atropurpurea' has bronze foliage; 'Multicolour' (sometimes sold by the apt name 'Rainbow') has bronze-green leaves with cream and pink variegations.

Astilbe x arendsii
The feathery plumes of flowers are available in many colours, including bright crimson, salmon-pink, pale pink and white.

Filipendula ulmaria (meadowsweet)
Frothy spires of creamy-white blossom rise above deeply cut, dark green foliage.

Gunnera manicata
This is a large plant resembling a giant rhubarb, with hairy leaves and a reddish flower spike.

Hemerocallis cultivars (daylily)
The brightly coloured, trumpet-shaped flowers are available in many colours including bright orange and lemon yellow with strap-like leaves.

Hosta sieboldiana
Bold, heart-shaped glaucous leaves are topped with sprays of lilac blossom.

Iris ensata
Clematis-like flowers are borne in a range of colours, including purple-blue, pale rosy-lavender and deep violet above the broad, grassy foliage.

above Hemerocallis 'Buzz Bomb' (daylily)

Lysimachia nummularia (creeping jenny)
An evergreen plant, this forms a carpet of yellow, star-shaped flowers.

Osmunda regalis (royal fern)
This tall, statuesque fern has feathery, bright green fronds.

Primula bulleyana
Clusters of bright red flowers are held in candelabras above soft green, oval leaves.

plants for special places

Plants for difficult places

Shrubs for exposed places

Berberis spp.

Buddleja davidii (butterfly bush)

Cotoneaster spp.

Cytisus spp. (broom)

Elaeagnus spp.

Erica spp. and cvs (heath)

Ilex spp. (holly)

Pinus spp. (pine)

Potentilla spp.

Ribes spp. (ornamental currant)

Santolina spp.

Senecio spp.

Spiraea spp.

Viburnum spp.

Weigela spp.

Plants for shady walls

Berberidopsis corallina (coral plant)

Camellia spp. and cvs

Celastrus spp. (bittersweet, staff vine)

Clematis alpina and cvs; *C. montana* (some); *C. viticella* (some) and most large-flowered, late-flowering hybrids

Cotoneaster spp.

Daphne spp.

Euonymus spp. (spindle tree)

above Abutilon vitifolium

Forsythia spp.

Garrya spp.

Hedera helix (common ivy)

Hydrangea anomala subsp. *petiolaris* (climbing hydrangea)

Jasminum spp. (jasmine)

Kerria japonica

Lonicera spp. (honeysuckle)

Mahonia spp.

Parthenocissus henryana (Chinese Virginia creeper); *P. quinquefolia* (Virginia creeper); *P. tricuspidata* (Boston ivy)

Ribes spp. (ornamental currant)

Skimmia japonica cvs

Tropaeolum speciosum (flame creeper)

Plants for sunny walls

Abutilon spp. (flowering maple)

Actinidia kolomikta

Buddleja spp. (some)

Campsis radicans (common trumpet creeper)

Ceanothus spp. (California lilac)

Chimonanthus spp. (wintersweet)

Choisya spp. (Mexican orange blossom)

Cistus spp. (rock rose, sun rose)

Clematis armandii, C. cirrhosa, C. forsteri, double and semi-double cvs (such as 'Daniel Deronda', 'Mrs James Mason and 'Vyvyan Pennell') and most large-flowered hybrids

Escallonia spp.

Fallopia baldschuanica (mile-a-minute plant, Russian vine)

Garrya spp.

Hedera helix (common ivy; variegated forms)

Ipomoea spp. (morning glory)

Jasminum officinale (common jasmine)

Lathyrus spp.

Lonicera x *brownii* (scarlet trumpet honeysuckle)

Lonicera periclymenum (common honeysuckle, woodbine)

Magnolia spp.

Parthenocissus henryana (Chinese Virginia creeper); *P. quinquefolia* (Virginia creeper); *P. tricuspidata* (Boston ivy)

Passiflora caerulea (passion flower)

Pyracantha spp. (firethorn)

Rosa spp. and cvs (rose)

Santolina spp.

Senecio spp.

Solanum crispum (Chilean potato tree)

Tropaeolum tuberosum

Vitis coignetiae (crimson glory vine)

Wisteria floribunda (Japanese wisteria); *W. sinensis* (Chinese wisteria)

Shrubs for sun

Buddleja spp.

Chaenomeles spp. (flowering quince, japonica)

Cistus spp. (rock rose, sun rose)

Cytisus spp. (broom)

Erica spp. and cvs (heath)

Philadelphus spp. (mock orange)

Potentilla spp.

Santolina spp.

Senecio spp.

Spiraea spp.

Syringa spp. (lilac)

Weigela spp.

Plants for sunny borders

Achillea spp. (yarrow, milfoil)

Agapanthus spp. and cvs

Alstroemeria ligtu (Peruvian lily)

Centaurea spp. (knapweed)

Cistus spp. (rock rose, sun rose)

Choisya spp. (Mexican orange blossom)

Cytisus spp. (broom)

Dianthus cvs (pink)

Eryngium spp. (sea holly)

Escallonia spp.

Genista spp. (broom)

Geranium spp.

Helianthemum spp. (rock rose, sun rose)

Hemerocallis cvs (daylily)

Iris germanica

Kniphofia cvs (red-hot poker)

Lavandula spp. (lavender)

Linum perenne (perennial flax)

Oenothera spp.
(evening primrose)

Rosmarinus spp. (rosemary)

Spartium junceum
(Spanish broom)

Santolina spp.

Verbascum spp. (mullein)

Shrubs for shade

Berberis spp. (barberry)

Camellia spp. and cvs

Cornus spp. (dogwood)

Cotoneaster spp.

Daphne mezereum (mezereon)

Elaeagnus spp.

Euonymus spp. (spindle tree)

Forsythia spp.

Gaultheria spp.

Hypericum calycinum
(rose of Sharon)

Ilex spp. (holly)

Kerria japonica

Mahonia spp.

Prunus laurocerasus
(cherry laurel)

Ribes spp. (ornamental currant)

Salix spp. (willow)

Sarcococca spp. (Christmas box,
sweet box)

Skimmia japonica cvs

Spiraea spp.

Symphoricarpos spp.
(snowberry)

Viburnum spp.

Perennials for shade

Acanthus spp. (bear's breeches)

Aconitum spp. (monkshood)

Ajuga spp. (bugle)

Alchemilla spp. (lady's mantle)

Aruncus spp.

Asperula odorata (woodruff)

Astilbe spp. and cvs

Astrantia spp. (masterwort)

Bergenia spp. (elephant's ears)

Brunnera spp.

Convallaria majalis
(lily-of-the-valley)

Corydalis spp.

Dicentra spp.

Epimedium spp. (barrenwort,
bishop's mitre)

Euphorbia amygdaloides var.
robbiae (Mrs Robb's bonnet)

Geranium endressii

Helleborus spp. (hellebore)

Hosta spp. and cvs

Liriope spp. (lilyturf)

Lysimachia clethroides
(loosestrife)

Meconopsis spp.

Pachysandra terminalis

Polygonatum spp.
(solomon's seal)

Primula spp.

Prunella spp. (self-heal)

Pulmonaria spp. (lungwort)

Sanguinaria spp. (bloodroot)

Symphytum spp. (comfrey)

Thalictrum delavayi (meadow rue)

Tiarella spp. (foam flower)

Trillium spp. (trinity flower,
wood lily)

Trollius spp. (globeflower)

Vinca spp. (periwinkle)

Viola spp. (pansy

Bulbs for shade

Allium moly (golden garlic)

Anemone blanda

Camassia spp. (quamash)

Cyclamen spp.

Ornithogalum nutans
(star of Bethlehem)

Plants for alkaline, chalky soil

Agapanthus spp. and cvs

Aster spp.

Aubrieta cvs

Campanula spp. (bellflower)

Clematis spp. and cvs

Daphne spp.

Deutzia spp.

Dianthus cvs (pink)

Eranthis spp. (winter aconite)

Erica winter- and spring-flowering
European spp. (heath)

Erysimum cvs (wallflower)

Hebe spp.

Hypericum spp. (St John's wort)

Papaver spp. (poppy)

Saxifraga spp. (saxifrage)

Syringa spp. (lilac)

Plants for acid soil

Calluna vulgaris cvs (heather, ling)

Camellia spp. and cvs

Clethra spp. (sweet pepper bush)

Enkianthus spp.

Erica most spp. and cvs (heath)

Gaultheria spp.

Gentiana sino-ornata (gentian)

Hamamelis spp. (witch hazel)

Kalmia spp.

Magnolia spp.

Pieris spp.

Rhododendron spp.
(including azaleas)

above Hosta 'Frances Williams'

above Magnolia

Perennials for dry soil

Acanthus spp. (bear's breeches)

Achillea spp. (yarrow, milfoil)

Alchemilla spp. (lady's mantle)

Anthemis spp.

Artemisia spp. (mugwort, wormwood)

Astrantia spp. (masterwort)

Aubrieta cvs

Bergenia spp. (elephant's ears) (some)

Campanula spp. (bellflower)

Corydalis spp.

Crocosmia cvs

Dierama spp. (angel's fishing rod)

Echinops spp. (globe thistle)

Erigeron spp. (fleabane)

Eryngium spp. (sea holly)

Geranium spp.

Kniphofia cvs (red-hot poker)

Liatris spp. (gayfeather)

Linaria spp. (toadflax)

Linum spp. (flax)

Lychnis spp. (catchfly)

Macleaya spp. (plume poppy)

Nepeta spp. (catmint)

Oenothera spp. (evening primrose)

Physalis spp. (ground cherry)

Sedum spp.

Sempervivum spp. (houseleek)

Solidago spp. (golden rod)

Vinca spp. (periwinkle)

Bedding plants for dry soil

Ageratum houstonianum (floss flower)

Agrostemma spp. (corn cockle)

Borago officinalis (borage)

Cosmos spp. and cvs

Digitalis spp. (foxglove)

Echium spp.

Eschscholzia californica (California poppy)

Gazania cvs

Gypsophila spp.

Helichrysum spp.

Lathyrus spp.

Linaria spp. (toadflax)

Linum spp. (flax)

Nigella damascena (love-in-a-mist)

Tagetes cvs (marigold)

Shrubs for dry soil

Berberis spp. (barberry)

Buddleja spp.

Calluna vulgaris cvs. (heather, ling)

Cistus spp. (rock rose, sun rose)

Cotoneaster spp.

Cytisus spp. (broom)

Genista spp. (broom)

Hebe spp.

Helianthemum spp. (rock rose, sun rose)

Hypericum spp. (St John's wort)

Lavandula spp. (lavender)

Lavatera spp. (mallow)

Myrtus spp. (myrtle)

Olearia spp. (daisy bush)

Osmanthus spp.

Santolina spp.

Sarcococca spp. (Christmas box, sweet box)

Tamarix spp. (tamarisk)

Yucca spp.

Plants for clay soil

Ajuga spp. (bugle)

Alchemilla spp. (lady's mantle)

Astilbe spp. and cvs

above Ligularia

Astrantia spp. (masterwort)

Brunnera spp.

Cimicifuga spp. (bugbane, cohosh)

Dicentra spp.

Dodecatheon

Fritillaria meleagris (snake's head fritillary)

Hemerocallis cvs (daylily)

Heuchera spp. (coral flower)

Hosta spp. and cvs

Iris spp. (many)

Lamium spp. (deadnettle)

Leucojum aestivum (summer snowflake); *L. vernum* (spring snowflake)

Ligularia spp.

Liriope spp. (lilyturf)

Lysimachia spp. (loosestrife)

Lythrum spp. (loosestrife)

Mimulus spp. (monkey flower, musk)

Monarda spp. (bergamot)

Myosotis spp. (forget-me-not)

Narcissus cyclamineus

Ornithogalum nutans (star of Bethlehem)

Persicaria spp. (knotweed)

Polygonatum spp. (solomon's seal)

Primula spp.

Pulmonaria spp. (lungwort)

Ruscus spp. (broom)

Sidalcea spp. (false mallow, prairie mallow)

Symphytum spp. (comfrey)

Thalictrum spp. (meadow rue)

Plants for warm, sheltered borders

Agapanthus spp. and cvs

Amaryllis belladonna (belladonna lily)

Ballota pseudodictamnus

Centaurea cineraria

Crinum spp.

Gazania cvs

Helichrysum petiolare

Nerine bowdenii

Osteospermum ecklonis

Tanacetum ptarmiciflorum

Tigridia spp. (peacock flower, tiger flower)

Shrubs and climbers for sheltered places

Berberidopsis corallina (coral plant)

Buddleja fallowiana

Callistemon spp. (bottlebrush)

Camellia sasanqua

Campsis spp. (trumpet vine, trumpet creeper)

Clerodendron spp.

Clianthus spp.

Convolvulus cneorum

Eccremocarpus spp. (Chilean glory flower)

Hebe spp.

Indigofera potaninii

Jasminum officinalis (common jasmine)

Mutisia clematis

Olearia 'Henry Travers' (daisy bush)

Passiflora caerulea (passion flower)

Piptanthus nepalensis (evergreen laburnum)

Teucrium fruticans (shrubby germander, tree germander)

Trachelospermum jasminoides (confederate jasmine, star jasmine)

Tropaeolum tuberosum

Perennials for seaside gardens

Achillea spp. (yarrow, milfoil)

Agapanthus spp. and cvs

Alstroemeria spp. (Peruvian lily)

Anemone (some)

Armeria spp. (sea pink, thrift)

Artemisia spp. (mugwort, wormwood)

Bergenia spp. (elephant's ears)

Catananche caerulea (blue cupidone, cupid's dart)

Centaurea spp. (knapweed)

Crocosmia cvs

Dianthus cvs (pink)

Dierama spp. (angel's fishing rod)

Echinops spp. (globe thistle)

Erigeron spp. (fleabane)

Eryngium spp. (sea holly)

Euphorbia spp. (spurge)

Festuca spp. (fescue)

Gazania cvs

Geranium spp.

Gypsophila paniculata (baby's breath)

Heuchera spp. (coral flower)

Kniphofia cvs (red-hot poker)

Linaria spp. (toadflax)

Lychnis spp. (catchfly)

Oenothera spp. (evening primrose)

Penstemon cvs

Primula vulgaris (primrose)

Scabiosa spp. (pincushion flower, scabious)

Sedum spp.

Tradescantia Andersoniana Group

Veronica spp. (speedwell)

Shrubs and climbers for seaside gardens

Berberis spp. (barberry)

Buddleja spp.

Carpenteria californica

Caryopteris x *clandonensis*

Ceanothus spp. (California lilac)

Choisya spp. (Mexican orange blossom)

Cistus spp. (rock rose, sun rose)

Clematis spp. and cvs

Cotoneaster spp.

Cytisus spp. (broom)

Eccremocarpus spp. (Chilean glory flower)

above Hebe 'Autumn Glory'

Elaeagnus spp.

Escallonia spp.

Euonymus japonicus (Japanese spindle)

Fremontodendron spp. (flannel bush)

Fuchsia magellanica

Garrya spp.

Genista spp. (broom)

Hebe spp.

Hedera spp. (ivy)

Hibiscus syriacus

Hydrangea spp. and cvs

Hypericum spp. (St John's wort)

Juniperus spp. (juniper)

Lathyrus spp.

Lavandula spp. (lavender)

Lavatera spp. (mallow)

Leycesteria spp.

Myrtus spp. (myrtle)

Olearia spp. (daisy bush)

Osmanthus spp.

Passiflora spp. (passion flower, granadilla)

Phormium spp.

Potentilla spp.

Pyracantha spp. (firethorn)

Ribes spp. (ornamental currant)

Romneya coulteri (tree poppy, matilija poppy)

Rosmarinus spp. (rosemary)

Sambucus spp. (elder)

Santolina spp.

Skimmia japonica cvs

Solanum spp.

Spartium junceum (Spanish broom)

Symphoricarpos spp. (snowberry)

Tamarix spp. (tamarisk)

Tropaeolum spp. (some)

Viburnum tinus (laurustinus)

Weigela spp.

Yucca spp.

Plants for special positions

Climbers for arches

Akebia quinata (chocolate vine)

Campsis radicans (common trumpet creeper)

Clematis spp. and cvs

Humulus lupulus (hop)

Lonicera spp. (honeysuckle)

Rosa cvs (some, such as 'Albéric Barbier' (creamy-white), 'Emily Gray' (yellow) and 'New Dawn' (pale pink)

Vigna caracalla (corkscrew flower, snail bean)

Vitis spp. (vine)

Fragrant plants for walls

Actinidia kolomikta

Akebia quinata (chocolate vine)

Azara microphylla

Itea ilicifolia

Jasminum officinalis (common jasmine)

Lathyrus odoratus (sweet pea)

Lonicera spp. (honeysuckle)

Magnolia grandiflora (bull bay)

Osmanthus delavayi

Trachelospermum asiaticum

Wisteria sinensis (Chinese wisteria)

Plants for screening

Clematis montana, C. viticella

Fallopia baldschuanica (mile-a-minute plant, Russian vine)

Hedera helix (common ivy)

Humulus lupulus 'Aureus' (golden hop)

Hydrangea anomala subsp. *petiolaris* (climbing hydrangea)

Lonicera periclymenum (common honeysuckle, woodbine)

Parthenocissus henryana (Chinese Virginia creeper)

***above** Galanthus nivalis (snowdrop)*

Bulbs for containers

Begonia Tuberhybrida Group (tuberous begonia)

Chionodoxa luciliae (beauty of the snow)

Crocus chrysanthus

Cyclamen hederifolium

Galanthus nivalis (snowdrop)

Hyacinthus orientalis (hyacinth)

Iris reticulata

Muscari armeniacum (grape hyacinth)

Narcissus tazetta

Tulipa kaufmanniana (waterlily tulip)

Shrubs and trees for containers

Acer palmatum var. *dissectum*

Buxus sempervirens (box)

Convolvulus cneorum

Cordyline australis (New Zealand cabbage palm)

Hydrangea macrophylla

Laurus nobilis (bay)

Rhododendron yakushimanum

Skimmia japonica cvs

Perennials for containers

Acanthus mollis

Agapanthus campanulatus

Dianthus 'Doris'

Diascia vigilis

Euphorbia characias subsp. *wulfenii*

Hosta 'Gold Standard'

Nepeta x *faassenii* (catmint)

Phormium tenax (New Zealand flax)

Primula vulgaris (primrose)

Stachys byzantina (lamb's ears)

Bedding plants for containers

Argyranthemum frutescens (marguerite)

Begonia Semperflorens Cultorum Group

Bidens ferulifolia

Brachyscome iberidifolia (Swan River daisy)

Helichrysum petiolare

Impatiens walleriana (busy lizzie)

Isotoma axillaris

Pelargonium cvs

Petunia cvs

Verbena cvs

Viola cvs (pansy)

Plants for windowboxes

Begonia Semperflorens Cultorum Group; *Begonia* Tuberhybrida Group

Fuchsia (compact bush and cascading cvs)

Glechoma hederacea 'Variegata' (variegated ground ivy)

Hedera helix (common ivy; small-leaved forms)

Impatiens spp. (balsam, busy lizzie)

Lobelia erinus cvs

Lobularia maritima (sweet alyssum)

Pelargonium zonal and ivy-leaved cvs

Petunia cvs

Tagetes patula cvs
(French marigold)

Verbena cvs

Viola cvs (pansy)

Early-spring plants for the rock garden

Adonis amurensis

Androsace carnea (rock jasmine)

Anemone apennina

Aubrieta cvs

Aurinia saxatilis (gold dust)

Chionodoxa luciliae (beauty of the snow)

Erythronium dens-canis (dog's tooth violet)

Muscari armeniacum (grape hyacinth); *M. botryoides*

Narcissus bulbocodium (hoop-petticoat daffodil); *N. triandrus* (angel's tears)

Omphalodes cappadocica; *O. verna* (blue-eyed mary, creeping forget-me-not)

Saxifraga Kabschia types (saxifrage)

Tulipa tarda; *T. kaufmanniana* (waterlily tulip)

Mid-spring plants for the rock garden

Adonis vernalis

Aubrieta cvs

Aurinia saxatilis (gold dust)

Draba aizoides (yellow whitlow grass)

Fritillaria meleagris (snake's head fritillary)

Primula auricula

Pulsatilla vernalis; *P. vulgaris* (pasque flower)

Ramonda myconi

Tulipa greigii

Late-spring plants for the rock garden

Aethionema 'Warley Rose'

Armeria juniperifolia (sea pink, thrift); *A. maritima* (sea thrift)

Dianthus spp. (pink)

Dryas octopetala (mountain avens)

Erinus alpinus (fairy foxglove)

Gentiana acaulis (trumpet gentian); *G. verna* (spring gentian)

Geum montanum

Iberis gibraltarica

Iris cristata

Linaria alpina (alpine toadflax)

Lychnis viscaria (German catchfly)

Potentilla neumanniana

Pulsatilla alpina (alpine pasque flower)

Trillium sessile (wake robin)

Viola riviniana (dog violet)

Early-summer plants for the rock garden

Achillea chrysocoma

Androsace sarmentosa (rock jasmine)

Aster alpinus

Geranium dalmaticum

Gypsophila repens

Helianthemum nummularium

Leontopodium alpinum (edelweiss)

Phlox adsurgens; *P. douglasii*

Saxifraga Aizoon Group (saxifrage)

Thymus serpyllum

Midsummer plants for the rock garden

Campanula carpatica; *C. garganica* (Adriatic bellflower)

Gentiana septemfida

Hypericum olympicum

Sempervivum spp. (houseleek)

Late-summer plants for the rock garden

Ceratostigma plumbaginoides

Oenothera macrocarpa (Ozark sundrops)

Persicaria vacciniifolium

Sedum kamtschaticum var. *floriferum* 'Weihenstephaner Gold'

Silene schafta

above Saxifraga Aizoon Group (saxifrage)

Autumn plants for the rock garden

Colchicum autumnale (meadow saffon); *C. speciosum*

Crocus kotschyanus; *C. laevigatus*; *C. speciosus*

Cyclamen cilicium; *C. hederifolium*

Erica carnea (winter heath, alpine heath)

Gentiana sino-ornata

Sternbergia lutea (autumn daffodil)

Zauschneria californica (Californian fuchsia)

Zephyranthes candida (rain flower)

Winter plants for the rock garden

Anemone blanda

Crocus chrysanthus

Cyclamen coum

Galanthus nivalis (snowdrop)

Helleborus niger (Christmas rose)

Hepatica nobilis

Iris reticulata

Narcissus cyclamineus

Plants for special effects

Groundcover plants

Acaena spp. (New Zealand burr)

Aegopodium podagraria 'Variegatum'

Ajuga spp. (bugle)

Alchemilla spp. (lady's mantle)

Asarum spp. (wild ginger)

Asperula spp. (woodruff)

Aucuba japonica (spotted laurel)

Brunnera spp.

Convallaria majalis (lily-of-the-valley)

Cornus canadensis (creeping dogwood, dwarf cornel)

Epimedium spp. (barrenwort, bishop's mitre)

Euonymus fortunei cvs

Euonymus japonicus (Japanese spindle)

Euphorbia amygdaloides var. *robbiae* (Mrs Robb's bonnet)

Gaultheria spp.

Hedera spp. (ivy)

Hosta spp. and cvs

Hypericum spp. (St John's wort)

Lamium spp. (deadnettle)

Lysimachia nummularia (creeping jenny)

Pachysandra terminalis

Pulmonaria spp. (lungwort)

Rhododendron spp.

Sarcococca spp. (Christmas box, sweet box)

Tiarella spp. (foam flower)

Vaccinium vitis-idaea (cowberry)

Vancouveria spp.

Vinca spp. (periwinkle)

Grasses for a modern look

Calamagrostis x *acutiflora* 'Karl Foerster'

Festuca glauca (blue fescue, grey fescue)

Helictotrichon sempervirens (blue oat grass)

above Nepeta x *faassenii* (catmint)

Imperata cylindrica 'Rubra'

Leymus arenarius

Melica ciliata (melick)

Milium effusum 'Aureum' (Bowles' golden grass)

Miscanthus sinensis 'Morning Light'; *M. sinensis* 'Strictus'

Molinia caerulea subsp. *arundinacea* 'Transparent'

Pennisetum villosum (feathertop)

Flowers to attract bees and butterflies

Ageratum houstonianum (floss flower)

Aster novae-angliae (New England aster)

Buddleja davidii (butterfly bush)

Hedera helix (common ivy)

Lavandula angustifolia (lavender)

Limnanthes douglasii (poached-egg plant)

Mentha spicata (spearmint)

Monarda didyma (bergamot, bee balm)

Nepeta x *faassenii* (catmint)

Sedum telephium (orpine)

Thymus serpyllum

Plant attributes

Climbers for foliage

Actinidia kolomikta

Hedera helix (common ivy)

Parthenocissus henryana (Chinese Virginia creeper); *P. quinquefolia* (Virginia creeper); *P. tricuspidata* (Boston ivy)

Vitis coignetiae (crimson glory vine)

Climbers for flowers

Campsis radicans (common trumpet creeper)

Clematis spp. and cvs

Fallopia baldschuanica (mile-a-minute plant, Russian vine)

Hydrangea anomala subsp. *petiolaris* (climbing hydrangea)

Jasminum officinale (common jasmine)

Lonicera x *brownii* (scarlet trumpet honeysuckle); *L. periclymenum* (common honeysuckle, woodbine)

Passiflora caerulea (passion flower)

Solanum crispum (Chilean potato tree)

Wisteria floribunda (Japanese wisteria); *W. sinensis* (Chinese wisteria)

Plants with silver foliage

Artemisia 'Powis Castle'

Cerastium tomentosum (snow-in-summer)

Convolvulus cneorum

Cynara cardunculus (cardoon)

Eryngium giganteum (Miss Willmott's ghost)

Hebe pinguifolia 'Pagei'

Lavandula angustifolia (lavender)

Pyrus salicifolia 'Pendula'

Santolina pinnata subsp. *neapolitana*

Stachys byzantina (lamb's ears)

Tanacetum ptarmiciflorum

Plants with golden foliage

Acer shirasawanum 'Aureum'

Fuchsia 'Golden Treasure'

Gleditsia triacanthos 'Sunburst'

Hedera helix 'Buttercup'

Hosta 'Sum and Substance'

Humulus lupulus 'Aureus' (golden hop)

Lonicera nitida 'Baggesen's Gold'

Lysimachia nummularia 'Aurea' (golden creeping jenny)

Milium effusum 'Aureum' (Bowles' golden grass)

Origanum vulgare 'Aureum' (golden wild marjoram)

Shrubs with gold and green foliage

Aucuba japonica 'Crotonifolia'; *A. japonica* 'Variegata'

Cornus alba 'Spaethii'

Elaeagnus pungens 'Maculata'

Euonymus fortunei 'Emerald 'n' Gold'

Ilex x *altaclerensis* 'Golden King'; *I. aquifolium* 'Golden Queen'

Shrubs with silver or cream and green foliage

Cornus alba 'Elegantissima'

Euonymus fortunei 'Emerald Gaiety'

Euonymus fortunei 'Silver Queen'

Ilex aquifolium 'Argentea Marginata'

Ilex aquifolium 'Handsworth New Silver'

Ligustrum ovalifolium 'Argenteum'

Weigela florida 'Variegata'

Shrubs with golden foliage

Berberis thunbergii 'Aurea'

Calluna vulgaris 'Gold Haze'

Choisya ternata 'Sundance'

Erica carnea 'Foxhollow'

Fuchsia magellanica var. *gracilis* 'Aurea'

Ligustrum ovalifolium 'Aureum'

Lonicera nitida 'Baggesen's Gold'

Philadelphus coronarius 'Aureus'

Ribes sanguineum 'Brocklebankii'

Sambucus racemosa 'Plumosa Aurea'

Shrubs with purple or red foliage

Berberis thunbergii f. *atropurpurea* and *B. thunbergii* 'Red Chief'

Cordyline australis Purpurea Group

Corylus maxima 'Purpurea'

Cotinus coggygria 'Royal Purple'

Phormium tenax Purpureum Group

Prunus x *cistena*

Salvia officinalis 'Purpurascens' (purple sage)

Sambucus nigra 'Guincho Purple'

Shrubs with silver or grey foliage

Artemisia arborescens

Brachyglottis Dunedin Group 'Sunshine'

Caryopteris x *clandonensis*

Convolvulus cneorum

Hebe pinguifoia 'Pagei'

Perovskia atriplicifolia (Russian sage)

Santolina chamaecyparissus (cotton lavender)

Trees and shrubs for berries

Berberis thunbergii

Cotoneaster horizontalis (herringbone cotoneaster)

Crataegus monogyna (common hawthorn)

Daphne tangutica

Ilex aquifolium (common holly, English holly)

Ligustrum lucidum (Chinese privet)

Rosa glauca (rose)

Sorbus hupehensis (Hubei rowan)

Symphoricarpos albus (snowberry)

above Philadelphus

Fragrant flowers

Choisya ternata (Mexican orange blossom)

Convallaria majalis (lily-of-the-valley)

Cosmos atrosanguineus (chocolate cosmos)

Daphne tangutica

Dianthus 'Mrs Sinkins'

Erysimum cheiri (wallflower)

Philadelphus 'Sybille'

Rhododendron luteum

Rosa cvs (many)

Sarcococca hookeriana

Fragrant foliage

Aloysia triphylla (lemon verbena)

Geranium macrorrhizum

Laurus nobilis (bay)

Lavandula angustifolia (lavender)

Mentha spicata (spearmint)

Myrica gale (bog myrtle, sweet gale)

Myrtus communis (common myrtle)

Rosmarinus officinalis (rosemary)

Salvia officinalis (common sage)

Santolina chamaecyparissus (cotton lavender)

daily chores

Watering

If you want your plants to grow healthily and without check, they must have access to a constant supply of water or they will wilt and growth will be temporarily halted. If water is not made available to them soon after wilting, their leaves will turn crisp and brown, and the plants will eventually die.

When to water

You are most likely to need to water plants – particularly herbaceous and bedding plants – in spring and summer when the weather is warmer and plants are actively growing. In dry weather sandy soils will dry out much quicker than heavier clay soils, so you will need to start watering earlier.

Keep a sharp eye on fruit and vegetable plants, which require more watering than ornamentals, especially when the fruit is forming. Drought will have a serious effect on your harvest.

Autumn and winter are the prime planting seasons for deciduous trees and shrubs, and it is a good idea to water them in well unless the ground is extremely damp at planting time. This is not necessary so much to keep the plant growing as to settle the soil particles around the roots in readiness for growth the following spring.

Watering cans

The simplest way to apply water to your plants is with a watering can. Choose a can with a long spout, that feels well balanced when it is full and that has a long reach. Galvanized steel cans are durable but expensive. Plastic is cheaper but not so long lived. Both materials will split if water is allowed to freeze in them in winter. Spray heads or 'roses' are supplied with most cans, and these vary from fine to coarse. Use a fine rose on seeds and seedlings to avoid knocking the plants over or washing away seeds with big droplets, and keep the rose with larger holes for established perennials and shrubs.

When you are using a watering can fitted with a rose to water trays of seedlings, begin pouring to one side of the plants then pass the can over them, maintaining a steady, light flow. Move the can away from the plants before stopping the flow of water. This technique avoids any sudden surges of water, which can both damage tender plants and displace compost.

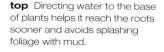

top Directing water to the base of plants helps it reach the roots sooner and avoids splashing foliage with mud.

right An oscillating sprinkler makes light work of watering: experiment with the position to get the most efficient coverage.

Hosepipes

If you have a convenient outside tap, a hosepipe is quick and easy to use. It may be left running on a patch of soil and moved around at intervals, or it may be held over a particular plant or group of plants. Take care not to allow strong flows of water to wash away soil and expose the roots of plants.

Buy a strong hosepipe, which will not kink when bent and which will retain its suppleness over the years. Hosepipes reinforced with nylon thread are especially strong. Cheap hosepipes eventually crack and leak, especially if they are used in cold weather. You'll be able to buy a wide range of clip-on connectors and nozzles.

Seep hoses are microscopically porous, designed to be trailed around beds for water to slowly seep out along their length.

Sprinklers

There are two main types of sprinkler, both of which can be attached to a hosepipe. The oscillating type consists of a perforated tube, which rocks backwards and forwards, distributing its water over a square or rectangular area. The rotating sprinkler ejects water from one or more nozzles, which are forced around by the water pressure. This type of sprinkler covers a circular area. Both sprinklers may be controlled to a certain extent by the water pressure – the higher the pressure the larger the area they will cover.

Sprinklers may be less effective on ornamental plants than on vegetables, especially in summer. The foliage of some ornamentals will deflect much of the spray, and heavy blooms and foliage can be weighed down and damaged by the water, so once the blooms appear you may prefer either use a watering can or a hosepipe to deliver water to the base of individual plants.

Reducing the need to water

If you want to cut down on time-consuming watering and at the same time help preserve water reserves, remember the following guidelines.

- Plant drought-resistant plants, which will better cope with water shortage in warm weather. Mediterranean plants, such as rosemary, lavender and other silver-leaved shrubs, are ideal.

- Use mulches, such as gravel or bark chips, on beds and borders to prevent evaporation (see pages 158–9). Top-dress containers in the same way.

- Incorporate plenty of water-retaining organic material into the soil when planting. Use potting composts that retain moisture when planting up containers.

above Lavender is a drought-resistant plant.

- Choose plastic or other non-porous containers to hold moisture for longer, and stand the pots in saucers.

- Incorporate water-retaining gel crystals into potting compost for tubs, hanging baskets and windowboxes.

- When you do water, water well and deeply to encourage plants to form deep roots. If you supply only a little water, plants will form roots near the surface where they can get at it and will be more vulnerable to drought in future.

below Mulching borders can prevent water evaporating.

Mulching and feeding

When feeding and mulching plants it is helpful to think about where they grow in the wild: plants of dry rocky habitats are not going to want a lot of rich nutrients, while fast growers and those with large, lush leaves to support will need a richer diet.

Mulching

A mulch is a layer of organic material, such as leaf mould or bark chips, or inorganic material, such as black polythene, which is laid over the surface of the soil. Use labour-saving mulches to reduce the amount of watering you need to do, and to prevent weed seeds from germinating in your beds and borders. This really is a great way of saving time.

A layer of organic matter, 5–8cm (2–3in) thick, spread around plants growing in beds and borders will slowly decompose and help to enrich the soil. Although inorganic mulches do not enrich the soil, they still keep the moisture in and prevent weeds growing. Gravel makes an excellent mulch around plants that like a dry environment, cutting down on the weeding and preventing damp from accumulating around the base of the plants.

Mulches are best spread in spring. First remove any perennial weeds, including their roots, because they will regrow through the mulch. Water the soil if it is not already moist, then lay the mulch on top. Any mulch that is left in autumn can be forked in.

Feeding

Plants that are grown both in open ground and in containers must always be kept supplied with nutrients so that they can continue to grow vigorously. Outdoors, the rain – topped up with regular watering when necessary – will leach (wash) plant foods from the soil and from containers. In addition, the nutrients will be used up by developing plants, and they will need a further supply of nutrients as they grow.

Check on the nutrient requirements of different plants: they do not all need the same amount or type, and it is a mistake to think that, if some is good, more must be better.

left Bark is clean and pleasant to use and makes an attractive blanket mulch. It will also in time rot down to improve the soil.

top Gravel is an effective weed suppressor and helps shield vulnerable stems from damp soil that might cause rot.

Fertilizers

There are many different types of fertilizers, but they fall into two categories – organic and inorganic. Organic fertilizers come from natural sources, such as plants, animals and rocks, whereas inorganic products are manmade from chemicals. The former are often slower to break down and need the help of soil bacteria to make them available to plants, which increases the number of beneficial bacteria in the soil. Slow-release fertilizers, as their name implies, release their goodness in small amounts over a long period.

Fertilizers are concentrated plant foods, and contain different levels of the major nutrients that plants need to grow – nitrogen (N), phosphorus (P) and potassium (K). When you look at the packaging of a fertilizer you will find these levels expressed as N:P:K – 4:4:6, for example. Choose a fertilizer with a high level of nitrogen if you want leafy growth, one high in phosphates to promote root growth and one high in potassium to encourage fruit and flowers. It usually says on the packet what a product can be used for, so check when you buy.

top Fertilizers formulated to be watered on come either in powder or concentrated liquid form. Mix carefully according to the instructions.

Types of mulches

Black polythene (plastic)
Advantages: Cheap and effective; can be used under gravel or bark
Disadvantages: Unsightly

Chipped bark
Advantages: Looks natural in most positions in the garden
Disadvantages: Some of the bigger chips can look ugly

Farmyard manure
Advantages: Excellent soil conditioner
Disadvantages: Must not be used fresh; may contain weed seeds

Grass cuttings
Advantages: Readily available, best used at backs of borders
Disadvantages: Unsightly; must not be used in too deep a layer

Gravel
Advantages: Attractive
Disadvantages: Not suitable for all borders as becomes mixed into the soil

Leaf mould
Advantages: Very natural, excellent soil conditioner
Disadvantages: Not readily available unless home-made

Spent mushroom compost
Advantages: Excellent soil conditioner
Disadvantages: No good for acid-loving plants as it contains lime

below Chipped bark

Supporting and protecting

Gone are the days when gardeners would patiently tie in regimental rows of dahlias and delphiniums, but some unobtrusive support for plants that need it will avoid your garden looking like it has been steamrollered after every windy or rainy day.

Moving trees and shrubs

If you need to move a tree or shrub, the best time to do so is between early winter and late spring.

Cut a vertical slit in the soil around the plant with a spade. Make the slit 30–60cm (12–24in) away from the stem, depending on the plant's size. Take out a trench 30cm (12in) wide and one spit deep, starting from the slit and working outwards. Sever any roots that extend into the trench. Thrust the spade under the rootball at an angle of 45 degrees, cutting the roots. When it will move, ease the rootball onto a sheet. Dig a new hole 30cm (12in) wider all round than the rootball. Add leaf mould or peat substitute and two handfuls of bonemeal and replant the tree or shrub in the hole.

Staking and supporting

Newly planted trees will need staking until they have grown enough roots to support themselves. Other garden plants produce large heavy blooms and therefore need constant support.

Staking trees

Dig the planting hole and check that it is large enough for the tree's roots. Then knock a stake into the soil until one-third of its length is buried. The stake should be either a length of 50 × 50mm (2 × 2in) timber, treated with a preservative other than creosote, or a larch pole similarly treated. Position the stake to the windward of the tree. The top should be just below the lowest branch.

With the stake firmly in place, plant the tree. Then fix one tree tie 5cm (2in) from the top of the stake and another 30cm (12in) above soil level. Check the ties regularly and loosen them as necessary as the trunk thickens up.

Supporting annuals and perennials

Support plants that have straight stems, such as delphiniums, either with stout bamboo canes or 2.5cm (1in) wooden stakes pushed into the ground alongside them. Fasten the stems to the supports with soft twine or raffia. Make sure that the support does not touch the flower or it might damage it.

Support bushy but floppy herbaceous plants, such as heavy-headed daisies, by pushing twiggy branches among them while they are small. As the plants grow they mask the branches but are held steady by them.

You can also buy purpose-made systems of plastic-coated metal. These come in a variety of sizes and can be linked in circles at different heights or are designed

left Tree ties should be easily adjustable and include a spacer to keep the young tree from rubbing against its stake.

top Provide support for tall plants, such as delphiniums, before they need it; don't wait until they start to flop.

to be supported on one or two posts and pushed up and down. Make sure you put them in position before the plants get too large – successful supports should not be visible once the plants are at full height.

Protecting plants from the elements

Even in a sheltered garden, gusts of wind and sudden changes in temperature can undo all your hard work. If you know that your garden is susceptible to damaging weather, take the appropriate evasive action before it's too late.

Wind protection

Wind can cause an enormous amount of damage in the garden, particularly to newly planted trees and shrubs. The plants may be completely blown over, or they may become desiccated, which causes the foliage to wilt and turn brown. Erecting screens or low hedges within the garden will help to shelter those areas that are most vulnerable.

Frost protection

The crowns of tender perennial garden plants are susceptible to frost. Protect them in autumn by placing a piece of wire netting over each crown. Cover this with dry straw or bracken and fasten another layer of

netting over the top to make a warm blanket. You can protect larger plants and shrubs by surrounding them with a cylinder of wire netting filled with either straw or bracken.

If your garden is only rarely affected by frosts, you can protect plants with temporary 'floating' mulches, which are sheets of horticultural fleece that can be laid over especially delicate plants when particularly cold weather is forecast.

Overwintering

In winter the care of hardy perennials that remain in their flower beds and herbaceous borders is relatively straightforward because they need little tending. At the end of the season, when the foliage has begun to die, cut them back almost to the ground, although you may prefer to leave any that produce seedheads, for the wildlife to harvest over the winter. In any case, remove any dead foliage from the soil nearby to prevent any possible rotting from the waste material left around the plant and to discourage insects and slugs and snails from overwintering there.

Some tubers, corms, rhizomes or bulbs – dahlia tubers and gladioli corms, for example – may need to be lifted entirely from the soil and placed in a dry, airy, frost-free place during the winter months.

left Hebes are quite hardy but can succumb to winter wet in cold areas. A little straw should provide sufficient protection.

top Horticultural fleece sheets or bags are invaluable for providing emergency protection from frost.

Pruning and training

There are many plants in the garden that will benefit from judicious and regular pruning. This will encourage healthy growth and, in the case of flowering plants, strong new growth on which flowerbuds are borne.

Plants that need pruning

Woody plants are the prime candidates for pruning, and these come in the form of ornamental shrubs (including conifers), climbers, hedges and topiary, and trees, as well as fruit trees, bushes and canes. Roses are deciduous flowering shrubs, and they need regular pruning to keep them healthy and capable of creating a new display of blooms each year.

Pruning tools

Pruning tools should be functional as well as comfortable to use. They must be kept sharp if they are to function effectively and efficiently. Wash and wipe them after use and, if they are not to be used for a few weeks, oil metal parts lightly.

Secateurs

Good secateurs are vital for pruning (see page 46). Try out several in your hand to find a pair that are a good size for you. You can also get left-handed models. Plastic-coated handles are more comfortable in cold weather than metal ones, and it can be a good idea to get secateurs with brightly coloured handles so that you can spot them easily on grass or soil.

Branch or tree loppers

Use these for cutting shoots high on fruit trees or climbing plants. They cut shoots up to 2.5cm (1in) thick and from branches 3m (10ft) high. They are ideal for pruning large fruit trees that have been neglected or those that have been grafted onto vigorous rootstocks.

The right cut

The position of a cut in relation to a bud is important and will influence subsequent growth. The illustration on the right shows the correct position of a cut: slightly sloping, with the upper point just above a bud. If the cut slopes downwards and towards the bud (a), there is a danger that it might be damaged. If the cut is too high (b), the stub will die back and allow diseases to enter. Cuts that are positioned extremely close to the bud (c) may leave it unsupported and damaged.

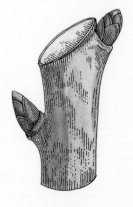

correct position of a cut

incorrect positions of cuts

Loppers

These are like long-handled secateurs and will cut wood to 3.5cm (1½in) thick. Loppers are easy to use, but are soon strained if used continuously to cut excessively thick and tough shoots.

Saws

Folding saws are usually 18cm (7in) long, extending to 40cm (16in) for use, although there are larger models. The teeth cut on both the push and pull strokes, and most folding saws will cut wood to 3.5cm (1½in) thick.

Most straight-bladed, fixed-handled saws will cut branches 13cm (5in) thick. Saws with curved blades, Grecian saws, cut on the pull stroke. Because the blade is tapered and pointed, it is usable in narrow spaces.

Knives

Pruning knives are mainly reserved for paring cut surfaces smooth, and are essential when bark-ringing trunks or notching and nicking buds. They come in many sizes. It is a false economy to buy a cheap knife because the blade will need repeated sharpening and may not be firmly secured in the handle.

Hand shears

These are ideal for trimming hedges and beds of heathers. Rubber-clad handles absorb the wrist-juddering action of repeated opening and closing.

Powered hedge-clippers

To clip a long hedge you will require some powered clippers. For an area far from an electricity supply you can choose either petrol-powered clippers or electric ones powered by a generator. Most clippers for small-scale cutting are run on electricity. Cordless types will avoid a trailing flex: check they will have enough power to do the job without recharging.

Pinching out

Pinch out the growing tip of plants such as fuchsias in order to encourage the growth of sideshoots and a bushy habit.

Deadheading

Deadheading is nothing more complicated than the removal of flowerheads as soon as they have died. It is, however, important to carry it out as often as you can throughout summer. Many perennials and biennials will flower again if you deadhead them as soon as the first flowers have died. Removing dead flowers from the plant not only makes them look better but also minimizes the chances of diseases affecting the plant.

Caring for tools

To preserve your tools it is vital to clean off any gardening dirt with an oily cloth every time you pack them away. This will keep them clean and serviceable and prevent rust. Keep knives and secateurs sharp and well oiled to prolong their lives and avoid accidents. Tools that are not needed in winter should be cleaned, oiled and kept in a dry place.

If you have children, keep your tools, especially ones like knives and pruning saws, in a locked shed.

top left A pair of secateurs is an invaluable garden tool. Sharpen them regularly to ensure they give a good, clean cut.

top For small branches that are beyond the capability of secateurs or loppers, you will need a pruning saw.

above Snapping off the dead heads of rhododendrons will prevent them from putting their energy into seed production.

Pruning deciduous shrubs

Shrubs are among the most popular garden plants. When they are correctly pruned, they will produce colourful flowers each year that will last for several weeks. Not all deciduous shrubs need annual pruning, but those that do can be divided into three types according to their flowering time: 'winter', 'spring to midsummer' and 'late summer'.

above On an early-flowering shrub, cut out shoots that have already flowered.

above Pruning a late-flowering shrub.

Winter-flowering deciduous shrubs

Shrubs in this group need little pruning other than shaping when they are young and the removal of branches that cross the plant's centre, creating congestion and reducing the maturing and ripening influence of the sun. Always cut out pest- and disease-damaged shoots; if these are left, they will encourage the decay to infect and damage other parts. This group includes plants such as *Hamamelis mollis*.

Prune winter-flowering deciduous shrubs as soon as the display is over. This gives shrubs the maximum amount of time in which to produce new shoots and for them to ripen before the onset of cold weather in the following autumn or early winter. It is easier to control the size of winter-flowering shrubs than any other type.

Early-flowering deciduous shrubs

Shrubs that flower between late spring and midsummer should be pruned as soon as their flowers fade. This group includes shrubs such as *Deutzia* spp., *Kolkwitzia amabilis* (beauty bush) and *Weigela* spp.

First, cut out thin and weak shoots and those that cross a shrub's centre. Then cut out to within a couple of buds of their base all shoots that have borne flowers. The removal of flowered shoots leaves young ones that will bear flowers during the following year. If shrubs have been neglected for several seasons, many can be rejuvenated by cutting back the complete shrub. However, this usually means foregoing flowers for one season.

Late summer-flowering deciduous shrubs

When shrubs flower in late summer, they should not be pruned until late spring of the following year. If they are pruned immediately after the flowers fade, the young shoots that subsequently develop would be damaged by frosts during winter. If you leave pruning until the following year, the fresh young shoots will not be exposed to frost. Plants in this group include hardy fuchsias, *Ceanothus* spp. and *Spiraea japonica*.

First, cut out dead and diseased shoots, then those that cross the centre of the shrub. At the same time, cut out thin and weak shoots. Next cut to just above a bud all those shoots that produced flowers during the previous year. Pruning varies slightly according to the individual shrubs.

Pruning evergreen shrubs

Evergreen shrubs are clothed in leaves throughout the year, with old leaves continually falling off and new ones being formed. Once they are established, these shrubs need no more pruning than the cutting out of weak, diseased and straggly shoots in spring. Never prune evergreen shrubs in winter, because any young shoots that subsequently develop could be blackened and damaged. This could mean that pruning has to be performed again in spring, to cut out these newly developed and blackened shoots. In exceptionally cold areas, it is better to defer pruning until early summer.

If an evergreen shrub is grown for its spring or early-summer flowers – *Berberis darwinii* (Darwin's berberis), for example – which blooms during late spring and early summer, delay pruning until after the display has faded.

Rejuvenating shrubs

Large, overgrown evergreen shrubs, such as *Aucuba japonica* 'Variegata' (spotted laurel), can be rejuvenated by cutting back all stems to within 30cm (12in) of the ground in spring. If the shrub is exceptionally large and old, cut the stems 60–90cm (2–3ft) high. You will probably need heavy-duty, double-action loppers or a curved saw.

above Cut back hard to encourage stems for winter colour.

Pruning for winter colour

Many shrubs are grown for their attractive stems to provide colour during winter. These include *Cornus alba* (red-barked dogwood), *C. stolonifera* (red osier dogwood) and *C. stolonifera* 'Flaviramea'. In spring use loppers to cut down all stems to within 5–8cm (2–3in) of the ground. This will encourage the development of fresh stems that will create a bright feature during the winter months.

Pruning hydrangeas

Mop-head forms of *Hydrangea macrophylla* are superb garden shrubs, which flower from midsummer to autumn. Leave the flower stems and old flowerheads in place until late winter or early spring, then cut out all shoots that produced flowers during the previous year. This radically thins out the shrub, allows light and air to enter and encourages the development of fresh shoots, which will bear flowers later in the year.

Pruning lavender

Lavender flowers from mid- to late summer and is pruned by lightly trimming over the plants in late summer, using a pair of sharp hand shears. Do not cut into young shoots; just trim off the old flowers. If a plant has become straggly, cut the stems hard back in late spring to encourage the development of new shoots from the plant's base. Lavender hedges are clipped to shape in spring.

left *Berberis darwinii* does not need regular pruning. If necessary, cut it back in early summer immediately after it has finished flowering.

Pruning climbers

Some climbers need regular pruning to encourage the production of flowers. to ensure that the plant remains vigorous and to keep them nicely shaped. Many, however, do not need pruning, at all, except to remove dead wood as necessary. For deciduous climbers that flower in spring or early summer, prune back the growths produced the previous year immediately after flowering. Deciduous climbers that flower in summer and autumn on growths formed in the current season should be pruned in early spring.

Renovating honeysuckle

Even the name honeysuckle evokes thoughts of canopies and arbours drenched in fragrant flowers. Unfortunately, in many ways some honeysuckles – including *Lonicera japonica* (Japanese honeysuckle), *L. periclymenum* 'Belgica' (early Dutch honeysuckle) and *L. periclymenum* 'Serotina' (late Dutch honeysuckle) – are too undemanding for their own good and will continue to flower for many years without having to be pruned. In time, however, the weight of their leaves and stems can often break their supports.

If a honeysuckle does become a mass of old stems, in spring cut back the complete plant to within 38–50cm (15–20in) of the ground.

Where it is just a mass of thin, tangled shoots, cut back the dead shoots from the base and use hand shears to trim thin shoots back to new growths.

Pruning wisteria

Wisteria are perhaps the most spectacular and best known of all flowering climbers for covering walls and pergolas or even climbing into trees. In late spring and early summer they are covered in pendulous clusters of fragrant blue or white, pea-shaped flowers. Although wisteria can be grown as standards, they are more often trained against a supporting framework of horizontal wires.

Pruning established wisterias

Once a framework has been formed, the most important objective is to keep the climber in check – lateral shoots may grow up to 3.6m (12ft) in a single year, and unless this exuberant growth is pruned the plant can soon become a jungle of stems and may grow too large for its allotted area. Severely pruning a wisteria in winter will only encourage even more rapid growth. However, by cutting it in summer it is usually possible to restrain the plant without encouraging massive growth.

In late or early winter, cut back all shoots to within two or three buds of the point where they started growing in the previous season. Where a plant becomes too large, also prune it in midsummer, cutting the current season's young shoots back to within five or six buds of the plant's base.

Pruning clematis

Gardeners often worry about pruning clematis, fearing that it is complicated and confusing. To make life easier, for pruning purposes clematis are divided into three groups, which are based on the age of the growth on which the flowers are produced.

Types of clematis

Group 1 contains early-flowering species and hybrids that bear flowers from late spring to midsummer on shoots produced in the previous year. This means that in any one year, as well as flowering on the previous year's growth, the plant is also producing shoots that will bear flowers later in the same year, creating a second and welcome flush of colour in late summer and sometimes into early autumn.

Group 2 includes vigorous spring- and early summer-flowering types that bear flowers on short shoots arising from growths that developed in the course of the previous year and on the tips of the current season's growth.

Group 3 includes the late-flowering, large-flowered cultivars, some small-flowered cultivars and late-flowering species. These clematis bear flowers in summer and autumn on shoots produced in the same season. Clematis in this group begin new growth in spring each year by developing fresh, young shoots from the ends of old shoots. If these plants are left unpruned, therefore, the bases of the plants will soon become bare and unsightly.

Pruning an old climber

Eventually – especially if they have been neglected over several years – many climbers develop a tangled web of old wood. Slowly, the climber's ability to flower is diminished and it becomes full of congested, old, non-flowering shoots. Cut back in spring.

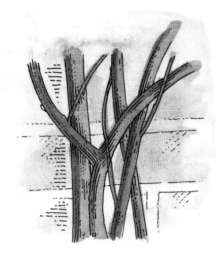

1 Cut out as much of the old, congested growth as possible. Usually it is a matter of repeatedly snipping out small pieces of tangled shoots.

2 Use sharp secateurs to cut old, dead, twiggy shoots to a healthy stem.

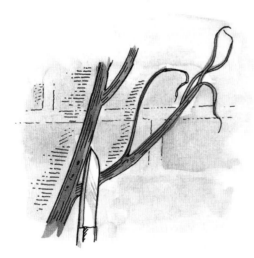

3 At the same time, cut back diseased shoots to strong and healthy shoots. If left, they will spread infection and disease.

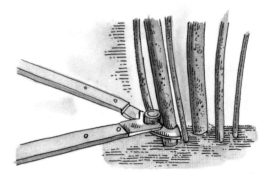

4 Some climbers continually develop new stems from their bases; the old ones eventually become thick, unproductive and congested. Use strong loppers to cut off these shoots at their base.

Pruning clematis

Group 1

Clematis include: *C. alpina* and cvs, such as 'Frances Rivis'; *C. armandii* and cvs, such as 'Apple Blossom'; *C. cirrhosa*; *C. macropetala* and cvs, such as 'Markham's Pink'; *C. montana* f. *grandiflora*, *C. montana* var. *sericea*, *C. montana* var. *rubens* and cvs, such as 'Alexander', 'Elizabeth' and 'Tetrarose'.

1 In late winter of the first year after being planted prune plants by cutting the stem to slightly above the lowest pair of healthy, strong buds. This severe pruning encourages the development of strong shoots that will help to form the climber's framework. In the summer, space out and secure these stems to a permanent framework of wires or a wooden trellis. The initial training of shoots is important to ensure that light and air can reach the shoots.

Group 2

Clematis include: Florida group cvs, such as 'Duchess of Edinburgh' and 'Vyvyan Pennell'; Lanuginosa Group cvs, such as 'Carnaby', 'Elsa Späth', 'Général Sikorski', 'Marie Boisselot' and 'Nelly Moser'; Patens Group cvs, such as 'Barbara Jackman', 'Daniel Deronda', 'Lasurstern', 'Mrs N. Thompson' and 'The President'; and other large-flowered cvs, such as 'Henryi' and 'Niobe'.

1 In late winter after being planted cut back the stem to the lowest pair of strong, healthy buds. In late spring and early summer young shoots will grow rapidly and need to be trained and secured to a framework of wires or a wooden trellis. Shoots will also develop from ground level and these, too, should be trained to the framework. Occasionally, a few flowers are produced during the first year.

Group 3

Clematis include: Jackmanii hybrids, such as 'Comtesse de Bouchaud', 'Ernest Markham', 'Hagley Hybrid' and 'Perle d'Azur'; *C. florida* and cvs, such as 'Flore Pleno'; *C. tangutica* and cvs, such as 'Bill MacKenzie' and 'Golden Harvest'; *C. texensis* and cvs, such as 'Duchess of Albany, 'Étoile Rose' and 'Gravetye Beauty'; and *C. viticella* and cvs, such as 'Ville de Lyon'.

1 In late winter after planting cut back the main shoot to the lowest pair of strong buds. Rigorously cutting back the plant in this way encourages the development of fresh shoots. In the following summer healthy young shoots develop and must be trained and secured against a wire or wooden framework. Pruning in this way encourages the development of strong shoots from ground level.

2 In the late winter of the second year cut back by half the lengths of the main shoots that developed during the previous year and were secured to a supporting framework. Ensure each shoot is cut back to slightly above a pair of strong, healthy buds. If shoots low down on the climber develop flowers early in the year, cut them back to one pair of buds from their base. In the summer months, fresh shoots will grow; space them out and secure to the supporting framework.

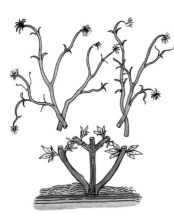

3 In the early summer of the following and subsequent years use secateurs to cut back all growths that produced flowers earlier in the year to one or two buds from their point of origin. Within this group, *C. montana* and *C. montana* var. *sericea* are very vigorous and are sometimes left unpruned. This eventually creates a tangled plant; rejuvenate by cutting to near ground level in late winter. Where plants are allowed to scale trees, leave them unpruned.

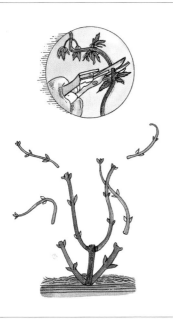

2 In late winter of the second year cut back by half all the main shoots which were produced during the previous year. Sever them just above a pair of strong, healthy buds. In the following summer, train the new shoots and space them out on the supporting framework. In this second season plants usually develop a few flowers on new growth, often into autumn. Creating a strong framework of shoots is absolutely essential.

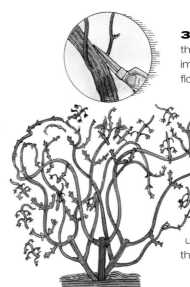

3 In early and midsummer of the third and subsequent years, immediately after the first flush of flowers has faded, cut out one-quarter to one-third of mature shoots to within 30cm (12in) of the plant's base. When plants are grown against a wall, the shoots can be readily reached and the method of pruning indicated above is ideal. However, when plants are grown on a pergola, stems cannot be untangled and plants are therefore best left unpruned.

2 In late winter of the second year cut back each shoot to its lowest pair of strong buds. This also includes shoots that developed from ground level during the previous year and are starting to form a bushy plant. In the following summer, space out vigorous shoots and secure them to a supporting framework. From mid- to late summer flowers will appear on shoots produced earlier in the same season.

3 In late winter of each subsequent year cut all growths back to leave a pair of strong buds at their base. Shoots will grow from these buds and bear flowers from midsummer to autumn. Tie shoots to a framework. On a neglected plant, cut half of the stems back into older wood to encourage the development of shoots from ground level. The following year, cut back the other half.

Pruning roses

Entire books are devoted to the topic of pruning roses, and the fact that a kind of mystique has developed around the subject of when and how roses should be pruned and with what seems to deter many people from growing roses at all. The aim of pruning is to remove dead, diseased, crossing and old shoots and to open up the plant to light and air and to encourage the production of healthy flowering shoots. Always deadhead roses regularly and in autumn cut back any long, whippy stems by about one-third to prevent wind-rock. In most areas the main pruning should be done in late winter or early spring, but always wait until the last frosts so that plants do not suffer dieback. The main groups are treated slightly differently, and the pruning requirements are summarized here.

Climbers and ramblers

After flowering cut out at least one-third of the flower-bearing shoots on rambling roses. Climbers should be tackled in late winter or early spring, when sideshoots should be shortened to leave three or four buds. Cut back main stems if necessary to keep the plant within its allotted space.

Species and related hybrids

After flowering, cut back to ground level between one-third and one-quarter of the old shoots.

Old shrub roses

Hybrid perpetuals can be pruned fairly hard. In early spring cut back the main stems to within about 30cm (12in) of ground level and take right back to ground level about one-third of the oldest stems.

Cut back the stems of other old once-flowering, shrub roses by about one-third and take about one-quarter of the oldest stems of established roses back to ground level after flowering. Repeat-flowering roses should receive the same treatment but in late winter to early spring.

Modern shrub roses

Prune once-flowering plants after flowering, cutting back the main stems by about one-third and sideshoots to 10–15cm (4–6in). On established plants some of the very oldest stems should be cut right back to ground level. Repeat-flowering roses can be pruned in late winter to early spring.

Modern bush roses

Cut back the stems of large-flowered roses to 25–30cm (10–12in) above ground level in late winter or early spring. Leave the stems of cluster-flowered roses slightly longer – 30–45cm (12–18in). You can cut one or two of the oldest stems right back to ground level on established plants of both kinds.

Miniature and patio roses

Keep plants neat by cutting back stems by about one-third in late winter to early spring. Assiduous deadheading should be enough on the smallest of plants to keep them tidy, but always take the opportunity of pruning to inspect plants closely and remove any damaged or diseased stems.

Pruning cuts on roses

Pruning cuts on roses are made individually with sharp secateurs. Take care that you do not leave short stubs at the plant's base, which are not only unsightly but can cause disease. Cuts should slope slightly from an outward-facing bud. Incorrect pruning cuts are:
1 too far away from the bud, leading to dieback;
2 caused by using blunt secateurs;
3 too close to the bud.

correct position of a cut   1   2   3

Shaping hedges

Bare-rooted hedging plants should be planted from late autumn to early spring; container-grown plants can be planted wherever the soil is workable. Straight after planting, cut back their leader and sideshoots by about half.

The following year, between late autumn and early spring, do the same thing again. This may seem drastic, but it is necessary to produce a mass of shoots from the base; hedges with thin bases are always an eyesore. In the third winter, cut back all new shoots by one-third. The following spring the shoots will be bushy and start to form a solid screen.

Water young hedges regularly and feed them in spring and midsummer to encourage the development of strong shoots.

Coniferous hedges

When the leading shoots of conifers reach 15–30cm (6–12in) above the desired height, cut off their tops about 15cm (6in) below this point. This leaves sufficient space for the hedge's top to create a bushy and well-filled top at the desired height of the hedge.

Evergreen hedges

When they are planted, evergreen hedges must be treated in the same way as the deciduous hedges.

Large-leaved evergreen shrubs need little initial pruning other than cutting back long shoots to just above a leaf-joint. However, cutting back the tips to a point slightly above the leaves encourages the development of stronger shoots. At the same time, you should cut out any diseased or damaged shoots.

If, during the second season, large-leaved shrubs are not creating a sufficiently bushy outline, cut a few shoots back to encourage new side growth.

Pruning trees

Trees require less regular pruning than shrubs, although during their formative years it is essential that crossing branches are removed.

Most deciduous trees are pruned in winter when they are dormant. Flowering cherries and other types of *Prunus*, however, must be pruned in spring or early summer, when the sap is rising, to prevent diseases.

right × *Cupressocyparis leylandii* (Leyland cypress) is not a suitable hedging plant for any but the very largest of gardens.

Shaping a hedge

To establish a uniform height, stretch a taut string between stout poles for a short distance. For longer hedges, however, it is easier to use a template, made from hardboard or heavy-duty cardboard, known as a batter.

In areas where there is a risk of heavy snowfalls, the top of the hedge should be sloped so that snow falls quickly and easily off the top.

It is essential that conifers are checked every year to ensure they have only one leading shoot. If two are allowed to grow, the conifer develops a forked top, which is unsightly and may split.

Occasionally, an established tree needs to be pruned because it has become too large and it is intruding on other plants, or into a neighbour's territory. When you are choosing a tree, it is useful to find out what its size will be after 15 or 20 years' steady growth so that you do not later have to cut it back and mar its appearance.

care-free containers

Using containers

Containers adds a new dimension to gardening, revitalizing dull areas and introducing instant colour and interest. Choose among pots, urns, planters, troughs, tubs and windowboxes made from a range of materials. Placing a few containers on patios, terraces and balconies will bring the garden close to the house, and, when secured to walls or windowsills, they can introduce a vertical element.

Moving displays

The greatest advantage of container gardening is that the containers can be moved around the garden as you wish to create a series of different effects. Moreover, you can replace the plants in them when they have passed their best, or even if you decide that you want a change of colour so that you can be assured of a continuous display of flowers. Whenever possible, position the container before you fill it with soil and plants. Always take great care when you are moving containers – even a moderately sized one filled with damp compost will be heavy – and if necessary ask for help.

Size is everything

Large containers are versatile. Make an expanse of paving more interesting by placing the largest container you can find in the centre as a focal point. To be wholly successful, the container must be large enough and the plant or plants in it bold enough to make a statement. To make an area of paving appear smaller, place large, plant-filled containers in each corner. This is also a good ploy if you have an irregularly shaped terrace, because the large pots in the corners will create a sense of unity and detract from the irregularity. Large, free-standing containers, such as urns and tubs, can be used to create focal points in lawns or to add height, and a pair of matching containers will help to create an imposing entrance way. The distinctive and dramatic shape of urns means that they look best alone or in pairs rather than as part of a cluster. Use an urn to highlight a special garden feature, to mark a focal point or to lead the eye to a point of interest. Urns look especially handsome positioned at the top or bottom of a flight of steps.

In many respects, small containers are more difficult to place than large ones. Several small containers scattered about a garden will not make much of an impact and can look fussy. In addition, a group of small containers is difficult to maintain. They do, however, come into their own when they are placed around the edges of larger containers to soften their outlines or arranged on shelves or an étagère and filled with trailing plants or colourful pelargoniums.

Grouping containers

Try to create different levels when you group containers. Not only does a tiered effect look more interesting than a

top Osteospermums and pelargoniums both like plenty of sun and are drought-tolerant, which makes them excellent container companions.

right above Heathers and hebes look pretty when in flower but, being evergreen, their interest continues all year.

right below Slow-growing conifers are suited to growing in containers and give permanent form and colour when no flowers are in bloom.

uniform row of pots, but each planting will be displayed to best effect and create a terrace-like cascade of foliage. Do not mix too many different types of containers in one group. Choose containers of a similar style or one type of material, such as terracotta.

Considering backgrounds

When containers are to be displayed against a white background, choose contrasting flowers. In spring, for example, combine blue forget-me-nots, golden-yellow or red wallflowers, pink daisies, bright yellow *Crocus chrysanthus*, blue or red hyacinths and yellow daffodils. To subdue the contrast and link the planting with its backdrop, add a few white flowers, such as the dainty white form of the Siberian squill, *Scilla siberica* 'Alba'.

To create displays that shine out against a dark background, select plants such as white, cream or yellow hyacinths, yellow *Crocus chrysanthus*, yellow-variegated ivies, vivid yellow polyanthus, white tulips and bright yellow daffodils.

It can be difficult to find colours that are sympathetic to red-brick walls, but try a combination of pale blue forget-me-nots, white hyacinths, bronze and cream wallflowers, blue grape hyacinths, yellow-variegated ivies, yellow polyanthus and white tulips. For a rich contrast with grey stone walls, go for vibrantly coloured blooms such as red wallflowers, dark blue forget-me-nots, pink tulips and pink or blue hyacinths.

Quick tips for plant combinations

- As well as considering colour, mix together plants with contrasting flower shapes and textures.

- Mix low-growing plants, such as forget-me-nots, with taller ones, such as tulips or daffodils.

- Aim for a range of growth habits by combining trailing or hanging plants with upright ones.

- Cover the container with bushy and trailing plants to create dominant patches of colour.

- Avoid using too many different plants – otherwise your container will lack definition and form.

Choosing containers

The range of containers is huge. There are not only purpose-made ornamental ones, such as hanging baskets, wall-baskets, windowboxes, troughs, tubs and urns, but also more unexpected items, such as sinks, old wheelbarrows, tyres and growing-bags. Almost anything can be called into service, and the scope for originality and novelty is endless.

If an object can hold sufficient suitable compost to support plants and has one or more holes for drainage at its lowest point, it becomes a candidate for creating anything from a splash of colour in the border or a focal point on a lawn or patio to a garden in microcosm.

Some of the largest containers, such as tubs and windowboxes, can be used for plants throughout the year. Hanging baskets are traditionally reserved for summer, although even then you needn't confine your choice to conventional ornamental plants. For a change, plant them with low-growing, cascading roses or with attractive and succulent strawberries and tomatoes. Small urns are best used for spring- and summer-flowering displays.

Your choice of container will always be a matter of personal taste, but the right scale and shape are of the utmost importance when it comes to creating a pleasing effect. When you are buying, bear the following points in mind:

- A container with a significant volume of growing medium will dry out less rapidly than a smaller container; it will also be capable of sustaining larger, more vigorous plants.
- Look for containers with large or heavy bases to give stability, especially if they are to stand near to where people will be passing to and fro.
- Some containers, especially stone ones, can be extremely heavy to lift and move. Although this is a bonus in terms of stability, such containers are not easily brought home in a car, and you may have to arrange special delivery. Some vases are made in sections, but even their individual parts can be weighty and awkward to transport.
- Drainage is essential. There should always be one large hole or several smaller holes in the base of the container.
- Containers made in natural materials will usually look best, but will be more expensive, especially if hand-crafted.

Materials

Choose a material that is in keeping with the overall style of your garden. Stainless steel will not be appropriate in a cottage-style design, and terracotta may not be suitable in a high-tech, minimalist one.

Terracotta

Terracotta is a sympathetic material, which fits in well with both the garden and the plants it contains. Plants also grow well in it. Because it is porous it is difficult to overwater plants, and it is cool in summer and warm in winter. Some terracotta pots are not frostproof and can shatter in a cold winter; you will have to move these under cover in periods of very cold weather.

Cement and stone substitute

Stone containers are still available, but they are expensive. Many of the reproduction ones, which are made of cement or stone substitute, are good imitations. Choose with care, however, because the cheaper versions are poor quality even though they, too, will eventually weather. Containers that are made of cement will also eventually age, although perhaps not as gracefully as stone will do.

Ceramics

A wide range of ceramic containers has recently appeared on the market. Most are glazed in a variety of colours and carry a range of incised or slip decorative patterns. Green, blue and brown glazes are among the most popular, but other colours can also be found.

Plastic

Most plastic pots look what they are – plastic – but they have one great advantage over pots in other materials in that they are light, which makes it easier to move them from one place to another, even when they are full of compost. One disadvantage is that the sides are not porous and it is easy to overwater.

Stainless steel

The gleaming sides of stainless steel containers can look striking in the garden. The great disadvantage of these containers is that, when they are standing in direct sun, the soil inside gets hot, so make sure you stand them in shade to protect the plants' roots. Similarly, in winter, you will need to move them under cover or wrap them in hessian or bubble plastic to protect the roots from the penetrating cold.

Container shapes

As with materials, there has been an explosion in the number of different shapes and sizes in which pots are available. The basic shape of the everyday flowerpot still takes a lot of beating for its simplicity, and many plants, such as pelargoniums, are displayed perfectly in them. A row sitting on a wall or ledge can look fantastic. Many of the other shapes are derived from classic styles, particularly the larger urns, but the use of glazed ceramics has led to the introduction of some new shapes.

Tubs, pots, urns and planters

These containers vary widely in shape and size and the types of plant that suit them. Large tubs are ideal for shrubs as well as summer-flowering bedding plants and spring-flowering bulbs. Urns are smaller and hold less compost. They are usually more decorative in character and are often best used for summer-flowering plants and displays of bulbs in spring.

Clay pots and planters are informal and functional by nature. Plastic and glass-fibre alternatives are available, however, and these can be used in place of the traditional stone types. They are less costly, lighter and have considerable potential, especially when they are displayed at some distance, filled with cascading plants to mask their synthetic origins.

Stone urns tend to be rather formal in appearance and need an architectural plant, such as a yucca. Wooden tubs are less formal and are better suited to a patio or small back yard.

Windowboxes and troughs

Wood is the most common material for windowboxes and troughs. It can be painted, stained or left untreated for a rustic, natural look. Terracotta is also popular because its texture and colour harmonize naturally with plants. Because of their weight, either position these containers on strong, concrete or brick windowsills or use them at ground level as a trough.

Reconstituted stone is also heavy and therefore best positioned at ground level. Its surface has a natural, stone-like appearance and soon mellows. Concrete troughs are suitable only for use at ground level. Glass fibre and plastic are ideal for raised positions because they are not only durable and rot-proof but light.

top left A cottage-garden favourite, nasturtium, is given a modern twist when planted in clean-lined steel.

right An original container in a city garden features the eye-catching *Imperata cylindrica* 'Rubra' (dragon's blood grass).

Planting your containers

For healthy plants and prolific flowering, make sure your containers get the very best start by using the right type of compost. Keep this well watered and regularly deadhead the flowers and weed the containers. Summer-flowering plants will also need feeding regularly.

Composts for containers

Plants in containers need well-drained yet moisture-retentive compost. The planting medium must also be fertile for summer-flowering bedding plants, which need to develop rapidly and sustain their growth throughout the summer. Spring bulbs, planted in late summer or autumn, do not need such high fertility.

For a suitable compost, use a mixture of equal parts soil-based and multipurpose compost. The multipurpose compost retains moisture, while the soil-based part provides nutrients, especially the minor ones. The addition of vermiculite further assists the retention of moisture. Proprietary composts especially designed for use in hanging baskets are available and make it easier to get the mixture right. Because the roots of plants in containers cannot extend beyond the confines of the pot to search for nutrients in the soil, it is worth using a proprietary compost that will have a good balance of everything plants need.

Drainage

It is essential that containers have adequate drainage, otherwise the planting medium will get waterlogged and the plant roots will rot. Make sure that the containers have at least one large central drainage hole or several smaller ones and place a layer of crocks (broken pieces of clay flowerpot or something similar) on the bottom of the container before filling it with compost. Containers should always be raised from the ground on bricks or flat stones so that any excess water can drain out.

If you prefer, use a layer of well-washed pea shingle instead of crocks for more permanent displays, such as those involving shrubs or small trees.

top A layer of coarse gravel, broken crocks or small pebbles in the bottom of a pot will provide the good drainage that is essential in a container.

left The *Impatiens* (busy lizzies) and heavy-headed begonias in this windowbox will need regular feeding through the summer.

right This *Acer palmatum* 'Dissectum' will take years to outgrow its handsome pot, and makes a focal point among the summer flowers.

Planting

When you are planting a container, it is a good idea to place the plants, still in their pots, on top of the soil in the partly filled container so you can experiment with different arrangements before you plant them. Once you have decided on the best composition, press each pot lightly into the soil and remove it, leaving an indentation so you can see where to make the hole.

The planting holes should be big enough to accommodate the roots with a little room to spare. Carefully remove the plants from their pots: place your hand flat over the surface of the pot with the stem of the plant between your two fingers. Carefully ease off the pot. If the rootball is particularly solid, gently tease it apart to loosen it slightly before planting. Once planted, firm the compost around the plant and water it in well.

Choosing plants for containers

Urns, tubs and planters stand on flat surfaces, such as walls, paths and patios, while windowboxes, wall-baskets and hanging baskets adorn vertical surfaces. It is, therefore, essential to choose appropriate plants for each type, both to show off the plants to perfection and to suit the container.

The shape of the container will also affect plant choice. Rectangular containers present planting challenges similar to those offered by windowboxes, but the difference in their position affects the angle at which they are viewed. While windowboxes are seen at eye level or even higher, containers stand on the ground, are raised on legs or a plinth or set on or against walls.

Raising a container offers opportunities to use trailing plants, which are best seen from the sides. When containers are mainly seen from above, choose plants with bright faces that peer upwards. In containers at ground level, low-growing herbaceous perennials create attractive features.

Most containers have a face side from which they are mainly viewed, but those on the tops of low walls may be viewed from both sides. Always make sure that the most noticeable sides are well clothed with plants. If they are bare, especially in midsummer, when troughs should be overflowing with colourful blooms, they will look unattractive and may even make the garden as a whole appear neglected and even unkempt.

Grouping plants

The way plants are grouped in containers is just as important as the grouping of the containers themselves. Although what you choose to grow is a matter of individual taste, there are a few points that it is helpful to bear in mind.

Free-standing containers

One well-chosen plant can often look better than a mixed planting, but if you do mix plants aim to have one main plant in the centre surrounded by smaller plants. Always aim for as bold an effect as possible and make sure the planting is in scale with the container.

Low-growing plants will look lost if planted alone in a wide-topped vase or urn, for example, but, if they are dominated by a tall central plant, the whole design comes into proportion.

Medium-sized, main-feature plants can be grown with strongly growing trailing plants to keep the display in proportion.

Trailing plants will help to soften harsh outlines, but remember to leave exposed any container with a particularly pleasing shape, especially if it has prominent decoration.

Windowboxes

To counteract the long, narrow shape of a windowbox, you should make every attempt to avoid planting in straight rows. An air of informality can be given to the display by varying the heights of the main plants and by softening the effect with filler plants. One way to make an attractive planting is to group main-feature plants first and put fillers in between them.

A succession of seasonal displays will give interest over a long period, and you can make up small individual pots in advance and insert them into the container as the plants come into flower. Most gardeners find it more convenient to rely on two main displays – in spring and summer – which are planted in the previous autumn and spring.

When you are selecting plants for windowboxes remember that they need to look attractive when seen from both indoors and out. To achieve this a series of low, bushy plants, which will make mounds of colour along the top of the container, is the first requirement.

Intersperse these with plants that have sprawling or trailing stems. which can be directed towards the front and sides of the box. This will help to soften the outline of the window box.

Hanging baskets

When you are grouping plants in a hanging basket, surrounding one taller central plant by smaller growing kinds usually works well, but having several plants of a single kind can be equally effective. The side plants in a basket will usually be trailing types, while taller, bushier plants should be set in the top so that the finished planting creates a ball of colour.

Watering

The relatively small volume of compost and large number of plants in containers and hanging baskets make it essential to water the compost regularly during summer and to keep it evenly moist at other times of

Planting bulbs

Bulbs can be used on their own for an eye-catching seasonal display or they can be interspersed with other plants, so creating a splash of temporary colour before the other plants come into their own. For a spectacular display of spring flowers, plant the bulbs in two layers, one on top of the other.

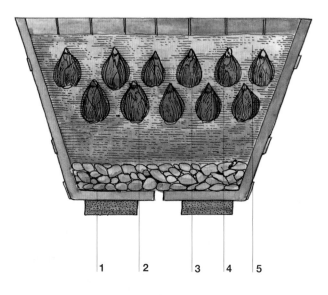

1 Place a 5cm (2in) layer of pebbles or a layer of crocks at the bottom of the container.

2 Space out the lower level of bulbs on firm compost, 20cm (8in) below the rim of the tub.

3 Position the top level of bulbs between the necks of the lower ones and firm the compost down over them.

4 After the bulbs are planted, the noses of the top bulbs are covered with 10cm (4in) of compost.

5 Leave the top of the compost about 2.5cm (1in) below the rim of the container. This will settle later.

year. At all times avoid waterlogging, which will encourage the plants to rot.

Hanging baskets tend to dry out more quickly than containers because more of their surface is exposed to the air. Plants sometimes appear to wilt during early afternoon on exceptionally hot days even though the compost is moist, and this is because they cannot absorb moisture quickly enough. The plants usually recover by the evening. If you discover a neglected hanging basket, cut back any severely wilted stems and immerse the compost in a bucket of water. Leave it until the soil has taken up water, remove it to drain and place in a cool position until the plants recover.

Moisture-retaining gel can be mixed with the compost before planting, and this will help keep the compost damp. Follow the instructions on the packet.

Feeding

Summer-flowering bedding plants need feeding regularly from early to late summer, at about three-week intervals. Spring-flowering displays composed of bulbs and biennials, such as wallflowers and daisies, do not need to be fed, but do use fresh and fertile compost. Only feed winter-flowering displays in late spring and midsummer.

A liquid fertilizer is the most widely used and convenient way of feeding plants. In this form, it is readily available for absorption by the plants. Sticks and pills of concentrated plant fertilizer are popular and provide nutrients over a long period of time. They are clean and quick to use, but the chemicals are not so readily available to plants as those applied in water and they are suitable only for summer-flowering plants.

Granular and powdered fertilizers are more widely used in gardens, where they can be dusted on the soil's surface, lightly hoed in and then watered. Dissolve them thoroughly in clean water before using them for containers.

Encouraging bushiness

Tall, lanky plants can be encouraged to put out more sideshoots if you nip out their growing points while they are still young. Fuchsias, for example, benefit from having their tips pinched out after three sets of leaves have formed. Try to position the break just above a leaf so that you do not leave a short stem, as this will die back and decay.

left A dainty late narcissus, *N.* 'Hawera', contrasts prettily with the large blooms of the double tulip 'Angelique'.

top A bold display teams a short-stemmed lily with dwarf campanulas, double and single pink marguerites and ivy.

Planting a hanging basket

Start planting a hanging basket in mid- to late spring in warm areas, but wait until early summer in cold regions. Planting can be earlier if a greenhouse or conservatory is available to give the plants protection during cold nights in spring, when frost is forecast. They need a reasonably sunny position.

1 Rest the basket on top of a large bucket to hold it firm. Line it with a sheet of black plastic or moss.

2 Fill the bottom half with compost and lightly firm it with your fingers. Trim off the excess plastic.

3 If you wish, make some planting holes in the sides of the basket and insert your chosen plants through the holes.

4 Arrange the plants in the basket and pack in compost to just below the rim.

5 Firm the compost around all the plants and then water them thoroughly.

6 Hang your planted basket in your chosen position for maximum effect.

Siting a hanging basket

Few things are more redolent of warm summer days than hanging baskets filled to overflowing with colourful blooms. Make the most of them by thinking carefully about the position.

- Arrange matching hanging baskets on either side of a frontdoor so that cascading plants slightly cut across the uprights of the frame. This will make the door area appear larger and more distinguished. Make sure, however, that the baskets cannot be accidentally knocked by visitors and that water does not drip on other plants or make a path or steps slippery.

- Windows can be treated in the same way as the frontdoor, with foliage and flowers breaking up the framework on the outer edges. If the window also has a windowbox, make sure that water from the hanging basket does not drip on to it.

- If there is a large expanse of bare wall between two windows, brighten the area by securing a hanging basket halfway along it. Where a house has three equally spaced windows, use two hanging baskets of flowers for symmetry.

above Swags of *Brachycome* (Swan River daisy) and verbena.

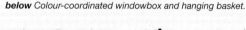

below Colour-coordinated windowbox and hanging basket.

- Large areas of wall benefit from a few well-placed baskets. Take the colour of the wall into account when selecting flower colours.

- Verandas can often be swathed in climbers, but they also look superb with hanging baskets suspended from above. Because part or all of the basket will be under cover, regular watering is essential, but take care to prevent drips.

- Carports are stark and functional. Position a couple of hanging baskets on either side of the front. Include white flowers and silver-leaved plants, which show up well at night.

- Roof gardens benefit from a little colour at head height, but make sure that the basket is not positioned in a particularly windy position.

- If you add a hanging basket to a balcony, make sure that strong wind cannot damage the plants and that water does not drip on the people below. Use plastic baskets with drip-trays built into the base.

Seasonal displays

The simplest and easiest way to use containers is to plan a series of plantings, one for each season. You can either opt for a single-colour theme, such as white and silver, or create a splash of colour using a combination of plants.

Year-round interest

Foliage plants are particularly helpful in container plantings, which tend to have short periods of interest if they rely on seasonal plants. Foliage provides a permanent background structure against which flowers can come and go.

Grey-leaved plants, such as *Helichrysum petiolare* and *Senecio cineraria* (cineraria), will 'cool' the impact of strong hues, and bring out the best in pastel pinks, mauves and misty blues. Golden tones have affinities with yellow flowers and mid-green leaves, and intensify the richness of deep blues and violets. Variegated foliage is decorative in its own right and adds interest and texture to mixed plantings.

Summer and autumn

Most summer interest is created by brightly coloured annuals. Red, pink and purple are popular summer colours, and when they are mixed with interesting foliage the result is lively and eye-catching. Many summer displays will last well into autumn, but fuchsias and sedums can be relied on well into the autumn.

When composing your planting, choose plants with contrasting flower shapes. Masses of tiny blooms create a hazy effect, which will soften the edges of a container and contrast well with larger, bolder plants.

Winter and spring

Winter containers should concentrate on shape and form to create bold, striking outlines. Foliage comes into its own, along with small berried shrubs. These can be supplemented with winter-flowering bulbs in mild areas.

Spring interest is mainly created by bulbs and biennials. Yellow is a favourite spring colour, either on its own or combined with white, cream and, perhaps, a hint of blue. For greater impact, add a splash of yellow to vibrant reds, blues and white.

Scented displays for winter

The foliage of some conifers has an intriguing aromatic quality when it is bruised. *Chamaecyparis lawsoniana* 'Ellwoodii' smells of resin and parsley, *C. pisifera* 'Boulevard' also has a resinous bouquet, and *Juniperus communis* 'Compressa' is apple scented. It is easier to appreciate the honey-scented *Iris danfordiae* or violet-scented *I. reticulata* when they are planted up in containers, and both give a wonderful winter display.

left Planting containers up for summer is a chance to try out new colour combinations and the effect of different schemes.

top The neat, glossy leaves of *Buxus sempervirens* (box) look good all year and respond well to clipping to shape.

Great ideas for seasonal containers

Colour themes for spring

- For simple impact, fill the windowbox with bright yellow narcissi – ideal for this type of container.

- Underplant red *Tulipa fosteriana* or *T. greigii* with a sea of blue **forget-me-nots**. Include a few *Muscari* (grape hyacinths) for darker accents and texture. Edge the box with **double daisies**.

- For an alternative version of the ubiquitous red-white-and-blue theme, try combining a range of **hyacinths** with **daisies** and **forget-me-nots**.

- Mix **wallflowers** in tapestry colours, or choose reds and yellows to accompany **tulips** and **daffodils**.

- For vibrant colour intersperse multicoloured **polyanthus** with some miniature **trumpet daffodils**.

- For a subtler two-colour scheme, plant yellow **polyanthus** in a sea of blue *Muscari* (grape hyacinths).

Summer sunshine schemes

- For a fragrant summer container, plant *Lobularia maritima* (sweet alyssum) with cool, sweetly scented **pansies**. For height in the centre use the fragrant *Nicotiana alata* (tobacco plant) and deep-purple *Heliotropium arborescens* (heliotrope), which is said to smell of cherry pie.

- Try *Argyranthemum frutescens* (marguerites), trailing **petunias** cascading over the front and edges of the container, *Ageratum houstonianum* (floss flower), dwarf **marigolds** and **ivy-leaved pelargoniums**.

- For a cascade, combine **Swiss Balcon** or **Continental pelargoniums**, **godetias**, trailing and compact **impatiens**, **ivy-leaved pelargoniums** and *Bassia scoparia* 'Childsii' to add some height to the display. A graceful, ferny **grevillea** can also be planted to give height, although it will have to be moved on to a larger container after a season.

Autumn effects

To make the most of your containers in autumn, consider using some of the following, which will last until the nights draw in.

- Colourful **ornamental cabbages**, in shades of pink and cream, will make an unusual and eye-catching display in autumn.

- **Fuchsias** will carry on flowering well into autumn with their exotic blooms in shades of red, pink, purple and white.

- *Heliotropum arborescens* (heliotrope) bears large heads of tiny, dark purple, sweetly scented flowers. It is a good choice for base planting.

- There are several cultivars of *Nicotiana alata* (tobacco plant), both tall and short, with deliciously scented white, green, pink or red flowers.

- **Pelargoniums** are always a favourite in containers, whether they are trailing or upright and with flowers in red, pink or white.

- *Sedum spectabile* (ice plant) has large, flat heads of pink flowers spread above fleshy stems and greyish-green leaves. It is excellent for colour in late summer and autumn.

Winter highlights

Evergreen shrubs really come into their own for winter containers. Conifers are an obvious choice, but there are other evergreen shrubs that are equally useful.

- *Chamaecyparis lawsoniana* 'Ellwoodii', a slow-growing conifer that forms a dark green column, will grow to 3m (10ft) tall. For a golden colour choose 'Ellwood's Pillar'.

- *Chamaecyparis pisifera* 'Boulevard' is a slow-growing cypress with intense silver-blue foliage, which forms a neat cone, eventually to 10m (30ft).

- *Cotoneaster integrifolia* has a creeping habit, with small, narrow leaves and white flowers in early summer. In autumn and early winter these are followed by bright scarlet berries.

- *Gaultheria procumbens* (checkerberry, wintergreen) is an evergreen, with creeping stems and bright red berries in winter. Make sure it is planted in ericaceous compost.

- *Juniperus communis* 'Compressa' is a dwarf, compact conifer, to 80cm (32in) tall, with dark green, silver-backed, needle-like leaves. This is a miniature form of the Irish juniper and is widely grown in containers of all kinds.

looking after the lawn

Creating a lawn

A beautiful, well-maintained lawn is an asset in many gardens and will do much to enhance the intrinsic beauty of both the garden and the house. Despite the chore of mowing, there is no doubt that a lawn can add an air of peace and maturity to a garden, providing a splendid foil for flowers and foliage. It is also an important area for both children and adults to play.

Shape and size

Too often, insufficient consideration is given to the shape of a lawn. It is usually thought of as a square or oblong carpet when, in fact, an irregular, slightly curving shape would be more effective and attractive. To be both useful and aesthetically pleasing, a lawn must not be too small. Anything less than 3m (10ft) square usually looks rather insignificant and is really not worth the cost of a mower. In such a situation a paved or gravelled area would be more sensible, especially if it is planted with a few tough but aromatic groundcover plants tumbling out of the crevices and softening the overall effect.

Starting from scratch

A new lawn can be made either by sowing seeds or laying turf. Turf is more expensive but provides a usable lawn relatively quickly. Although some suppliers of turf provide more than one type of grass, sowing seeds allows you to choose the species of grass, which should be selected with the use to which the lawn will be put in mind. If, for example, the grass will be used primarily by children for playing, a sturdy mixture, such as a rye grass selection, should be used. If you want a decorative lawn with a fine texture, look for bent or fescue seed. There are also different seed mixes for different climates and soil types and for lawns that are in shade or in full sun. Don't just buy the first packet of lawn seeds you come across.

left A curved lawn and wall provide a feeling of flowing movement in this area.

top Edging a lawn with paving provides easy access to the garden whatever the weather.

Alternatively, if you would like a garden meadow area get a flower seed and grass mix, although these do not normally do well on soils that are strongly acid or strongly alkaline.

Preparing the site

The ideal site is one that is open to the sky and with no large trees nearby. Because the lawn is likely to occupy more than half of your garden, however, it is seldom possible to choose a site that is entirely suitable for the grasses that will compose it. At the least, choose an area that will not be in shade for more than half the day in summer. Grass does, of course, grow in shade and there are some special mixtures for growing under trees, but they form loose turf, which does not stand up to hard wear.

The soil should be reasonably well drained. You will not get a good lawn to grow in waterlogged soil. If the ground is simply badly drained because the soil is compacted much can be done by digging in plenty of well-rotted manure and grit. However, if the soil is permanently wet – because of a high water table, for example – you may need to install a drainage system, which is a permanent but expensive solution.

Sloping lawns can look effective, but horizontal lawns are the norm, and easier to care for. If it is to be used as a play area or for sunbathing, you will want a flat, level area. Whichever you choose to create, the surface must be level enough for a mower to negotiate it easily. This is the primary consideration when preparing the site. If your garden is new, remove any builder's rubbish and make sure there are no half-buried lumps of concrete or bricks. At this point, if the soil is thin, chalky or sandy, apply a dressing of garden compost or well-rotted manure. Afterwards, turn over the top layer or use a rotavator to incorporate the organic matter.

Level any bumps and hollows, and tread down the surface to finish. Rake thoroughly down the plot, then across, removing all the larger stones. Ideally, allow the soil to settle for at least a month, preferably twice as long. Any weeds that appear during this period must be removed.

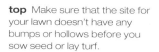

top Make sure that the site for your lawn doesn't have any bumps or hollows before you sow seed or lay turf.

right Creating a lawn from scratch can seem daunting, but time spent preparing the site will pay dividends.

Sowing seeds

Grass seeds are light and not easily sown evenly by hand. If you can, borrow or rent a spreader. If you decide to sow by hand, mark out the lawn in 1m (1yd) wide strips with string and stakes. If the soil is very fertile and has been weeded once or twice beforehand allow about 15g (½oz) of seeds per square metre (yard). If the soil is less rich and has not been weeded before sowing, double this quantity.

Mark off a square metre (yard), weigh the appropriate amount of seeds and do a trial sowing to see what the density looks like. Thereafter, it should be possible to continue at that rate along each strip.

When the entire lawn has been sown, gently rake the surface with long, steady strokes, first down and then across to cover as much of the seeds as possible. Cover the area with netting or black cotton raised up on short sticks if birds are troublesome. (Use cotton rather than nylon, which can trap birds by their legs.) Nothing need be done until the seedlings are well grown if the soil is moist. If the surface dries out before germination, use a fine spray or lawn sprinkler.

Looking after seedling grasses

When the seedling grasses are about 2.5cm (1in) high give them a light rolling, which will help to firm the little plants and encourage branching from the base. A week later, mow the lawn, setting the cutting blade high. About two months after germination, or in the spring following an autumn sowing, you can apply a lawn fertilizer, following the directions on the label for quantity and timing. Water regularly in dry weather and remove any broad-leaved weeds by hand.

Laying turf

Starting a lawn from turf is more expensive than sowing seeds, especially if you buy good-quality turves. Turf is lawn grass that has been seeded and grown on a farm, cut loose from the ground in regular rectangles, with about 2.5cm (1in) soil attached, and rolled or stacked. It provides an almost instant lawn and prevents erosion on slopes. Only buy turves from a reputable supplier, or you may find that the turf contains perennial weeds or has been allowed to dry out before it is delivered to you.

Prepare the site as for seeds, and make sure the work is complete before the turves are due to be delivered to you. Also make sure you have somewhere convenient to stack the turves while you are working on the lawn. Early autumn or spring are the best times for laying. Apply a lawn fertilizer to the ground before laying and rake it in. Stand to one side of the lawn site and lay a row of turves along one edge, butting them end to end. Now place a plank across the laid turves and put down the next row, staggering them like rows of bricks in a wall. Move the plank over and lay the next row and so on until the job is complete. Standing on the plank will spread your weight as you work and also prevent you from compacting the prepared soil. Walking along the plank will firm the turf as it is laid; any turf that misses the plank should be tapped down with the back of a spade.

If the lawn has curving edges, shape the turf by trimming with a sharp serrated knife; don't try to shape the turf around the curve. Don't worry about odd points or edges of turf protruding over the outline of the lawn – these can be trimmed with an edging tool when you have finished laying all the turves. Fill any cracks between the strips of turf with a mixture of fine soil and sand and work it in with the back edge of a rake. Water thoroughly.

Looking after new turves

Autumn-laid turf will not need mowing until the following spring. Spring-laid turf will need to be cut after about three weeks. Make the first cut a high one, but thereafter mow as required. The procedures for feeding, watering and weeding are the same as for a seeded lawn.

left Turves are laid in staggered rows, like bricks. Remember to use a board to stand on, to spread your weight and avoid compressing the new lawn.

Sowing seeds

To help you distribute seeds evenly by hand, mark off the area into squares or strips about 1m (3ft) across, depending on the extent to be covered. If you are using a seed mixture, give it a stir in a bowl or bucket to ensure that the heavier seeds are not left in the bottom of the packet.

1 Divide the quantity of seeds into two and, if you are sowing by hand, broadcast one batch walking lengthways across the site and the other batch walking crossways.

2 After sowing the seeds, lightly rake over the entire seedbed, taking great care not to bury the seeds too deeply, otherwise they may not be able to germinate.

Laying turf

Unless the soil is already rich, a few days before you begin, apply a dressing of fertilizer to the ground. If you have applied a dressing of fertilizer, rake it in and incorporate it really well into the soil. This will encourage the turves to knit together.

1 Mark out the exact shape of your lawn by hammering in pegs at intervals and stretching a length of string, twine or garden line between them.

2 Lay the turves in straight lines, making sure that each turf is as close as possible to the preceding one. Allow an overlap of 2.5–5cm (1–2in) at the edge.

3 Stagger rows of turf by laying half turves. Do not walk on newly laid turf but lay down planks as pathways. These will help to spread your weight. When you have finished laying the turves, use an edging tool to trim back the edges and leave you with a neat, sharply defined edge.

What does your lawn need?

Apart from regular mowing, looking after your lawn takes little time but can make a big difference to the overall appearance of your garden. You will need to carry out a few basic tasks throughout the year, but these will take little time and will keep the grass in tip-top condition.

Fertilizers

Lawns must be fed if they are to remain healthy. Towards the end of spring apply about 100g per square metre (4oz per sq yd) of lawn fertilizer evenly over the grass. Follow the directions on the packet and do not apply too much or you may cause the grass to scorch or to grow unevenly. In summer apply the lawn fertilizer again, but this time use about 50g per square metre (2oz per sq yd).

In autumn lay a special lawn dressing. It's very important to make sure that you use something that is formulated for autumn application because it will have a low percentage of nitrogen in relation to phosphorus and potassium. While you are doing this, also apply a fine top-dressing of peat (or, preferably, peat substitute) over the lawn at a rate of about 100g per square metre (4oz per sq yd) and lightly brush this into the surface.

Watering

Freshly laid turf and newly sown seeds should be watered until the grass is established. Thereafter, watering is a matter of preference and will probably depend on whether your water supply is metered. Even grass that turns yellow in dry weather often recovers as soon as it rains again, and bear in mind that a closely mown lawn is more likely to need watering because the soil is more exposed to the hot sun than it would be if the grass was left slightly longer.

If you do water, make sure that the water is applied gradually and in sufficient amounts to soak about 2.5cm (1in) into the soil. If you simply sprinkle water quickly over the grass, the water merely cakes the surface and runs off. Fine sprinklers, which give an even distribution, are better than harsh jets.

Scarifying

In the course of a season a certain amount of debris – known as thatch – accumulates on a lawn, including dead grass, moss and worm casts. If you have been applying fertilizers and top-dressings to the ground these, too, may not have worked into the soil. The process of scarifying will remove this material.

Use a spring-tine rake or a lawn rake with plastic tines. First rake in one direction and then at right angles so that the whole area is covered. Gather up the moss as you go so you do not scatter it from one area to another. If you have a 'bowling-green' lawn, this should be done about once every fortnight from spring through to late summer. Lawns that are growing well on well-aerated, fertile soil need less frequent attention. Thoroughly rake again before applying the autumn fertilizer.

top A lush, weed-free lawn is not difficult to achieve and will enhance your entire garden.

right above Grass roots find it hard to thrive in highly compacted soil, so aerating a lawn from time to time with a fork will be beneficial.

right below Use a broad-tined lawn rake to scarify the surface of your lawn and you will probably be amazed at the amount of moss and debris it brings up.

Aerating

Aerating the soil will promote healthy growth. The easiest way is to spike it with an ordinary garden fork, pushing the tines about 8cm (3in) into the ground and levering backwards on the handle so that the turf is raised slightly; repeat this every 15cm (6in) over the lawn. If you've got a large lawn, consider hiring a machine that will scarify and aerate at one go.

Aeration is usually an autumn job, although it can be done whenever necessary. If the underlying soil is badly compacted, work over the surface to make a series of holes, then brush some horticultural sand or a mixture of sifted soil and sand over the grass.

Weeding

Specially formulated lawn weedkillers can be applied in spring and early summer, a few days after the application of fertilizer. For persistent coarse weeds, you should repeat applications every two to three weeks. If there are only a few weeds, hand weeding will be more efficient. A daisy grubber is useful for removing daisies, plantains, dandelions and similar rosette-forming weeds. Alternatively, use a proprietary 'spot weeder', which is simply a small canister of weedkiller fitted with a pad, charged with the chemical, which is dabbed on the centre of each weed. Some spot weeders are available in aerosol form.

Edging

Nothing detracts more from the appearance of any otherwise well-maintained lawn than straggly edges. Trim the grass growing horizontally over the edge of the lawn with a mechanical edge-trimmer or a pair of long-handled shears. You can use ordinary garden shears, but this is tiring work if you have more than a metre (yard) or so to cut.

If the lawn is next to a flower bed, you can cut the edge with a special edging tool or a sharp spade, but this gradually eats into the soil. It is often easier to lay a line of flagstones or pavers between the flower borders and the lawn. Leave a channel about 5cm (2in) wide and 8cm (3in) deep so that the verges of the lawn can be trimmed easily.

If you are laying a path next to a lawn, try to make sure that the path is at least 1cm (½in) below the level of the lawn so that the lawnmower can be run up to and over the path.

Mowing

Cutting a lawn regularly keeps the grass short enough to be neat and attractive without hindering its growth. Mowing too close weakens the grass and allows moss and lawn weeds to become established; on the other hand, where lawns are allowed to grow too long, coarser grasses become increasingly dominant while the finer grasses deteriorate. The best approach is to mow regularly but not too closely.

How often?

How often you need to mow the lawn depends partly on how quickly the grass is growing and partly on the type of lawn you have. Increase or decrease the frequency of mowing according to the rate of growth, and this will vary from season to season and will be influenced not only by the weather but also by how often you feed the grass, how well drained the ground is, the type of grass being grown and the general health of the turf itself. As a general rule, start mowing the lawn once a fortnight in early spring if the grass is dry and has begun to grow.

During the growing season a fine lawn should be mown every two to three days to keep it looking its best. An average lawn, with a mix of grass species, will need to be cut at least once a week, preferably every three to five days. Other types of lawn should be mown at least once a week. In dry weather or when it is cool, when

the grass will be growing more slowly, you will not need to cut it so often.

From early winter onwards, you only need to mow the lawn occasionally in dry weather if you want to keep your lawn looking neat.

What happens to the mowings?

If your lawnmower has a grass box it will automatically collect the mowings. Otherwise, use a lawn rake with plastic tines to collect them.

The grass clippings can be left on the lawn if the weather is particularly hot and dry, when they will act as a mulch and help to preserve the moisture.

top Long-handled shears make the work of trimming the edges of a lawn very much easier.

left When choosing a mower take into account the area to be mown, the type of grass and the quality of lawn you want.

Choosing a mower

The range of lawnmowers can look a bit daunting when you see them all lined up in the garden centre or store, but there are only two basic styles, which are classified according to the cutting design of the mower.

Cylinder machines have a ring of blades curving around a central spindle that revolves when the machine is used, bringing each blade in turn across a fixed plate. A scissor-like action is created as each blade crosses the plate, and the blades of grass that are trapped between the two are cut cleanly. Whether motor-powered or hand-operated, cylinder machines give the neatest finish, as long as the lawn surface is level and the grass is dry.

Rotary mowers are always motor-operated. They have horizontally set, propeller-like blades, which cut the grass as much by their high speed as by their sharpness. They are best suited to hard-wearing lawns or shallow, rough banks, where they will also deal effectively with grass that has been allowed to become overgrown. Rotary machines are either on wheels or they operate on the hovercraft principle. If the lawn surface is uneven or the rough banks are steep, the hover type is the only mower that will do the job efficiently. It can also be used when the grass is wet.

Mowing tips

Don't make mowing the lawn more of a chore than it needs to be. Observe the following simple guidelines, and you will cut down on the work involved:

• Always plan the direction of mowing to minimize overlapping, reversing and abrupt changes of direction.

• Make an effort to eliminate bumps and depressions. It's much easier to mow a level area.

• Mow when the grass is dry. Wet mowings clog the machine and grass box and lengthen the mowing time.

• Scatter worm casts before mowing.

• Try to avoid mowing when cold winds are blowing because the leaf tips may be wind-scorched.

• Rake before mowing if the grass contains weeds.

• Avoid repeated backward and forward movements, which result in an uneven cut.

• Always mow at right angles to the line of the previous mow to help to control weed grasses.

A perfect finish

A neat finish with contrasting light and dark stripes can be obtained by using a mower with a rear-mounted roller. Work across the lawn and then mow each succeeding parallel strip in the opposite direction to the previous one.

Repairing lawns

All lawns suffer damage from time to time – a broken edge, a worn patch or a bump or hollow that has resulted from the ground settling after initial turf laying or seed sowing. These troubles are not difficult to rectify, and should be dealt with in spring.

Neglected lawns

If you move into a property with an established garden, you might be faced with a lawn that has been neglected and that now looks unkempt and weedy. It will be quite easy to renovate if you carry out the following steps.

First, mow it, setting the blade of the mower at the highest setting to prevent it being fouled by over-thick grass. A rotary mower is best, but if the grass is very long and thick you might have to use a power clipper.

After mowing, work the lawn over with a spring-tined rake to remove the thatch of dead grass and moss. If it's winter, wait for a mild spell. Apply an appropriate lawn fertilizer in late winter and water in if necessary. Dig out the worst of the broad-leaved weeds and apply a lawn weedkiller. If you take over the lawn in the spring to early autumn period, apply the fertilizers and weedkiller immediately after raking. If there are bare areas after weeding and using the weedkiller, loosen any compacted soil, rake it smooth

Mending broken edges

If the edge of your lawn is damaged, there is an easy way to mend it – all you need to do is rotate the damaged section of turf.

1 Remove a section of turf at least 15cm (6in) wide from around the damaged area. Be careful to keep your spade flat when you remove the slice of turf.

2 Rotate the turf so that the opposite edge is on the outside. Sow some seeds of a grass that matches the existing type of grass into the bare patch created by the damaged edge.

and sow seeds or insert a plug of turf. A neglected lawn that receives treatment should be virtually back to normal again after one growing season.

Broken edges

You can easily repair a broken edge by removing a section at least 15cm (6in) wide from around the damaged area and reversing the turf, so that what was the inside is now on the outside. Be careful to keep your spade flat when you remove the slice of turf and cut the shape first by pressing the spade into the grass against a straight piece of timber.

Sow some grass seeds into the bare patch created by the damaged edge, taking care to match the seed type with the existing type of grass. Alternatively, insert a small piece of turf from another part of the lawn into the space.

Dealing with bumps and hollows

Bumps and hollows make mowing difficult but can be easily dealt with. Bumps can be levelled by lifting the turf, taking out the surplus soil and then returning the grass. For a small bump you can often simply peel back a small area. Larger bumps are better tackled by making an X-shaped cut in the grass so that you can easily get to the soil below.

If there is a depression to fill, first cut a straight line through the centre of the depression, then cut two parallel lines at each side, like a capital H. Roll back the two freed pieces, putting extra soil beneath them and firming well. For very large depressions it is best to remove the turf in strips, fill the hollow with good-quality soil and then relay the turf. Water the replaced turf.

Bare patches

Reseed a bare patch in spring or autumn. You can get small proprietary packs of grass seeds, sold specially for dealing with small areas. These are widely available in garden centres. Choose a grass species that is the

same as, or a close match to, the existing grass and follow the instructions on the pack.

All you need do to prepare a bare area for reseeding is to lightly prick it over with a fork, while at the same time removing any weeds. Firm it by treading with your heels. Finally rake the surface with a steel rake to make sure the surface is really level and that there is a depth of about 2.5cm (1in) of fine, loose soil in which to sow the seeds. Finish off by drawing the rake in one direction across the patch to give a series of mini-furrows in which the grass seeds will drop. After sowing, lightly rake the soil at right angles to the furrows, so that they are filled in and the seeds are covered. Don't forget to keep the area well watered if the weather is dry. To prevent birds from eating the seeds, stretch some strong black thread over the sown area, supporting the cotton on short canes or wooden pegs.

top left A sprinkling of daisies may look pretty, but daisies, clover and dandelions can run riot in a lawn.

right above Over time, lawns often develop lumps and dips. Smoothing out problem spots will make mowing easier.

when disaster strikes

Dealing with weeds

It's a cliché, but it's true: a weed is a plant growing where it is not wanted. Weeds compete with garden plants for light, water and nutrients, and they also create a micro-environment around plants in which diseases and pests, such as mildew and aphids, can flourish. All in all, weeds should be removed.

Types of weed

As with other plants in your garden, there are two main types of weed, annuals and perennials. Annuals are plants that complete their lifecycle within a single growing season, and they are often able to undergo more than one lifecycle in a season. Annuals also produce large quantities of seeds, so that the weed seed population in the soil is constantly replenished and the weeds keep reappearing. When you are digging in winter, skim off annual weeds and dig them into the bottom of each trench, along with organic manure or garden compost. Subsequent cultivations should kill any weed seedlings that emerge. Like other perennials, perennial weeds live from year to year and usually have underground organs – stems or roots – that enable them to survive through the winter. Weed control begins with winter digging before you plant up beds and borders. Cut down any woody perennials, such as brambles, and dig out all the roots – even a tiny bit of root will regrow into a plant. Double dig the whole of the garden in the first instance and remove all perennial weed roots and rhizomes. Burn or dispose of them all and don't use them for compost making.

Staying in control

It sometimes seems as if weeds appear in the garden overnight. No sooner have you cleared one area of your garden and moved on to the next when you turn around to find weeds popping up in the ground you've just cleared. There is no denying that weeds are well equipped to survive. They are also often more robust than some of the hybridized strains that have been developed for their ornamental value. Be vigilant and keep on top of the weeding. Doing it little and often is the key to success.

Hand weeding

In a well-planted bed or border, hand weeding can be the only practicable solution. Use a hand fork to loosen the soil around the weed so that you can remove it and its root. Dandelions, for example, have deep taproots, and unless you remove it completely it will reshoot from sections left in the soil.

Hoeing

Hoeing is most useful in vegetable garden, where there are rows of well-spaced seedlings and plants so that you can get between the plants you want to keep and easily remove those you don't

top Weeding by hand is slow work, but it enables you to spot self-sown plant seedlings you would like to preserve.

above Hoeing weeds from the surface is easy and satisfying, and the weeds will soon wither once severed from their roots.

want. If you use a hoe in an ornamental border, take care that you do not disturb shallow-rooting forms and make sure that do not accidentally lift the roots or cause damage, which will be quickly colonized by disease organisms. Choose a warm, drying day so that the weeds wilt and die quickly after hoeing. When you are hoeing, make sure the blade is sharp so that the weeds are severed from their roots rather than pulled up with them. Keep the hoe in the upper layers of the soil so that you do not bring more weed seeds to the surface, where they will germinate and cause further problems. The dry soil produced by surface hoeing acts as a mulch, which itself inhibits weed growth.

Mulching

Weeds can also be controlled by using mulches. Use non-organic mulches, such as black polythene or weed-suppressing membrane, for best results. Heavy-duty black polythene forms a complete physical barrier to weed growth; it also warms up the soil and conserves moisture. It is usually necessary to bury the edges of the polythene to stop it blowing away and to prevent birds and small animals getting trapped underneath, and you need to cut holes in it through which to plant. You can cover the polythene or fabric with bark chips or gravel for a more sympathetic look.

Organic mulches, such as garden compost, perform similar functions but have the advantage that they can be dug into the soil at the end of the season, thus improving both its structure and its fertility. However, they are not quite so effective against weeds.

Using chemicals

Weedkillers will kill most, if not all, weed growth, both above and below ground, leaving the site free of weeds and ready for cultivation and planting. However, persistent weeds, such as bindweed and stinging nettles, may need several applications. It is possible to use a non-persistent contact weedkiller against annual weeds but it must be applied at a low level with a dribble bar when there is no wind and no danger of drift. It is inactivated rapidly on contact with the soil but kills any green tissues with which it comes into contact, so it must be handled with care. More toxic and persistent weedkillers should not be used in the

home garden especially where you are growing fruit or vegetables. Whenever you are using chemicals of any sort, it is very important that you always follow the manufacturer's instructions carefully.

Neglected gardens

The problems confronting any gardener who is faced with the task of taking over a neglected garden differ enormously. For sites that are to be used for permanent features, such as lawns or shrubberies, it is best to dig the site and, in doing so, to bury any established annual weeds. Remove small patches of perennials by digging them out, roots and all.

If a garden has been neglected for several years, vigorous perennial weeds are likely to dominate. In borders or beds many smaller plants may already have succumbed to perennial grasses, and areas of turf may have been reduced to coarse grass, weeds and moss. Reclamation can be particularly difficult after any extended period of neglect. In beds and borders, for example, few garden plants other than bulbs remain in sufficiently good condition to merit careful removal before dealing with weeds. If there is only a small area of infested ground, forking out the roots or rhizomes of perennial weeds is possible. Over larger areas this method is usually much too arduous, except perhaps for the dedicated gardener. The only effective approach is to dig over the whole garden by hand or to use weedkillers. Don't be tempted to use a rotavator, which will simply chop up the perennial weed roots into little pieces, every bit of which will regrow.

right A completely overgrown garden can seem daunting, but there may be horticultural treasures hidden in the jungle.

What are pests and diseases?

Healthy plants are much more resistant to pests and diseases than unhealthy ones, so the best thing you can do to avoid problems in the first place is to keep your plants growing strongly. If disaster does strike, adopt an integrated approach, using chemicals only as a last resort.

Avoiding problems

Preventing damage by pests and diseases is best achieved by a combination of different measures, all of which are designed to produce healthy, well-nourished plants. Then, even if there is an attack by a pest or disease, the plants will be less likely to suffer severe damage.

It is the plants under stress from drought, poor soil conditions or lack of nutrients, on the other hand, that are more likely to be severely weakened or even killed by attacks from insect pests or diseases in the air or soil. Good soil preparation, therefore, is the first stage in control.

Look after your soil

The incorporation of plenty of organic matter (see page 27) will help to open up heavy, clay soils and improve the moisture-retaining capacity of light, sandy soils. Well-conditioned soil will encourage the development of vigorous root systems that are capable of supporting strong, healthy plants.

Manures, fertilizer and lime also have a part to play in the control of various problems. For example, club root disease, which attacks members of the cabbage family – flowering types such as honesty and wallflowers as well as vegetable types such as cabbages, sprouts and cauliflower – is most troublesome on wet, acid soils. Good digging to improve aeration, together with the use of lime to reduce acidity, will lessen the chance of a severe attack of club root.

Liming can be of benefit to cauliflowers for another reason, too. Under acid conditions the element molybdenum can become deficient, and this lack can result in a condition in cauliflower known as whiptail, in which the leaves are reduced to whip-like strips. On the other hand, potato scab disease prefers alkaline conditions, so the use of manure or compost and acid fertilizers would help to reduce damage from that source.

top Keep a sharp look-out for slug and snail damage: they can strip a plant of its leaves in remarkably little time.

above Give pots and trays a thorough wash before planting them up, as they can harbour minuscule bugs and grubs that will make short work of young plants.

Slightly acid conditions are generally best for root crops, because if there is too much lime the alkalinity tends to make boron unavailable. Lack of boron in root crops causes them to develop hollow or brown centres, a condition referred to as brown heart or heart rot. Carrots and other root crops also tend to produce forked roots if they are grown on freshly manured soil, so for a variety of reasons care is needed to relate the treatment of the soil to the plants that are to be grown. The easiest way to achieve this is to follow a set rotation of crops.

Rotate crops

Crop rotation is a familiar practice in the vegetable garden, planting different types in a particular patch each year to reduce the build-up of soil-borne disease or pest infestation. To a lesser extent, this is also a sensible precaution in the ornamental garden. Avoiding the same annual plants in the same bed year after year will help to prevent the any problems from becoming unmanageable. In the flower garden, for example, try primulas, wallflowers and pansies for spring bedding in different years to reduce the risk of club root building up with regular annual plantings of wallflowers. With summer bedding, try not to grow asters every year, in order to stop the disease aster wilt becoming troublesome.

Control weeds

Good weed control (see page 200) and careful attention to garden hygiene play a useful part in pest and disease control by removing alternative hosts and hiding places. Woodlice and snails abound under piles of old seedtrays and pots under greenhouse staging or among weeds at the bases of hedges or walls.

Many pests and diseases can live happily on weeds and then spread from there to treasured garden plants. In both the greenhouse and the outside garden it is a wise policy to have a really thorough clean-up at least once a year. Most old plant residues can be composted quite safely (see page 33), but if any plants are carrying diseases or are heavily infested with pests they are best burned or disposed of away from the garden.

Grow resistant plants

A further factor that can be used to reduce the likelihood of attack from pests and diseases is the choice of plant varieties you grow. Increasingly, plant breeders are producing varieties with in-built resistance – or, at least, reduced susceptibility – to certain problems. Thus, it is now possible to grow antirrhinums and leeks that are free from rust, asters that are not susceptible to wilt, lettuces, blackcurrants and gooseberries that remain free of mildew, carrots that are partially resistant to carrot fly, and roses that have reduced susceptibility to mildew, blackspot and rust. These new varieties are not proof against any of these troubles, however, so it is advisable to take other measures as described above.

Disease-resistant roses

Many people don't grow roses because they are vulnerable to a number of diseases, such as blackspot and mildew. The following roses have been found to show some degree of resistance to a range of pests and diseases:

- **'Alexander'**
- **'Elina'**
- **'Flower Carpet'**
- **'Freedom'**
- **'Gilda'**
- **'Hertfordshire'**
- **'Ingrid Bergman'**
- **'Indian Summer'**
- **'Little Bo-Peep'**
- **'Pink Chimo'**
- **'Princess Michael of Kent'**
- **'Red Trail'**
- **'Telford Primrose'**

below Rosa 'Alexander'

Barriers and traps

Even if you follow all the good advice for preventing attacks, it is likely that pests and diseases will affect your plants at some time. Try barriers and traps as the next line of defence.

Netting

Plants attacked by flying pests, especially vegetables, can be covered with special, fine netting, which will prevent the pests from laying their eggs on or around the crop or establishing themselves on the foliage. This netting is of particular benefit to carrots to exclude carrot fly and to the cabbage family (brassicas) to exclude cabbage white butterflies as well as cabbage root fly.

Netting can also be used to protect soft fruit from attack by birds, and indeed in some areas it is virtually impossible to grow a satisfactory crop of soft fruit without a permanent fruit cage. An alternative method used with some success to keep birds off outdoor crops is the use of humming or buzzing lines. A thin, tightly stretched plastic strip held taut over a row of vegetables or soft fruit will vibrate in the wind, and this is often sufficient to stop birds from damaging the crop below.

Carpets and cabbages

A further example of a useful barrier method is the use of circles of carpet underlay placed tightly around the stems of brassicas when they are planted out. These will prevent the cabbage root fly from laying eggs in the soil close to the plant stems.

top Sticky traps are an effective measure against flying pests in the greenhouse.

left Netting growing crops will not keep out small bugs, but it will prevent your vegetables and fruit from being devoured by birds.

right above If earwigs are a problem, an old but still very efficacious way of trapping them is to attract them into hay or straw in a flower pot on top of a cane.

right Grease bands are a useful way of trapping a number of pests that are attracted to trees, including caterpillars and ants.

Sticky traps

In the greenhouse and conservatory it is possible to trap quite a number of flying pests with coloured, sticky traps hung over the plants. Different pests respond to different wavelengths of light, and whitefly and aphids will be attracted to yellow traps, while thrips for some reason prefer blue.

Grease bands and glue

Trapping with bands of grease around tree trunks will protect apples and pears from damage by various caterpillars, including the winter moth. The female of this moth cannot fly and so has to reach the male by climbing up the trunk of the tree. A band of grease prevents this, and these are available either as a proprietary product, which is applied directly on to the tree trunk, or on a paper band, which is tied firmly around the trunk. Alternatively, it may be a proprietary band purchased ready-greased or a plastic band with the sticky part hidden underneath to avoid contamination by leaves and to prevent it from fouling birds, pets or the gardener.

A grease band barrier also discourage ants from climbing up into the tree where they have been found to move aphids around to new shoots and also to defend them from predators. The ants obtain supplies of sugary honeydew from the aphids and can move them to new areas of the tree when overcrowding starts to occur.

A ring of barrier glue can also be applied around the tops of containers to stop vine weevil adults reaching the compost where they seek to lay their eggs.

Earwig traps

Earwigs can be trapped in small flowerpots filled with dry grass or crumpled newspaper and placed upside-down on the tops of canes. The canes are pushed into the soil between dahlias or other susceptible plants and the pots can be emptied daily.

Defending fruit trees

A different type of physical barrier can be used to reduce codling moth numbers. The caterpillars of codling moths, which attack apples and pears, spend the winter hiding in convenient crevices, pupate in early spring and then emerge in late spring to early summer to fly, mate and lay their eggs.

If bands of corrugated cardboard are tied quite tightly round the tree trunks in midsummer, many codling larvae will seek to hibernate there. The bands can be removed in winter and burned, thus removing quite a proportion of the local population.

Pesticides

If a pest or disease attack is threatening to ruin your plants, you may want to resort to chemical pesticides. Use the minimum possible and apply them with care, following the manufacturer's instructions to the letter.

In many countries legislation now limits the manufacture, sale and use of chemicals to control pests, diseases and weeds. There are strict rules on what is allowed to be manufactured, sold and applied and on what claims are allowed to be put on product labels. These regulations apply equally to manmade and to 'natural' or 'organic' substances and completely ban the use of home-made infusions, because such concoctions have never been examined for safety to the environment, to the user or to the consumer of treated produce.

Using pesticides

Always choose the right product. Read the label before you buy, and if you are in doubt ask for help. Follow the instructions carefully, using the correct rate and noting any intervals that must be observed between spraying edible crops and harvesting them.

Spray thoroughly, remembering that many pests and diseases will be found underneath the leaves. Spray to wet the leaves but not so much that the spray runs off, and make sure that no spray enters ponds, ditches or streams.

If you have surplus diluted spray left over, apply it to gravel or to unsurfaced paths or to level, bare soil. Wash your hands and equipment after use, disposing of the water used for rinsing in the same way as surplus diluted spray.

Always store pesticides away from children and pets, in a cool, dry, ideally lockable, place. Always keep them in the original containers and never decant them into unlabelled containers.

Getting the timing right

When you are using insecticides, in particular, the timing is aimed at finding a particularly susceptible stage in the lifecycle of the pest and at avoiding any times when the pest is likely to be in a non-susceptible stage. If you are controlling aphids on fruit trees and bushes, for example, a winter tar oil spray can be applied to kill the overwintering eggs. Once hatched out, however, an insecticide application at any time the pest is present (except during flowering) would be effective because both adults and young nymphs are susceptible to the treatment. On the other hand, the caterpillar of the cabbage white butterfly must be controlled before it pupates and becomes a chrysalis – neither eggs nor chrysalis are controlled by spraying. Understanding a pest's lifecycle is key to preventing it from proliferating.

Keep up to date

Product labels are constantly being revised and amended, pests may become resistant to chemicals and certain recommendations may be withdrawn. When buying chemical pesticides, the label must be the guide. Only apply a product when the pest and the crop are listed on the label, unless there is a general recommendation such as 'controls all foliar insect pests on flowers, fruit and vegetables'. Remember, if in any doubt, seek advice from the manufacturer.

top The larvae of the large cabbage white butterfly (*Pieris brassicae*) can cause severe damage on host plants.

When to spray

- Early morning or late evening
- When bees and other insects are not on the wing
- When there is no strong sun
- When there is little wind
- When the leaves are dry
- When the treated plants are not in flower

Common pests and diseases

Pests

Aphids (greenfly and blackfly)
Virtually all plants can be attacked by one sort of aphid or another. They feed on the sap, which can weaken the plants, leaves may be curled, and they can also spread virus diseases. Aphids excrete sugary honeydew as they feed, which makes leaves sticky and, as sooty moulds colonize the honeydew, the leaves and stems turn black. Ants are attracted to the honeydew and to the aphids, which they stimulate to exude more honeydew. Ants can also move the aphids to new leaves and defend them from predators. Aphid infestations build up rapidly because the females produce living young without needing to mate.
Control: Natural predators, including ladybird larvae and adults, lacewing and hoverfly larvae and a number of other beneficial insects, help to keep aphid numbers in check. Where such biological control agents are late to arrive or are inadequate for the size of the aphid infestation, spray with an aphid-specific insecticide to avoid causing any harm to the predators.

Carrot fly
Maggots of the carrot fly (*Psila rosoe*) feed on the surface of carrot and parsnip roots and then bore more deeply into the flesh of these vegetables. Typically, the mines develop a rusty appearance, and early and severe attacks can ruin the crop. The first batches of eggs are laid in late spring and early summer with the second generation of adult flies appearing in late summer to lay some more batches of eggs.
Control: Sowing the seeds later than normal, around the time the first eggs are being laid in late spring, will avoid most of the damage from the first generation of carrot fly, because the maggots will hatch before the carrot seedlings are large enough to be attacked. Covering the crop with fine netting or horticultural fleece in mid-spring will exclude the egg-laying adults, and maincrop carrots should be lifted and stored as soon as they are ready to avoid losses from second-generation maggots. The carrots 'Ingot', 'Parano', 'Flyaway' and 'Sytan' have a reduced susceptibility to attack, and these should be grown as an additional safety measure. There are no suitable chemical controls available to amateur gardeners.

Caterpillars
Several different types of caterpillar attack garden plants, but it is mainly on vegetables such as cabbages that it becomes a problem. They feed on the leaves, boring into hearts and generally reducing the attractiveness and palatability of the crops. Cabbage white butterfly caterpillars are perhaps the best known, but there are several different butterflies and moths which are culprits.
Control: Netting over the crops during the period that the adults are in flight will prevent eggs being laid on the foliage, although in the average garden it may not be practical to guard against all the different species in this way. Regular hand-picking of the caterpillars is a practical alternative. The crops can be sprayed with the antagonistic bacterium *Bacillus thuringiensis*, which prevents caterpillars feeding within two hours of application, then kills them. Alternatively, spray with bifenthrin at the first sign of egg-laying or caterpillar feeding and before the boring types have had chance to bury themselves down away from the spray. If the plants are close to harvest use an organic spray, such as those based on fatty acids or rape seed oil. Repeat the bacterium or insecticides as necessary to maintain the level of control.

Earwigs
Earwigs (*Forficula auricularia*) feed on leaves, flowers and flowerbuds and in some years can cause quite serious damage. Feeding takes place at night, but by day the earwigs hide away and so are rarely seen at work.

Control: Trapping is perhaps the best way to control earwigs (see page 205). Shake out the traps each morning and kill the earwigs. Spray badly affected plants with bifenthrin.

Leatherjackets
Leatherjacket is the name given to the larva of the crane fly (*Tipula pallidosa* and other species). The greyish, legless larvae feed on the roots of garden plants and weeds from summer through to late spring, growing to 4.5cm (1½in) in length in the process.
Control: Keep the soil well drained. Dig over the ground in early autumn, especially if it has been fallow throughout summer. Water the soil or lawn and cover with black plastic or tarpaulin overnight; the larvae will work their way to the surface and can be exposed for the birds to eat the following day. In mid- to late summer apply the pathogenic nematode *Steinernema carpocapsae* as a biological control to parasitize the larvae.

Red spider mites
Red spider mite (*Tetranychus urticae*) can be a major problem on all plants, mainly those in a greenhouse or indoors. The tiny mites, barely visible to the naked eye, are pale green to slightly yellow and have two dark spots on their backs. They feed under the plant leaves, and their sap-sucking activities result in a pale stippling on the upper leaf surface. In severe attacks the mites produce a mass of fine webbing over the foliage and tops of the plants. When the day length falls below 14 hours in autumn, the mites develop the orange-red winter female forms, which mate and hide away in the greenhouse and other suitable places over winter.
Control: Red spider mites are encouraged in a dry atmosphere, so regular damping-down of the greenhouse floor and benches, as well as misting over plants with water, will help to prevent attacks. Spray with an insecticide based on a plant extract, such as oil seed rape, at regular intervals as soon as the pest is noticed. Because red spider mites have developed resistance to most pesticides, introduce the predatory mite *Phytoseiulus persimilis* to control the pest biologically.

above Aphid infestation

above Caterpillar damage

Sciarid fly (fungus gnat)

The sciarid fly (*Bradysia*) is attracted in numbers to the organic content of container composts where the eggs are laid. The sciarid larvae are small and colourless, apart from a small black head. They feed on organic matter, which can be peat or bark in the compost or plant roots, and in severe cases they burrow up into the plant stems. Young plants are killed by the root loss and other damage, while the adult flies, like tiny gnats, are a nuisance as they constantly fly up off the compost during watering.

Control: Sticky yellow plastic traps hung around the plants will trap quite a lot of adult flies. For more severe attacks, water the compost with the nematode *Heterorhabditis megidis*, which also kills vine weevil (see below), or introduce the predatory mite *Hypoaspis*.

Slugs and snails

Slugs and snails eat the foliage of many different plants, particularly seedlings, tender young plants and hostas. Snails live above ground, while most slugs live underground. When winter temperatures are mild, both will continue to eat plants right through the year.

Control: These pests hide out by day in moist nooks and crannies and under dying foliage. Remove piles of flowerpots, decaying matter and any other possible hiding places and keep the garden neat. A mulch of coarse grit will deter them, as will slug-deterrent gel, which can be smeared around container rims to stop slugs getting at the contents. One of the best methods of control is to go out after dark with a torch and pick off any slugs and snails you find. Slug pellets can be effective, but be sure to choose environmentally friendly products to avoid poisoning wildlife or pets. There is also an effective biological control (see page 213).

Vine weevils

The larvae of the vine weevil (*Otiorhynchus sulcatus*) can be extremely damaging to plants in pots, feeding on roots, corms and tubers. Cyclamen, begonia and primula are all attacked, but very few plants escape when the adult weevil is laying eggs. In heated greenhouses, conservatories and even homes, overlapping stages of the lifecycle – from egg through larva and pupa to adult – can be found, but in the garden the overwintering stage is a larva. The adult weevils notch plant foliage, adding to the damage done to the roots by the larvae.

Control: Treat the soil around susceptible plants with parasitic nematodes (*Heterorhabditis megidis* and *Steinernema carpocapsae*), which

above Slug attacked by nematodes

parasitize and kill the pest. Use chemical formulations based on imidacloprid or drench containers with a solution of cresylic acid.

Whitefly

The glasshouse whitefly (*Trialeurodes vaporariorum*) is probably the most troublesome of the pests attacking greenhouse and conservatory plants. The pests suck the plant sap and excrete honeydew, and all attacks are likely to be severe ones, and infested plants can be killed. Fuchsia, regal pelargonium, poinsettia and solanum are among the most favoured hosts of whitefly. The small white adults each lay up to 250 eggs, laying them on the leaves, and successive generations through spring to autumn build up very high population levels.

Control: From early summer onwards the temperatures will be high enough for the whitefly parasite *Encarsia formosa* to be effective. Trapping early-season whitefly on sticky, yellow plastic traps will help to keep levels down and also act as a monitoring system to give an indication of when spraying is needed. For spraying, use fatty acids or pyrethrins if *Encarsia* is to be introduced later when temperatures are suitable. For chemical control without biological help, use bifenthrin, bioallethrin, fatty acids, permethrin or pyrethrins, repeating frequently as necessary.

above Vine weevil damage

Diseases

Blackspot

Blackspot of roses (*Diplocarpon rosae*) first appears as a dark, rounded or diffuse spotting of the foliage of roses. The leaf turns yellow shortly after the initial attack and premature defoliation follows. Bushes can be seriously weakened by a severe, untreated, blackspot attack. The disease carries over from year to year on infected leaves and on fungal spots on the stems. Various strains of the blackspot fungus exist, and breeding for resistance is a tricky operation (see page 203).

Control: Pick up and burn all fallen leaves and in winter prune out any stems with the characteristic black spots on the wood. To protect plants from attack or to eradicate an existing infection, spray with a suitable fungicide, such as flutriafol or mancozeb, immediately after carrying out spring pruning.

Botrytis (grey mould)

Botrytis cinerea or grey mould is perhaps the most common fungus to be found in gardens, feeding on all manner of dead and dying material. Unfortunately, it also spreads into previously healthy tissue, making the disease a major problem, especially under warm and humid conditions. On roses and some other shrubby plants the fungus gains entry through pruning cuts and snags and causes dieback. It also attacks perennials, bulbs and bedding plants; the infected tissue turns soft and rots, and has a grey, fluffy coating of spores over the surface. It often follows injury to plants caused by pests, bad weather or a clumsy gardener.

Control: On shrubs and climbers, prune out diseased stems to 5cm (2in) or so below the visible signs of dieback. Take care when pruning not to leave any lengths of stem between the cut and the bud below. On other plants, remove the diseased parts and apply a few sprays of benomyl or carbendazim fungicide.

Club root

Club root, which is caused by the fungus *Plasmodiophora brassicae*, is probably the most serious of all the diseases affecting brassica plants, as well as attacking other plants in the cabbage family, including weeds. Attack through the soil causes the root tissue to swell up into large galls in which the fungus multiplies. In severe attacks the plants may die, and the fungus remains in the soil in diseased roots. Resting spores develop, which can persist in the soil for 20 years or more, and when brassicas are again planted in the same site motile spores are produced, which swim in the

above Honey fungus

soil moisture to infect the roots. Club root is encouraged by acid and wet soil conditions, and can be spread in soil on boots and tools, in manure from animals fed on contaminated plants and in flood water, where the spores are washed out of the soil to come to rest in a new site.

Control: Follow a crop rotation plan (see page 203) and lime the soil where the brassicas are to be grown. Aim for an alkaline soil, with a pH of 7.3 to 7.5. If the soil is on the wet and heavy side, try to improve drainage to a soakaway. Where club root has already occurred, raise seedlings in pots of proprietary compost and not in outdoor seed beds to ensure a good, healthy root system is established by planting-out time.

Dip the roots of young transplants in a preparation of carbendazim or thiophanate-methyl before transplanting to reduce the severity of attack and enable a crop to be grown in infected soil, but this will not reduce the level of infection in the soil. As soon as any crops are found to be dying from club root or at the end of cropping where disease has not proved fatal, dig out all the roots and burn them before they start to rot. Keep cabbage family weeds – such as shepherd's purse and charlock – under control. If you are buying or have been given young brassica plants, examine the roots very carefully to make sure there is no disease present.

Damping off

Damping off results in seedlings and young plants wilting and toppling over and frequently a constriction of the stems can be seen at soil level. Species of *Pythium*, *Rhyzoctonia* and *Phytophthora* fungi can be involved, and these are encouraged by wet compost or over-humid conditions.

Control: Always use new compost and new, or thoroughly cleaned, pots and seedtrays. Sow seeds thinly and prick out as soon as possible to avoid overcrowding. Water only when necessary, and add a copper fungicide to the water once a week as a preventative.

Honey fungus

Honey fungus (*Armillaria mellea*) can attack a wide range of trees and shrubs, including conifers, although some species are more frequently attacked than others. Shoots wilt and turn brown and death may follow in the same year that the first symptoms appear. Under the bark at the base of the dead or dying plant will be found a web of white fungal threads, the mycelium, and in the soil around will be found black, bootlace-like growths, known as rhizomorphs. It is these that give the fungus its alternative name of bootlace fungus. The rhizomorphs spread through the soil to infect other host plants. The old, dead plant will continue to rot and large clumps of honey-coloured toadstools then appear around the base.

Control: Claims are made for the successful use of phenolic drenches around both lightly infected and healthy trees, and these may be worth trying. The only alternative is to dig up and burn infected plants and leave the soil unplanted except for annuals, for some years, or to remove up to a cubic metre (yard) of soil and replace with new. Make sure that all traces of rhizomorphs are also removed.

Potato and tomato blight

Potato blight and tomato blight are caused by the same fungus, *Phytophthora infestans*. It attacks mainly during warm, wet weather in late summer and early autumn. When it infects tomatoes it causes the leaves to turn black and die while the fruit develop dark brown areas on the skins. A whitish fungal growth develops on the leaves to spread the infection further and the fruit rot as secondary fungi take over. Tomato stems also turn dark and the whole plant will then collapse. On potatoes it first shows as a browning of the leaflets, and this is followed rapidly by the whole leaf and then the entire plant dying.

Control: Only plant healthy potato tubers, and resistant cultivars, such as 'Kondor', 'Cara', 'Estima', 'Record', 'Romano' and 'Maris Peer'. Spray with mancozeb or Bordeaux mixture when weather conditions favour the spread of potato blight spores. Spray tomatoes whenever a nearby potato crop is being sprayed for potato blight control.

Powdery mildew

Large numbers of different powdery mildew species occur, each with a fairly restricted host range. Some, such as pea mildew (*Erysiphe pisi*), can be damaging on agricultural crops, but they also attack herbaceous plants in the same botanical family – lupins, for example, are susceptible to pea mildew. Affected plants become coated with a white, powdery coating of disease spores, and in severe cases the leaves can turn brown and die. General growth and flowering can be reduced. Powdery mildew tends to be most serious during spells of dry weather, with evening dews to moisten the foliage.

Control: Keep plants well watered in dry weather. Cut out badly infected growths, first enclosing them in a plastic bag to prevent masses of infective spores being spread around the garden as you carry them away. Spraying with a systemic fungicide based on benomyl, carbendazim, propiconazole or triforine will eradicate an existing attack and protect against new infections. Sulphur could be used as an alternative for protective purposes.

Silverleaf

The silverleaf fungus (*Chondrostereum*) attacks a wide range of trees and some shrubs, mainly entering through pruning cuts and other wounds. With many plants, attack causes the upper leaf surface to separate from the central leaf tissue, thus altering the light-reflecting properties and giving the foliage a silvery look. On rhododendrons and some other hosts, however, this typical silverleaf symptom does not appear. The silvered leaves are not sources of infection, but the affected branches will soon die back and later produce small, purplish, bracket-like fungal bodies on the surface. These produce spores to spread the infection.

Control: Cut out and burn all dead and dying wood, preferably by midsummer to avoid the main spore-producing period. The fungus *Trichoderma* can be used to combat infection.

above Powdery mildew

Integrated pest control

To obtain the best possible results – the maximum reduction of plant damage and losses – try to adopt a holistic approach, using as many different methods of pest or disease control as are available. This approach is known as integrated control.

A typical example of integrated control would be in the control of whitefly in the greenhouse. The season would start off by hanging sticky yellow traps above the plants to reduce early damage. Should an attack start to develop, the infestation could be kept under control with an insecticide spray based on fatty acids or pyrethrins until the average day and night temperatures are sufficiently high for the biological agent *Encarsia* to be introduced. Leave the necessary interval between the last spray and introducing the parasite.

Sticky traps would not be effective for red spider mite on cucumbers, however, so more applications of fatty acids or pyrethrins may be necessary before conditions are favourable for the predatory mite *Phytoseiulus*. It may also be necessary to control cucumber powdery mildew, and, although a benomyl fungicide would not upset the whitefly parasite, the mite predator would be adversely affected. In such a case, you should have chosen a cucumber variety that is resistant to mildew and therefore needs no spraying.

By combining as many cultural measures as possible – choosing as appropriate from soil treatments, crop rotations, weed control, resistant varieties, physical barriers and traps, biological control and pesticides – it should be possible to keep damage to a minimum.

The 'better' chemicals

If you have a major pest or disease problem you may decide to use chemicals. Choose the less toxic, plant-based insecticides, such as insecticidal soap, pyrethrum, derris, quassia and copper fungicide, and follow the manufacturer's instructions carefully.

Organic gardening

Thankfully, the days when gardeners spent most of their lives spraying chemicals over everything either to kill it or make it grow are largely over. Chemical sprays are still used, but in a more responsible fashion, and on the whole they are safer. However, a great many gardeners now realize that it is not necessary to spray every time a bug or weed appears in the garden. Many slight problems or infestations can be tolerated because they cause little or no long-term damage to the plants. Problems are considerably reduced by growing a good mixture of flowering plants, especially old-fashioned forms, which encourage hoverflies and ladybirds, both of which prey on aphids.

top The *Encarsia* wasp is a boon to keeping whitefly under control in the greenhouse, but it will only survive and breed in warm conditions.

above Ladybirds have long been welcomed as the gardener's friend; they will eat copious amounts of aphids.

right Cloches will keep flying pests away from growing crops and young plants. Bottomless plastic bottles make good individual cloches.

Another disadvantage of chemical pesticides is that, as well as killing the pest, they also kill its natural predators – if you don't spray, these predators may well build up enough to control the pest themselves, making spraying unnecessary in the first place.

Organic gardening is about more than just not spraying pests with pesticides. Organic gardeners prefer to avoid chemical fertilizers, too. There seems to be almost universal agreement now that well-rotted manure is the best possible conditioner for soils. It not only provides nutrients but also improves the structure of the soil. Although chemicals provide an instant fix as far as food is concerned, they do little for the soil, and if you want to apply extra nutrients, use an organic fertilizer, such as organic pelleted chicken manure. Although it won't help the soil's structure, it will encourage soil bacteria and bring the soil to life.

Most organic gardeners make their own garden compost and leaf mould to maintain a natural balance in the garden. All waste material, except perennial weeds, is composted so that the nutrients can be returned to the soil. If you throw away or burn waste material, think about all the nutrients that are leaving your garden with it. See page 32 for how to make compost and leaf mould.

Organic pest control

Organic control starts with physically removing any pests you find and regularly checking plants for grey mould or powdery mildew; remove and burn any infected leaves or shoots.

When digging, look out for the fat, cream-coloured leatherjackets and squash them. Do the same with vine weevil larvae when repotting container plants.

Remove aphids by hand or by spraying with a jet of water. Use an insecticidal soap to spray badly infected plants. Remove caterpillars by hand and drop them into paraffin, and remove the eggs laid by moths and butterflies on plants, especially cabbages.

In late summer and autumn millipedes tunnel into potatoes and other root crops. A healthy soil with deeply dug beds and plenty of manure will help to keep them at bay.

During the day cutworms eat through the base of a plant. Weed to reduce the risk of infestation and hoe around plants, searching for the grubs, as they live just below the soil. Drown them in paraffin.

Wireworms will be attracted by a potato, carrot or split cabbage stalk pushed into the ground. Fix it on the end of a stick, then periodically remove the stick and bait and destroy the worms.

Home-made sticky traps can be used to catch flea beetles and whitefly. Coat one side of a small piece of wood with heavy grease. Pass the board, greased side down, just over the top of infested plants. The flea beetles will jump up and stick to it. Hang up a grease-coated piece of yellow card to trap whitefly.

Use any of the barriers or traps outlined on pages 204–5 because they do not make use of chemicals and try some of the biological controls on page 212, which rely on natural predators to control pests.

Organic slug solutions

Large slugs will not harm living plants – it is the small black and brown slugs that attack growing plants. Protect small plants with cut-off plastic bottles pushed into the ground. Surround larger plants with lime or soot, which slugs don't like. The best method is to go out into the garden with a torch after dark, especially on warm, wet nights, and collect slugs and snails as they eat your plants. If you wish, kill them by dropping them into water with a smear of paraffin on the top.

Organic weed control

The secret to controlling weeds without using chemical weedkillers is to keep on top of weeds and remove any that do appear by hand before they get too large. However, if you are clearing ground for the first time, digging out large areas of nettles may not seem so attractive. Cover the weeds with sheets of black polythene or old carpet to exclude light and literally starve them to death. You may need to wait several months for the roots to finally die out, but it is better than hours of back-breaking digging.

Biological controls

Pests have been controlled by their natural enemies in gardens since gardens were first created, and there are still quite a number of agents that can be encouraged to help establish and maintain the health of your garden in the most natural way.

Principal among the gardener's friends are ladybirds and hoverflies, together with lacewings, which feed mainly on aphids and some other leaf-feeding pests. There are also ground beetles and many spiders that feed on a range of ground-level pests. Both ladybird adults and larvae feed on greenfly and consume around 5,500 in their lifetime. Only the larvae of the hoverfly eat pests, but each one can eat around 100 greenfly before being fully fed. Lacewing larvae are rather more effective, consuming some 1,500 greenfly, but they are cannibalistic once alternative food supplies run out, so make sure there is a plentiful supply of greenfly.

Wildflower refuge

A strip of soil around the garden that is sown with grasses and both pollen- and nectar-producing wildflowers will be of great help in supplying food and shelter to a surprising number of garden friends. Take care if you are using any insecticidal sprays for pest infestations that you do not over-spray onto the strip of wildflowers. Where possible, spray only those parts of the plants where the pest attacks are worst, leaving other parts for the natural predators to clear up.

The following natural predators will really help you out in your garden, eating the pests that prey on your plants:

- **Birds** eat grubs, caterpillars, slugs and aphids. Attract them with bird food, water for drinking and bathing, and nesting boxes.
- **Bats** come out at dusk to feed on aphids, cutworm moths, craneflies and other insects.
- **Frogs and toads** eat slugs, woodlice and other small insects. A garden pond will encourage them and will also appeal to another slug-eater, the slow worm.
- **Hedgehogs** will remove slugs, cutworms, millipedes, wireworms and woodlice for you. Give them an undisturbed wild corner with a pile of rotting logs, leaves and a tree stump to hibernate in.
- **Centipedes** feed on small insects and slugs and, like ground beetles, need groundcover.

Parasites and predators

Natural pest control is also possible in the greenhouse. For example, *Encarsia formosa*, a parasite of the glasshouse whitefly, was first identified in 1926 and is now widely used to protect commercial glasshouse crops. These natural predators are now also widely available to domestic gardeners from specialist, mail-order suppliers. Check that you can supply the correct conditions in terms of temperature, humidity and daylight before ordering them. When they arrive, you must read the instructions carefully before proceeding. *Encarsia formosa* is supplied on cards that are hung up in the greenhouse but not in direct sunlight. The specific conditions must be met or the chances are that the control agent will die before it has even started to do its good work.

top Even in a town garden there is often room for a small area to be left wild, to encourage natural predators.

Natural pest control

Aphids

In the average garden, ladybirds, lacewings and hoverflies play their part in keeping aphid populations in check, but there are also two further biological controls available for use in the greenhouse. *Aphidoletes aphidimiza* is a small, midge-like fly, whose larvae seek out and devour up to 15 aphids a day. *Aphidius matricariae* is a tiny wasp, which lays its eggs inside the aphids, producing around 100 eggs in all.

The fungal parasite *Verticillium lecanii* is also effective when it is applied as a spray. Various strains of this fungus have been selected, and it is capable of attacking and controlling whitefly and thrips as well as aphids.

Caterpillars

The bacterium *Bacillus thuringiensis* (Bt) is effective against virtually all types of caterpillar. The bacterium is supplied in dried form, which is mixed with water to activate it and then sprayed over the infested plants. Caterpillars stop feeding very quickly and die a few days later. It works equally well out of doors or under glass. The use of Bt in genetically modified crops means that, in many parts of North America, Bt-resistant pests have developed.

Leaf miners

Tomato leaf miners can cause great damage to greenhouse crops, but two biological agents are available to help in the forms of *Dacunsa sibirica* and *Diglyphus isaea*. The former lays up to 90 eggs inside leaf miner larvae over its eight- or nine-day adult life, while the adult of the latter feeds on the leaf miner larvae as well as laying eggs in the mines close to older paralysed host larvae.

Mealybugs

Some species of mealybug can produce as many as 500 eggs in their eight-week lifecycle. They feed on plant sap and excrete sugary honeydew, which soon becomes colonized by sooty mould fungi. Available to control these pests is a relative of the Australian ladybird, *Cryptolaemus montronzieri*. This predator is active only at temperatures above 20°C (68°F), and it works slowly, so control may not become evident for six weeks or so after introduction. The adult beetles live for many weeks and lay around 10 eggs each day. Another way to control mealybug is with the parasitic wasps *Leptomastix dactylopii* and *Leptomastidea abnormis*, which lay eggs in large nymphs and adult female mealybugs.

Red spider mites

The beneficial agent against red spider mites is a predatory mite, which seeks out and eats the spider mites at the rate of up to 20 eggs or nymphs a day. The predatory mite, *Phytoseiulus persimilis*, does need some care in the amateur greenhouse to get the best results. The main problem is that, ideally, there should be a small resident population of red spider mites at all times, sufficient to keep the predators alive but not sufficient to cause significant plant damage. A programme of repeat introductions will top up the predator levels, however. Red spider mite populations can increase 100-fold in one month and 1,000-fold in two months, so the first introduction of the predatory mite should be made as soon as possible after the pest mite is discovered.

Scale insects

Different species of scale insects can occur, and the soft scale types can be controlled biologically by *Metaphyrus helvolus*, which is a tiny midge-like creature. It controls the scale insects in two different ways as it lays up to six eggs a day, which hatch out and feed on the scales, while the adults also feed actively on the pests, eating up to two dozen each day.

Sciarid fly (fungus gnat)

These annoying, small, black flies rise up from the surface of the compost of container-grown plants when disturbed. The larvae, which hatch from eggs laid in the compost, are slender, creamy-white creatures with small black heads, and they feed on plant roots. The larvae are controlled by the vine weevil nematode, but a newer control is a tiny straw-coloured mite, *Hypoaspis miles*, which burrows down into the compost and devours the sciarid fly larvae. The mites can live for up to up to six weeks without feeding, and so can control any subsequent invasions by sciarid flies during that period.

Slugs

There can be as many as 200 slugs living and feeding in each square metre (yard) of soil, and each one is capable of laying up to 300 eggs. Their potential for damage is enormous, but fortunately a useful nematode has been identified, which can exert virtually complete control. The nematode, *Phasmarhabditis hermaphrodita*, penetrates the slug's body, carrying with it masses of bacteria. The bacteria attack and kill the slug, the nematodes feed on the by-products and both nematode and bacteria build up and escape to seek more prey. Slug feeding is inhibited within three to five days of the nematode attack, and one treatment will normally give at least six weeks' control.

Thrips

These slender black insects can be damaging to flower crops, causing bleached spots on the petals. They are controlled by two related mites, *Amblyseius cucumeris* and *A. mackenziei*, which feed on the young stages of the pest. The parasitic fungi *Metarhizium anisopliae* and *Verticillium lecanii* are also known to be of use.

Vine weevils

The adult weevils eat notches out of 'hard' leaves, such as those of rhododendrons and camellias, while the legless larvae feed on almost all plant roots. Attacks happen on plants growing in the garden as well as those in pots grown in the home or greenhouse. When eggs are laid in the compost of pot plants, the resulting larvae soon kill the plant by eating the roots so that the plant is unable to take up water and nutrients. The beneficial nematodes *Heterorhabditis megidis* and *Steinernema carpocapsoe* seek out and enter the bodies of vine weevil larvae and some other soil pests including sciarid flies, chafers, leatherjackets and cutworms. The nematodes carry a bacterium (*Xenorhabdus*), which kills the pest within two weeks. Nematodes and bacteria multiply within the host and then leave to seek further prey. The nematode is active at temperatures down to 12°C (54°F), so it can be used in the open garden from spring through to autumn.

Whitefly

The whitefly parasite *Encarsia formosa* is probably the most commonly used beneficial insect. The parasite, which is a tiny wasp, lays eggs in the scale stages of the whitefly. The scales turn black in 10–14 days as the contents are eaten by the larvae of the wasp, and the new adults escape about 21 days later to start the cycle over again. Each tiny wasp destroys 10–15 whitefly scales each day and can lay up to 300 eggs in its life.

gardening under glass

Why have a greenhouse?

A greenhouse is the perfect all-weather place to cultivate plants. Not only will it allow you to extend the range of plants you grow, but it will provide the right conditions to propagate and overwinter less hardy plants or even to grow tender ones.

Greenhouses will not necessarily protect plants from frost unless they are heated, but they will minimize the damage caused primarily by the lethal combination of low temperatures and penetrating winds.

Because a greenhouse will allow you to sow seeds or pot up plants much earlier in the year, it is especially useful if you are growing half-hardy annuals or vegetables such as lettuces and peas, and it also increases your chances of obtaining reasonable crops of half-hardy vegetables, such as tomatoes, peppers and aubergines.

If you have a greenhouse you will be able to overwinter seedlings and winter salad vegetables, such as endives, corn salad and lamb's lettuce, and this improves their quality enormously.

Choosing a greenhouse

Greenhouses may be built of wood, metal or PVC. Wood tends to look more attractive than metal and it is marginally warmer, easier to repair and better for fitting shelves. It is, however, heavy to construct and the frame will need staining or painting from time to time. Steel and aluminium are light and easy to handle, and metal frames can be fitted with larger panes of glass, giving better light penetration.

The most popular size for a practical greenhouse is about 3 × 2.4m (10 × 8ft). However, if you can afford it, it may be worth buying something a bit larger, particularly if you do not plan to heat it, because many almost-hardy plants can become very large and you will soon wish you had more space for them in winter. If you do plan to heat it, estimate the cost of fuel before buying. Always buy from a reputable firm. There are plenty of cheap greenhouses on the market, but they are likely to be a poor investment.

Before you buy, consult your local regulations in case you need permission. There are rarely any constraints on small greenhouses, especially if they can be described as portable – that is, easily taken down and re-erected – but it is always worth checking.

left A small traditional ridge-roofed greenhouse does not take up much room, but can transform your growing power.

top Tender basil seedlings and overwintering pelargoniums share the protection of an unheated greenhouse.

Base wall or all glass?

Some greenhouses have timber-board or brick bases. Base walls help to conserve warmth in a heated greenhouse, but they reduce the amount of sunlight and cut off a free supply of solar heat. A base-walled greenhouse is usually fitted with staging at about the height of the top of the wall so that it's convenient to work in and you can use the space under the staging for storage or any plants that require less light.

Some greenhouse designs have only partial base walling, the side admitting the most light being glass to the ground. Some models even have removable base panels. These can be clipped on in the winter to conserve heat and removed in summer.

Generally, a glass-to-ground house is the most versatile because of the amount of light admitted. It's always easier to provide shade at the height of summer, when it's needed, than to have to move plants around to take advantage of the available light. If you decide to fit the framework onto a brick or concrete base wall, have the base built by a professional bricklayer unless you are reasonably skilled.

Glass or plastic?

Glass and plastic each material have their own advantages and disadvantages.

With glass it is usually possible to maintain a more stable environment than under plastic, and any artificial warmth can be more easily retained.

Types of greenhouse

- **Traditional**: One of the most practical, the barn or 'tent' shape allows you to make maximum use of available space.
- **Dutch light**: Designed to make the most of the sun, this is a good choice for winter crops, but the sloping sides make working in it more difficult.
- **Tunnel**: This has the same advantages and disadvantages as the Dutch light.
- **Hexagonal/octagonal**: Can be highly ornamental, an important consideration in a small garden, and would give easier access and manoeuvrability for a wheelchair.
- **Lean-to**: A popular design for setting against the side of a wall or even a tall sturdy fence. Lean-tos are the cheapest to heat.

Although some of the more rigid plastics are fairly long lived, none of them is as permanent as glass. All plastics tend to become brittle with age, and they may warp or even crack. Some also lose transparency or yellow. In addition, plastics are often less aesthetically pleasing – they do not have the sparkling clarity of glass – and they are also much softer than glass and become scratched or abraded by wind-blown grit.

Condensation can form in all greenhouses, but it is more of a problem in plastic houses. Water collecting on a plastic surface does not form a transparent film as it does on glass. The droplets may cut down light entry and raise humidity excessively, which can lead to problems with mould and mildew.

Plastic does, however, score over glass if safety is a consideration and may be your choice if there are small children or elderly people around or if the structure is at risk from vandals – if it's on an allotment, for example. Don't forget that plastics can also be used to partially 'glaze' a structure, and could be fitted where glass is most likely to break.

The other great advantage of plastic is that it is light and easy to move. It is therefore useful in places such as a vegetable plot, where the entire structure can be moved as you annually rotate your crop.

top Greenhouses can be used to bring on early crops or, as here, to keep precious plants like citrus trees and olives free from the ravages of winter.

Equipping a greenhouse

Before you can use your greenhouse you will need to fit a certain amount of basic equipment, such as ventilators and staging. It is also worth thinking about installing an automatic watering system, and, if the greenhouse is to be used for raising tender plants, some form of heating.

Ventilators

When you are buying a greenhouse a basic number of ventilators is usually included in the price, but some suppliers consider them extras. Most alloy greenhouses can be fitted with as many ventilators as you like. It is better to have more than you need – you don't have to open them all together – with a good distribution all around the greenhouse to allow you to use them according to the direction of the prevailing wind.

Ideally, ventilators in the roof should be installed as high as possible, while those in the sides are at ground level. This arrangement allows warm air to flow out freely at the top while cool air is drawn in from below. However, when there is staging or base walls, the vents are normally positioned just above them.

The conventional hinged ventilator with a stay bar is still used in most timber houses, but some designs incorporate sliding vents. Alloy structures are now increasingly fitted with louvred vents, but make sure that these are tight fitting.

Doors

Sliding doors are now often fitted to both timber and alloy structures, but some designs leave much to be desired. Metal doors can freeze up in winter, and some have draughty gaps between the door and frame. Make sure that the door opening is wide enough to allow easy access for wheelbarrows and large plants in pots. Sliding doors act as useful extra ventilators, since they are more easily adjusted than the hinged type. If you have children, choose a lockable door for safety.

Guttering

This is a highly desirable but not always integral feature. The constant shedding of rainwater around the perimeter of a greenhouse can, occasionally, cause subsidence of the foundations because of the solvent action on the soil. Water can also seep inside, causing cold, damp conditions. Many alloy structures are now equipped with built-in guttering, but plastic guttering can be easily and inexpensively fitted to any type. The rainwater should be led away to a proper soakaway at a convenient distance or, better still, collected in a butt.

Staging and shelving

So that you can make the most of the available space, you will need some staging (benching) and shelving. Sometimes the staging is entirely or partially supplied with a greenhouse and is included in the price, but it may be considered as an extra. Timber greenhouses are often equipped with conventional slatted wooden staging. Alloy structures have metal supports topped with a variety of materials, including stout wire mesh on which pot plants can be stood.

top Ventilation is vital in all greenhouses, but especially so in one heated by oil or paraffin, as it is dangerous to allow fumes to build up.

right above A small thermostatically controlled propagator is very useful for creating an extra-warm area within a greenhouse.

right In a greenhouse used to grow and display tender plants, lush foliage can provide some of the necessary shade.

No matter what it is made of, the shelving is usually of similar construction. Check that any staging is strong enough to take a reasonable weight and that the greenhouse framework is also strong enough to support shelving laden with pots filled with moist soil.

It can be a good idea to set staging along just one side, leaving the sunnier side free for tall plants. Modern staging is often designed to be portable and may also be adjustable, both in terms of height and of shape and configuration, so that it fits neatly inside the greenhouse. It is also available in tiered or stepped forms, which are ideal for displaying plants.

Shading

Nearly all greenhouses need shading at one time or another. An unshaded structure in a bright position can become so hot in summer that all the plants will be scorched or even killed.

If you can, get blinds that are fitted to the outside of the greenhouse. Slatted blinds are best; flimsy plastic or textile blinds are likely to blow away in a strong wind. Interior blinds give protection from direct sun scorch, but do little to keep down the temperature.

The alternative to blinds is a shading paint, which is applied to the glass. Shading paints can be difficult to apply and are tiresome to remove at the end of the season. However, a recently introduced electrostatic type makes life easier. It is a powder that mixes instantly with water. It can be sprayed or brushed on and is quite fast, even in torrential rain; yet it wipes off easily with a dry duster.

Heating

For most of the year the sun should keep your greenhouse warm enough. However, in winter you may want some additional heat, which will probably involve laying electric cabling from your house.

If you plan to raise a few plants from seeds in spring, an electric propagator or two will probably be all you will need to hold the seedtrays and some plant pots. More sophisticated (and expensive) systems are available, however, and if you intend to overwinter plants and raise seedlings on a large scale you will need something more substantial.

Although it shouldn't cost too much to raise the temperature in a greenhouse by a few degrees, before you invest in an expensive system remember that there are many ways in which you can keep down the costs. A site not shaded by overhanging trees or nearby buildings or boundaries will ensure maximum free solar heat, even in winter. Providing shelter from strong winds will minimize heat loss. Make sure that you eliminate all sources of draughts, such as gaps in the framework, ill-fitting doors, vents and panes.

Unless you have a conservatory, double glazing is either prohibitively expensive or simply impracticable for technical reasons. However, lining the inside of the greenhouse with polythene is a simple and inexpensive way to achieve insulation that is almost as good. Clear polythene film or, better, 'bubble' plastic, which is sold specially for the purpose, can prevent up to 50 per cent of heat loss. When you are putting up the plastic, make sure that there is an insulating air gap of about 2.5cm (1in) between the glass and the plastic. You can get special clips to attach the plastic sheets to a metal framework, but if you have a timber house you will have to use drawing pins.

How much heat?

Any form of heating must have a heat output that matches the heat loss when the temperature outside is at its coldest. This can be roughly calculated from the size of the structure, the type and surface area of construction materials, the minimum temperature you want to maintain, and the lowest outside temperature expected. If you can provide this information, a good supplier of greenhouse heating systems will be able to recommend the right equipment. Don't buy until you have been through this process.

Electricity

For a long time, electricity was regarded as the most expensive source of heat, but there is virtually no waste and, once installed, it needs the minimum of attention. There is no contamination of the greenhouse atmosphere, which means that ventilation – and consequent heat loss – can be reduced considerably, making it compare favourably with paraffin and gas heaters.

There are four main styles of electrical heaters:
- Fan heaters give an excellent distribution of warmed air. However, be sure to install a model in which both the fan and the heater are controlled by the thermostat. In those models in which the fan runs all the time, the air continues to be circulated after it has been warmed and consequently cools down more quickly. These systems are more expensive to run, however, than other fan heaters.

- Tubular heaters are also popular. Distribute them evenly around the greenhouse, rather than having them together in one place. If possible, position them near the central pathway on both sides. Putting them close to the greenhouse sides is a waste of heat.
- Convector heaters are a good buy. They give a moderate circulation of warmed air in the same way as fan heaters.
- Warming cables have many uses. They can be used in beds or on a part of the staging to provide economical, localized warmth. They are invaluable for gentle forcing of winter vegetable crops, and they can even be used in cold-frames to warm small areas. This is especially useful for propagation.

Only buy and use an electrical heater that has been specially designed for use in the greenhouse. Domestic equipment can be extremely dangerous in damp conditions and should never be used.

Gas

In many parts of the world, piped natural gas is probably the cheapest fuel, while bottled gas is the most expensive. Both can be used to fuel greenhouse gas heaters, and modern appliances give a high degree of thermostatic control, which cuts down waste. However, you must provide constant ventilation.

Paraffin

The wick-type paraffin heater has fallen from favour because it is not easily controlled thermostatically, fuel is expensive and waste is inevitable unless you are always at hand to adjust the wick. Nevertheless, a paraffin heater is so reliable that it is a good idea to keep it, in case the main system breaks down or there is a power cut or an exceptionally cold spell when it can be used to provide a little extra warmth.

Good ventilation is crucial with a paraffin heater, because condensation is usually excessive. Choose a heater specially designed for use in a greenhouse. The best type is a blue-flame type with a circular wick; it gives efficient combustion and is less liable to produce smells and fumes. Make sure you learn how to light the burner properly and always follow the instructions.

left Electric heaters are more economical than once thought, and are easy to install and safe to operate.

right top Grow greenhouse plants in pots rather than in the soil itself, and provide yourself with a safe, flat floor to stand on.

Labour-saving devices

Save time and effort in the greenhouse by installing labour-saving devices that will cut down on your work and make sure your plants get the best possible care. The most important of these is thermostatically controlled heating. Always buy equipment, whether heaters or propagating frames, with the most accurate thermostatic controls you can find.

If you know that you are regularly away for long periods and leave your greenhouse or conservatory unattended, consider installing an automatic watering system. There are several types on the market, but one of the best systems uses special capillary matting, which is kept constantly moist. The matting is spread over the staging and the plant pots are pressed onto it so that moisture can pass into the potting compost from the matting. Various types of trickle irrigation, overhead misting and spraying systems are also available, but they have more restricted, and sometimes specialized, applications.

Ventilation can also be efficiently controlled by special greenhouse extractor fans operated by a thermostat. Make sure that they are designed to prevent back draught. The size of fan – and therefore the volume of air moved – will depend on the size of your greenhouse. Consult the supplier before buying and installing. Because fan-ventilated greenhouses are liable to dry out very quickly, consider installing automatic watering or humidity control at the same time. For the ordinary home greenhouse, automatic

ventilator openers controlled by temperature change are simple to fit. They need no electricity, require little attention and are widely available.

Beds and floors

In most types of greenhouse, it's best not to use the ground soil for growing. You will get reasonably good results for about two years, but after that there is a build-up of unbalanced fertilizers, waste biochemical products from plant roots and, possibly, pests and diseases. Because the soil is not exposed to weathering as it is in the open garden, soil sickness soon becomes a problem, even if you do practise some crop rotation. It's sensible, therefore, to grow everything in a suitable compost, which can be replaced every year.

When the ground soil is not used for growing, a greenhouse can be erected on almost any sound, flat surface. Concrete, asphalt, paving slabs and the like make suitable floors, although if there is no drainage water may collect in puddles. Where a greenhouse is erected on soil, as it usually is in the average garden, a simple effective floor can be made by levelling and firming the ground, and then strewing it with clean shingle or gravel, as used on driveways. This holds plenty of moisture during summer and will maintain atmospheric humidity without puddling. It is cheap and reasonably attractive, though not comfortable to stand on for long periods.

Routine maintenance

Keep your greenhouse in good condition and it will last for years:

- Keep the glass clean using water only and a hose and long-handled brush. If the dirt is really ingrained, use a solution of a proprietary descaler specially formulated for greenhouses.

- Replace any broken panes of glass immediately.

- Check that all gutters and downpipes are clear. This is particularly important if there are nearby deciduous trees.

- Check metal frames for signs of rust and, if necessary, treat these with a rust remover.

- Check that wooden frames are in good condition and replace any rotting wood. Re-apply a wood preservative when necessary.

Siting your greenhouse

Your greenhouse is going to be a permanent structure, so it is worth taking a little time and trouble to identify the best position for it within your garden. If you are going to get the greatest possible use from it make sure that it is accessible from a weatherproof path.

You might also want a site that is not too far from your backdoor so that you can get to it quickly in wet weather. In a small garden, of course, you may not have many options, but bear the following points in mind:

- Avoid overhanging trees and nearby buildings, which may cast shadows.
- Avoid windy, exposed sites, which will lead to heat loss.
- A wall, fence or hedge on the side of the prevailing wind but distant enough not to cast shade will make a useful windbreak.
- Choose an open, bright position whenever possible. If you want your greenhouse to have one shady side and one sunny side, position it so that it faces sunrise. If you want both sides to receive direct sunlight, rotate the structure by 90 degrees.
- For the convenience of providing services, such as water, electricity or gas, choose a site as close to the house as possible.
- Make sure that the ground beneath the greenhouse is firm and level.
- Avoid wet and waterlogged ground and places where frost is known to form.
- A square or rectangular greenhouse is best sited so that its ridge, or length, runs as near as possible from east to west. This allows maximum entry of sunlight in winter, when the sun is low in the sky, and hence maximum solar heat. In summer, a greenhouse positioned in this way will need shading on only one side.

Firm foundations

When you buy a greenhouse, the supplier will usually recommend the most suitable form of foundation for your circumstances. It is worth taking trouble over constructing a sound foundation because, if there is any movement or subsidence after the glazing is complete, the glass may crack and the entire structure may have to be re-erected.

If you are offered a greenhouse with integral kerbing, buy it. The kerb (or plinth) is formed of shaped sections of concrete, and a small greenhouse of this type, erected on flat, stable ground, will need no additional base.

Many modern alloy structures use a ground-anchor system. The frame is first erected on firm, level ground, and then holes about the size of a bucket are dug at intervals around the base of the frame. Alloy anchors are then bolted on so that they drop down into the holes, which are then filled with concrete. This is the method that most people find easiest to carry out if they are erecting the greenhouse themselves.

Another simple way to make a foundation for a small greenhouse is to dig a trench, about 15cm (6in) deep and 15cm (6in) wide, to match the base size, and then fill it with a rather liquid concrete mix. The mix will automatically find its own level without you having to check with a spirit-level.

top Lean-to greenhouses can be very smart in design and have the advantage of a solid wall against which to train fruit or vegetables.

Cold-frames and cloches

Without a greenhouse you can still protect early sowings and late crops with smaller, portable structures such as cold-frames, cloches and polytunnels. These can also be used to harden off plants before they are transplanted and to protect plants all through the year.

Cold-frames

Cold-frames are best used for raising and hardening off plants, for summer crops of half-hardy vegetables, such as cucumbers, tomatoes and peppers, and for winter salad crops. They are useful adjuncts to a greenhouse, relieving space by housing shorter plants. Frames can be economically warmed with electric warming cables and can even be used inside the greenhouse for creating an extra-warm area, like a large propagator.

Traditionally, cold-frames were permanent fixtures, with brick sides and glass 'lights' or lids. Modern frames tend to be portable, and constructed of wood, plastic or aluminium with a glass lid. Some have sliding tops, but hinged tops are more useful, as you can wedge them open to harden off plants while still protecting them from rain.

Whether they are used outdoors or in the greenhouse, cold-frames are best sited so that they get little direct sunshine.

Cloches

Cloches come in a variety of shapes and sizes. Glass are the most expensive and, breakages apart, are the most durable and give the best light transmission. They are, however, heavy to handle. Of the many plastic materials available, double-layered corrugated propylene creates excellent growing conditions, with plants thriving in the diffuse light.

You must use some method of anchoring your cloche or it may blow away. Use a pane of glass or sheet of plastic to close the ends or it will turn into a wind tunnel. Ventilation is essential in warm, close weather – moving the cloches a little apart is a simple solution.

Cloches are easily moved from one crop to another and are often placed end to end to cover a row. The disadvantages are the labour involved in lifting them to care for the crops beneath, and tall plants outgrow all but the largest cloches.

Polytunnels

Low polythene tunnels are cheaper than cloches but can be used in much the same way. They are made from polythene film, which is stretched over a series of low, galvanized wire hoops. The film is held in place with fine wire or string stretched from side to side. The ends are anchored in the soil and the sides can be rolled up for watering and ventilation. The film usually needs replacing after two years.

top Courgettes cannot survive being frosted, so individual bell cloches give just that little bit of reassurance until all danger is past.

above Cold-frames are very adaptable, as mini-greenhouses, as overwintering homes and as a halfway house for plants being hardened off.

through the seasons

Spring

Spring is the busiest time of year in the garden. There are seeds to be sown and new plants to be put into the beds and borders. Remember to keep note of the weather forecasts, though, because a mild spell will encourage early growth and germination, which could be knocked back by a sudden cold snap.

Early spring

Low rainfall and drying winds make good gardening weather, and you've no longer any excuse for delaying the digging. Make a point of skimming off the weeds first and burying them below ground as you go. This is also the time to tidy up the borders, so cut down any stems that you didn't cut back in autumn and apply a slow-release fertilizer to the soil.

Bulbs will be having a huge impact on the garden this month. Winter-flowering crocuses flower in profusion, and the blue, mauve and purple cultivars of *Iris reticulata* come into full bloom, together with chionodoxas, *Scilla siberica* (Siberian squill), *Anemone blanda* and the first narcissi (daffodils). Later-flowering cultivars of winter-flowering heaths (*Erica* spp.) come into bloom, taking over from those that started in winter. Forsythias open their yellow bells, and the yellow-flowered *Mahonia aquifolium* (Oregon grape) and bright red and pink *Chaenomeles* spp. (flowering quince, japonica) begin blooming. *Pulmonaria* spp. (lungwort) produce flowers of red, pink and blue.

You should be thinking about dividing rampant perennials in the borders, particularly Michaelmas daisies, rudbeckias, *Solidago* (golden rod) and *Saponaria* (soapwort). Replant young, healthy offsets and discard the old, woody crowns.

Begin to prick out seedlings of half-hardy annuals (summer bedding plants) before they jostle each other, otherwise they will grow tall and spindly and never fully recover. Hardening off (see page 44) should begin at an early stage.

Finish putting in border plants and bare-rooted trees and shrubs as soon as possible. Use your hand shears to snip off the dead flowerheads from winter-flowering heaths that have finished blooming to keep them compact. Take cuttings of delphiniums and lupins as soon as the shoots are about 10cm (4in) high. Make sure each has a solid base, and set them in pots of rooting compost in a cold-frame. Scatter general fertilizer around hardy border plants and roses and use a hand fork to mix it into the soil's surface.

Towards the end of the month, prune climbing roses and hypericums (St John's wort). This is also the time to deal with large-flowered (hybrid tea) and cluster-flowered (floribunda) roses, provided that

left Magnolia seeds have been lying dormant all winter, but with spring warmth and longer days they have burst into growth.

top Colour is so welcome after the winter that the brightest of colour combinations seem cheery rather than brash.

there are not going to be any more frosts, and while you've got your secateurs out prune the *Buddleja davidii* (butterfly bush).

Mid-spring

This is the time for hope and anticipation. Warm spring sunshine is often followed by night frosts, and, if you've not being paying attention to the weather forecasts and a favourite plant is frozen, try thawing it gently by spraying with tepid water; afterwards, cover it with a layer of bracken, horticultural fleece or sheets of newspaper.

Try to make time to visit as many nurseries as possible, especially those where ornamental cherries are in full bloom. The cherries are a great sight, from the showy double pink flowers of *Prunus* 'Kanzan' to the subtler charms of *Prunus avium* (gean, wild cherry); the cultivar 'Plena', one of the loveliest of all, has double white flowers now and good autumn colour to look forward to.

Daffodils and narcissi make a brave show this month, together with the early tulips, blue *Muscari* (grape hyacinth) and *Fritillaria meleagris* (snake's head fritillary). The yellow daisy-like flowers of the earliest *Doronicum* spp. (leopard's bane) make a sunny display and are joined by *Omphalodes cappadocica* (navelwort), epimediums (barrenwort, bishop's mitre), bergenias (elephant's ears) and the earliest-flowering ajugas (bugle). *Vinca* spp. (periwinkle) start flowering in earnest, as do evergreen forms of *Berberis* (barberry) and *Kerria japonica*, while the flowering crabapples (forms of *Malus*) and *Amelanchier lamarckii* (snowy mespilus) cover themselves in blossom and the early-flowering brooms (*Cytisus* spp.) burst into colour.

Most gardeners will find time in autumn to plant

spring-flowering bulbs, which are now at their best, but comparatively few plant the summer-flowering bulbs in spring – and by not doing so they miss a lot. In go corms of *Anemone coronaria* De Caen Group hybrids, with their single poppy flowers and black centres, and the richly coloured St Brigid Group hybrids. You can also plant the bulbs of *Galtonia candicans* (summer hyacinth) and of the exotic and brilliantly coloured *Tigridia* spp. (peacock flower, tiger flower).

Prune spring-flowering shrubs that have already bloomed, particularly the free-growing forsythia.

Sow seeds of hardy annuals to flower in summer and seeds of perennial border plants, such as *Papaver*

left Wait until the soil has warmed up before planting out shrubs. They will then soon send down new roots.

top Bluebells and a fine *Cytisus battandieri* (pineapple broom) are telltale signs that spring is well advanced.

orientalis (oriental poppy), lupins and one of the interesting new forms of *Heuchera* (coral flower). If you have not already done so, plant gladioli corms for the main summer display. Start staking quick-growing border plants, such as delphiniums. This is also a good time to put in evergreen trees and shrubs, including conifers.

Late spring

The weather can still be changeable. Wind will dry the soil, and a sudden drought may make watering necessary. Meanwhile, late frosts sometimes damage any too-early planting or tender shoots put out by plants that have responded to an early mild spell and some sunshine.

Late narcissi and daffodils are joined by regiments of colourful tulips and *Hyacinthoides non-scripta* (English bluebell) and *H. hispanica* (Spanish bluebell). The pretty cultivars of *Lamium maculatum* (deadnettle) produce the pink spikes, which go well with the variegated leaves. By now all the plants grown for their foliage – silver artemisias and *Stachys byzantina* (lamb's ears), the hostas in wide array, the brilliant ajugas (bugle), the variegated and yellow- and purple-leaved shrubs – will have begun to contribute colour to the scene. Masses of blossoms are

provided by types of *Prunus* spp. – Japanese cherries, plums and almonds – while *Crataegus* spp. (hawthorn), wisteria and *Clematis montana* will be starting to bloom.

The battle against rose pests begins early. Combined insecticides and fungicides have lightened the work of spraying, but if the bushes are to be kept clean they must be sprayed every ten days or so.

You will be busy in the herbaceous border, staking, supporting, pinching out any leggy growth, thinning out the Michaelmas daisy and delphinium shoots, transplanting, weeding and sowing a few annuals to fill the gaps. Delphiniums and other soft-stemmed plants must be defended against slugs and the fast-growing seedlings of border plants encouraged with a dressing of fertilizer. All bedding plants and seedlings growing under glass should be given as much air as possible.

left The warm weather doesn't only encourage good things to grow: mildews and fungus spores will also multiply fast.

top An archetypical spring picture: tulips and bluebells springing up through the new leaves of an acanthus.

Jobs for early spring

- Rake over areas of gravel and bark chips and top up if necessary.

- Carry out lawn repairs before mowing starts.

- Start mowing the lawn once a fortnight if the grass is dry and has begun to grow.

- Visit the garden centre to buy new flowering and foliage perennials and plant them if the soil is workable.

- Cut back all dead foliage from herbaceous perennials if you didn't do it in autumn.

- Mulch all bare soil with organic material to keep moisture in the soil and suppress weeds.

- Prune late summer- and autumn-flowering shrubs, such as *Buddleja* (butterfly bush) and hydrangeas.

- Plant new evergreen shrubs.

- Prune roses that are just starting into growth.

- Sow summer bedding plants in the greenhouse or on a windowsill.

- Apply a general-purpose fertilizer around all fruit trees and bushes. Give them a mulch, too.

- If the vegetable plot is still wet, put some cloches in place to help the soil dry out before you begin sowing.

- As soon as the soil is in a suitable state, make a start with vegetable sowings.

- Plant potato tubers.

Jobs for mid-spring

- Start mowing the lawn regularly if you haven't started already.

- Apply a granular lawn feed.

- Plant summer-flowering bulbs, such as *Allium* spp. (ornamental onion).

- Feed shrubs, trees, hedges and established flower beds with a slow-release fertilizer.

- Prune shrubs that have just finished flowering.

- Divide perennials if necessary.

- Sow seeds of lettuces, French beans, carrots and radishes.

- Sow hardy annuals straight into borders.

- Continue to plant herbaceous plants, summer-flowering bulbs, evergreen shrubs and conifers.

- Weeds will be in full growth by now – remove them little and often.

- There is still time to carry out lawn repairs and this is a good time to sow a new lawn or apply lawn fertilizer, mosskiller and weedkiller.

- Apply a liquid feed to spring bulbs after flowering.

- Apply mulches around all permanent plants, such as roses and shrubs.

- Continue with vegetable sowings of all kinds. Sow tomatoes in a greenhouse or on a windowsill.

- Thin out vegetables sown in early spring.

- Earth up potatoes and plant maincrop varieties. Support peas and tall broad beans.

Jobs for late spring

- Mow the lawn once a week.

- Plant dahlia and gladioli tubers outside.

- Prune shrubs that have just finished flowering.

- Continue to weed beds and borders little and often.

- Plant summer bedding plants in containers and beds outside.

- Divide pond plants if necessary.

- Sow seeds of hardy perennials, trees and shrubs, rock plants, spring bedding plants and summer-flowering biennials for next year.

- Discard spring bedding plants after flowering.

- If necessary, spring bulbs can be lifted and heeled-in on a spare piece of ground until the foliage has died down.

- Thin out hardy annuals if necessary.

- Make a start on hedge trimming.

- Plant out tomatoes, courgettes and sweetcorn in the garden when all risk of frost has passed.

- Continue with vegetable sowings, including sprouting broccoli, cucumbers, kale, marrows and swedes.

- Hoe regularly and water well in dry periods.

- Keep an eye open for pests and diseases.

- Plant tomatoes, capsicums, aubergines and cucumbers in the greenhouse.

Summer

Summer is a time to relax and enjoy the fruits of your labours, but don't forget watering and pest control. It's all too easy to allow plants, particularly if they are in tubs, to dry out in hot weather. Make a regular point of checking the garden, especially the vegetables, for signs of disease and insect damage.

Early summer

A host of hardy border plants, such as *Dianthus* (pinks), delphiniums, lupins, peonies, *Hemerocallis* (daylilies) and *Papaver orientale* (oriental poppy) burst into flower at this time, together with many of the hardy annuals sown earlier. New shrubs to flower include *Lonicera periclymenum* 'Belgica' (early Dutch honeysuckle), potentillas, weigelas, hypericums (St John's wort), *Hydrangea anomala* subsp. *petiolaris* (climbing hydrangea), *Solanum crispum* (Chilean potato tree), *Solanum jasminoides* (potato vine), *Buddleja alternifolia* and *B. globosa* (orange ball tree). One of the glories, of many gardens, however, will be

the roses, which make a tremendous show of summer colour – even those that were only planted the previous autumn and spring.

The sun will soon be at its strongest, and this is often the driest time. Watering becomes a more pressing task, and if you have not been able to mulch the borders you will have to work overtime with the hose once the sun has gone down.

Staking is another important job in early summer. A sudden storm can play havoc in the border and ruin a year's endeavour. All herbaceous plants will be growing freely and will benefit from a feed of fertilizer or a drink of liquid manure. Now that summer has come, pot-grown camellias and others previously kept indoors or in a greenhouse will benefit from being out in the garden.

left With everything growing so fast, don't forget to provide support in time for any plants that need it.

top Summer annuals and pot-grown summer bulbs will quickly fill any gaps left by spring bulbs or winter losses.

Complete the planting of beds and borders with tender plants, including dahlias, cannas and other bedding plants, as soon as you can. Trim back *Cytisus* spp. (broom), aubrieta and *Erica* spp. and cultivars (heath) as they finish flowering to keep them bushy. Check upright conifers to ensure that they have not produced competing shoots at the top. Remove dead flowers as they fade from roses, annuals and border plants.

Midsummer

Midsummer does not always have the highest temperatures and the hottest days of the year. We can generally count on some hot days, but the fine weather may break up with a thunderstorm accompanied by rain or hail. Meanwhile, the flower garden should be a riot of colour.

Buddleja davidii (butterfly bush) will be flowering now, together with hypericums (St John's wort), *Olearia × haastii* (daisy bush), *Phlomis fruticosa* (Jerusalem sage), the climbing *Schizophragma integrifolium* and many of the mid-season, large-flowered clematis cultivars, some with blooms as large as saucers.

Extra colour is provided in borders by white *Leucanthemum × superbum* (Shasta daisy), the pink, daisy-like *Echinacea* (coneflower), *Liatris* (gayfeather) and *Persicaria* spp. (knotweed). The peppery-scented border phloxes also begin to burst upon the scene, together with the brilliant purple *Salvia nemorosa*, dwarf dahlias and all the summer bedding planted out a few weeks ago.

At this time of year, deadheading must be done daily, otherwise bedding plants will soon lose interest in flowering and put all their energy into producing seeds, a tendency that's particularly evident in the short-lived annuals.

Plants are still making rapid growth and will benefit from a feed of liquid fertilizer. Established roses will relish a pick-me-up after their first flush. Spring cuttings of plants such as fuchsias, which are now well rooted, should be moved on to 15cm (6in) pots before they become cramped and pot-bound.

right above As summer progresses, purple phloxes and *Galega hartlandii* 'Alba' (white goat's rue) bush out and bloom.

right below Rosemary takes easily from semi-ripe cuttings at this time of the year, quickly developing into new plants.

Late summer

The weather is usually similar to midsummer. Atmospheric conditions are often the same and these are the months that will determine whether the year has a fine or wet summer. Although autumn has not yet shown signs of taking over, plants and trees have lost their youth and many are becoming overgrown and blowsy. If rainfall is low, regular watering will be called for, but the heavy dews will begin to help replace moisture that has been lost from plants by transpiration.

If you visit nurseries or garden centres, look out for hybrids of the lovely *Alstroemeria ligtu* (Peruvian lily), which will produce pink, coral, yellow or buff flowers through late summer. Other plants that are worth tracking down are the beautiful, if not fully hardy, *Hibiscus moscheutos* 'Southern Belle' from Japan and *Fuchsia arborescens* from America. Other plants worth finding are the dignified *Eremurus* (foxtail lily), the evergreen *Magnolia grandiflora* (bull bay), presenting its immense sweet-scented flowers from late summer into autumn, and *Romneya coulteri* (tree poppy, matilija poppy), which has grey-green foliage and petals of white, crinkled 'paper' that surround a golden centre.

Dainty *Anemone* × *hybrida* (Japanese anemone), *Solidago* (golden rod), *Sedum spectabile* (ice plant) and tuberous dahlias take over the display as earlier plants pass out of bloom. *Persicaria* spp. (knotweed) show their attributes now, and the charming *Cyclamen hederifolium* adds to the display. It is also the time when the spectacular trumpet vine *Campsis* × *tagliabuana* 'Mme Galen' opens its red trumpet flowers after a hot summer, and the bedding plants reach the peak of their display, as do some late cultivars and species of clematis.

You should be planting bulbs such as crocuses, fritillaries, dwarf bulbous irises, chionodoxas and narcissi for a display next spring. Also set out *Colchicum* spp. (autumn crocus) as soon as you buy them.

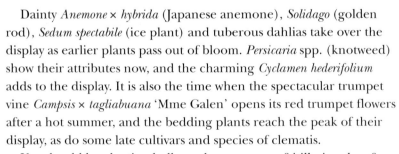

left In their first year, keep an eye on all shrubs and trees, and water them freely during spells of dry weather.

top Large-flowered clematis are a joy when allowed to ramble naturally rather than be strapped against a wall.

Jobs for early summer

- Top up the pond in warm weather if the level drops through evaporation.
- Mow the lawn once a week.
- Water containers and recently planted plants in dry weather.
- Weed beds and borders little and often.
- Sow more lettuces, radishes and other fast-maturing vegetables for a second crop.
- Feed bedding plants and vegetables regularly with a liquid feed.
- Prune shrubs after flowering.
- Keep an eye open for pests and diseases and deal with them as soon as possible.
- Remove dead flowerheads.
- Take softwood cuttings of shrubs and perennials.
- Thin out hardy annual seedlings.
- Provide support for growing herbaceous perennials.
- Protect strawberries from slugs.
- Provide support for peas and beans.
- Sow runner and French beans.

Jobs for midsummer

- Thin out pond weed if necessary.
- Mow the lawn once a week.
- Deadhead annuals and bedding plants to encourage them to flower again.
- Feed bedding plants and vegetables regularly with a liquid feed.
- Water containers and recently planted plants in dry weather.
- Weed beds and borders little and often.
- Trim evergreen shrubs and hedges.
- Lift and divide bearded irises.
- Continue to prune any shrubs that have finished flowering.
- Protect fruit from birds.
- Remove old leaves and unwanted runners from strawberries.
- Make sowings of spring cabbage, turnips, carrots, lettuces, winter radishes, beetroots, early peas and winter spinach.

Jobs for late summer

- Mow the lawn once a week.
- Water containers and recently planted plants in dry weather.
- Weed beds and borders little and often.
- Plant autumn-flowering bulbs.
- Propagate plants from semi-ripe cuttings.
- Continue deadheading, and maintain good pest and disease control.
- Continue feeding if you feel plants need a boost.
- Continue hedge trimming.
- Plant strawberries, either in a bed in the open ground, or in strawberry containers.
- Prune raspberries as soon as the fruits have been picked. Cut out old fruited stems to ground level.
- Lift onions and shallots, dry off and store.
- Sow spring cabbage, winter spinach and salad crops.
- Cut and dry herbs for winter use.

Autumn

Autumn is a lovely time of the year in the garden. The leaves begin to colour and the fruit to ripen. When the frosts begin to strike and the foliage to die back, our thoughts automatically turn to next year. Now's the time to think about planting bulbs and preparing the ground for new shrubs and trees.

Early autumn

Anemone × hybrida (Japanese anemones) are still giving a lavish display, while asters of all kinds are beginning to appear. *Callistephus chinensis* (China asters) do their best to hold attention, while *Aster novae-angliae* (New England aster) and *A. novi-belgii* (Michaelmas daisy) brighten the borders.

Many berrying trees and shrubs add extra colour at this time, including cotoneasters, gaultherias, cultivars of *Sorbus* (rowan, mountain ash) and *Pyracantha* spp. (firethorn). Some of the first glowing autumn leaf colour is provided by *Amelanchier lamarckii* (snowy mespilus). Many species and cultivars of the dainty autumn-flowering crocuses and colchicums begin to bloom, but the annuals are almost played out, and the days are visibly shortening as planting time is near.

Plan now for the spring with a tree (or a large shrub if space is really tight) that, planted now, will give a good show in the spring. Some of the loveliest are the small ornamental cherries and crabapples or, for something a little different, look for *Mespilus germanica* (medlar). These will also be highly rewarding next autumn. For gardeners on acid soil the choice could be *Camellia × williamsii* 'Donation', a striking Himalayan rhododendron or the slow-growing, red-barked *Arbutus unedo* (strawberry tree).

Other significant work to be done at this time is the potting up of 'prepared' bulbs in the home and greenhouse, the planting of daffodils, snowdrops and other early-flowering bulbs in beds and borders (or in the grass if there is a wild garden), adding perhaps a few of the brilliant tulip species that do not require autumn lifting.

If peonies have to be moved or divided, this is the best time to do it, although only do it if absolutely necessary. This is also a good time to move the winter-flowering *Iris unguicularis*. Lifted conifers and other

left Buying bulbs early will give you the pick of the best instead of the frustruation of making do with whatever is left.

top The exotic garden comes into its own late in the year, with the flowering of cannas and other late developers.

evergreens can be moved safely from now until mid-autumn. After planting, water them freely in dry weather. Prune rambling roses, removing or shortening the old stems and tying in the new ones to replace them. Many roses, especially ramblers, can be raised from cuttings taken now.

The tougher hardy annuals, such as *Calendula* (pot marigold), *Centaurea cyanus* (cornflower) and godetia, can be sown now to provide larger plants and earlier flowers next summer. Lift and pot any pelargoniums, tender fuchsias and cannas you want to save before the first frosts, and keep them in a warm greenhouse, or in a light place indoors, for the winter.

Mid-autumn

Flowers are scarce at this time, but the berried trees and shrubs, bright with autumn colour, take their place. The mahogany-coloured trunk and dazzling red leaves of *Acer griseum* (paper-bark maple), the orange but inedible fruit of *Arbutus unedo* (strawberry tree) and the gorgeous flame of *Liquidambar styraciflua* (sweet gum) play their part. If there is a trellis, archway or wall where the magnificent *Vitis coignetiae* (crimson glory vine), which is native to Japan and Korea, can ramble freely, it will provide a blaze of exciting reds and maroons. This climber is quick and willing to camouflage any structure as long as you give it a helping hand. The lace-like *Parthenocissus quinquefolia* (Virginia creeper) and its forms give the same dramatic effect and have the advantage of being self-clinging.

If you have a small garden and are considering an elegant tree, look out for *Betula pendula* 'Youngii' (Young's weeping birch) or even the taller but equally decorative *Betula pendula* (silver birch), known so aptly as queen of the woods.

The display of brilliant berries continues as the season progresses, and the brightly coloured crabapples (*Malus* spp.) add to the show, some of them hanging on long after the leaves have fallen. *Callicarpa bodinieri* becomes covered in tight clusters of amethyst-violet berries. Some autumn crocus and colchicum species continue to open their frail blooms, and many border plants, such as *Sedum spectabile* (ice

plant) and *Aster novi-belgii* (Michaelmas daisy), hold their display, while others make a second, smaller, but nonetheless welcome showing. The first glistening pink blooms of *Nerine bowdenii* open now, as do *Schizostylis coccinea* (kaffir lily), and if they have been regularly deadheaded most bedding plants continue to be colourful until they are cut down by the first frost.

Complete the work of planting all bulbs (except tulips) as soon as possible. Weed any hardy annuals sown in early autumn and thin them out to 8cm (3in) apart for the winter. Clear fallen leaves from low-growing plants. Make sure that you lift and store gladiolus corms and dahlia tubers once their top growth has been frosted.

right Despite being still full of colour and interest, there is an unmistakable sense of autumn in the air as seedheads become a feature in the garden.

Late autumn

This is the best time for planting hedges, and you can choose from among the slow-growing, dark and distinguished *Taxus* (yew); *Fagus sylvatica* (common beech), which keeps its russet leaves through winter (a copper beech planted here and there will make a colourful addition); *Ilex* spp. (holly), often a slow starter, but with a useful prickly and resistant quality; *Escallonia* cultivars, which are decorative shrubs, suitable for seaside gardens but in mild districts only; the easy-to-grow *Prunus laurocerasus* (cherry laurel) or ubiquitous *Ligustrum* (privet), which is both tolerant and inexpensive (nine broad-leaved privets to one golden privet makes an attractive hedge). Don't overlook *Crataegus* spp. (hawthorn), tough and fast-growing, which makes a fine boundary, or *Berberis* × *stenophylla*, which is decked with a mass of bright yellow flowers in late spring. Rhododendrons can also make excellent early-flowering summer hedges if you garden on acid soil. *Rosa rubiginosa* (sweet briar) forms a delightful scented barrier, while the cluster-flowered rose 'Queen Elizabeth' is excellent for medium-height informal planting.

As deciduous trees and shrubs shed their remaining leaves, the winter garden scene emerges, but provided it is well planted with evergreens it never looks empty and dead. The coloured-leaved conifers, especially, can provide plenty of variety. Also revealed when the leaves fall is the colourful bark of some trees and shrubs, including the coral-red shoots of *Acer palmatum* 'Sango-kaku'), which look attractive the whole winter through.

top *Euonymus alatus* and *Prunus sargentii* vie for top award for brilliance in this autumn scene. The spiky pink leaves are provided by phormiums.

above Maples are justly famed for their autumn colouring: this one is *Acer palmatum* 'Seiryyû'.

Jobs for early autumn

- Continue to mow the lawn once a week.
- Plant spring-flowering bulbs such as narcissi (daffodils) and crocuses.
- Buy and plant new shrubs and trees if the weather is cool and moist.
- Water containers and recently planted plants in dry weather.
- Sow some of the tougher hardy annuals for an early show next summer.
- Prune rambling roses.
- Pull up and discard summer bedding plants when the display is over.
- Prune trained forms of fruit trees.
- Lift and store maincrop carrots, beetroots and potatoes.
- Plant spring cabbages.
- Pick any green tomatoes and ripen them indoors. Clear tomato plants from the greenhouse.
- Sow greenhouse lettuces for winter salads; there are forms for both heated and unheated greenhouses.

Jobs for mid-autumn

- Sweep up fallen leaves from paving and gravel areas.
- Remove fallen leaves and other debris from the pond.
- Reduce lawn mowing to once a fortnight throughout autumn.
- Weed beds and borders if necessary.
- Plant ornamental containers with plants for winter and spring interest.
- Lift and store frost-tender plants.
- Apply timber preservative or paint to fences, gates and garden buildings.
- Clear out the bases of hedges, removing all rubbish and weeds.
- Continue planting spring-flowering bulbs and spring bedding plants.
- Cut down herbaceous plants as they die back.
- Continue deadheading roses if they are still flowering.
- Start digging the vegetable garden after clearing away old crops.
- Prune soft fruit, such as raspberries, blackcurrants and blackberries.
- Pick and store apples and pears.

Jobs for late autumn

- Clear away fallen leaves and dead foliage from the beds and borders.
- Cut down the dying foliage of herbaceous perennials if you don't want to wait until spring.
- Rake or sweep fallen leaves off the lawn.
- Clean and pack away garden furniture.
- Plant tulip and lily bulbs if you haven't done so already.
- Prune deciduous trees.
- Plant deciduous trees and shrubs, and climbers and roses.
- Make sure that tree ties are secure and that climbers are well tied in so that they withstand winter gales.
- Prune fruit trees, such as apples and pears.
- Plant new fruit trees and bushes.
- Sow broad beans under cloches.
- Continue with the digging in the vegetable garden.

Winter

Winter dormancy makes it possible to move plants that cannot be disturbed at other times of the year. You must, however, take care that the soil is not waterlogged or frozen. At these times it is better to keep off the soil and catch up with garden maintenance and tidying tasks instead.

Early winter

There is no reason why early winter should be the bleak, flowerless time it is in many gardens. There are several winter-flowering plants that deserve room in any garden. The sculptured white blooms of *Helleborus niger* (Christmas rose), sometimes tinted pink, and its interesting, hand-like leathery leaves make a wonderful winter show. The plant may be slow to settle down – new plants sometimes seem to disappear for a year and then reappear when all seems lost – but given semi-shade, a rich loamy soil that does not dry out and a taste of manure in the spring, it will respond. Other hellebores include *H. argutifolius* (Corsican hellebore), which has handsome foliage and clusters of dangling apple green cups, and hybrids of *H. orientalis* (Lenten rose), which have beautiful blooms in shades of purple, red, plum, white and primrose yellow. These plants flower a little later in early spring.

Iris unguicularis, which originates in Algeria, is another flower that no garden can afford to be without. Its foliage is untidy, but the lavender flowers that hide themselves in the tufts are beautiful. If picked in bud when they appear, looking like tightly rolled umbrellas, they will give a magical show when brought into the warmth of a room. This iris should be planted at the base of a sunny wall where it can remain undisturbed for many years; poor soil discourages flowering.

Another candidate for the winter garden is *Jasminum nudiflorum* (winter jasmine), providing bright yellow sprays during mild spells from autumn to spring. This is a willing grower, but it needs rich soil, shelter and regular tying in.

Don't overlook the winter heathers. *Erica carnea*, the

top The berries of *Skimmia japonica* 'Rubella' shine all the brighter for a dusting of snow. They will stay on the bush all winter.

above The green flowers of *Helleborus argutifolius* look too delicate to survive bad weather, but they appear reliably year after year.

alpine or winter heath, is low-growing and excellent groundcover. Cultivars such as 'King George' are smothered in rose-pink blooms from midwinter to early spring. Other good cultivars include 'Springwood Pink' and 'Springwood White', which have a slightly trailing habit and are suitable for furnishing a dull bank, while 'Celia M. Beale' is one of the earliest and largest of the whites for its size. *Erica × darleyensis* (Darley Dale heath) is seldom out of flower from early winter until the spring. Most ericas tolerate a moderately limy soil provided they are given a diet of moist peat substitute and a place in the sun.

Among other winter-flowering shrubs are the cultivars of *Prunus × subhirtella* (Higan cherry), with their white and pink blossom, the golden ribboned *Hamamelis mollis* (Chinese witch hazel) and the fragrant maroon and yellow *Chimonanthus praecox* (wintersweet). *Garrya elliptica* (silk-tassel bush) possesses trailing, green-grey catkins; they are particularly long and decorative in the male form. This shrub thrives on a shady wall in a sheltered position. Finally, there is the Japanese shrub *Corylopsis spicata*, which has attractive, bright yellow flowers with red anthers.

Take the opportunity of mild spells to prune leafless shrubs in need of attention. Also plant shrubs and trees if the ground is not too wet and sticky: if it is, heel the plants in a trench in a well-drained spot until you can get them into their final position. Tidy established borders, lightly forking over the soil between the plants. At the same time mix in old mulching material, and add a dressing of well-rotted manure if you can get hold of some. Give established hedges and areas planted with bulbs a boost by forking in a little bonemeal. Border plants, such as *Anemone × hybrida* (Japanese anemone), perennial anchusas and border phloxes, can be propagated from root cuttings taken now.

Midwinter

This is usually the coldest time of the year and is often thought of as a completely colourless time in the garden, but in a well-designed garden there will be several plants blooming now. *Jasminum nudiflorum* (winter jasmine) is generously spangled with bright yellow blooms that are continuously produced whenever the weather is mild, and some cultivars of *Erica* (winter-flowering heath) are smothered in tiny

blooms, shining even through the snow. In milder areas *Garrya elliptica* (silk-tassel bush) will continue to display its long, silver catkins to give a charming display. *Galanthus* spp. (snowdrop) will have appeared in many gardens, and *Iris unguicularis* continues to produce lilac blooms throughout the winter months.

More colour is provided by the bark of some trees and shrubs, none more eye-catching than the brilliant crimson young shoots of the dogwood *Cornus alba* 'Sibirica', while the coloured-leaved evergreens, such as the variegated forms of *Ilex* (holly) and *Hedera* (ivy) and the golden conifers, create an impression of sun even on overcast days.

top Caught between a forsythia and the sharp yellow stems of *Cornus stolonifera* 'Flaviramea' is a mature *Daphne mezereum* in full fragrant flower.

Late winter

Happily, the cold fails to deter *Hamamelis* spp. (witch hazel) or *Daphne mezereum* (mezereon) from opening their scented flowers now. The winter-flowering heathers continue to bloom profusely, regardless of frost and snow, while *Jasminum nudiflorum* (winter jasmine) and *Viburnum × bodnantense* open a fresh crop of flowers as soon as each cold spell passes. The first dainty blooms of the dwarf *Cyclamen coum* often appear now, and the enchanting yellow *Eranthis hyemalis* (winter aconite) get into their stride if it is sunny. The scented strings of pale yellow *Mahonia japonica* flowers open at the shoot tips, and the first winter crocuses open wide in any warming rays of the sun. The dwarf yellow *Iris danfordiae* and blue *I. histrioides* 'Major' also come into flower.

Retread the soil around newly planted trees and shrubs to firm it again when it dries out after heavy frosts. Check posts, pales, trellis and wires used as plant supports and replace or tighten any that are broken or loose before the plants break into new growth. The end of the winter is the time to prune those cultivars of *Cornus alba* (red-barked dogwood) that are grown for the bright winter colouring of their young shoots, to encourage a new crop the following summer. This is the time, too, to prune all clematis plants except the small-flowered ones, such as *Clematis montana*, that bloom early.

top So often misplanted, a stand of *Cortaderia selloana* (pampas grass) makes a fine sight on a frosty morning.

above It takes time, but *Eranthis hyemalis* (winter aconite) will slowly colonize a favoured site to form a golden pool.

Jobs for early winter

- Service the pond pump if you have one.
- Mow the lawn occasionally in dry weather if you want to keep it looking neat.
- Continue to plant deciduous shrubs, trees, climbers and roses.
- Clean, oil and store away garden tools.
- Dig empty beds and borders, and apply well-rotted manure or compost.
- Spray fruit trees and bushes with tar oil winter wash to kill eggs of pests.

Jobs for midwinter

- Get the lawn mower serviced and pack it away for the rest of winter.
- Buy hardy annual seeds from seed catalogues and garden centres.
- Plant new trees and shrubs or move existing ones.
- Plan some new features during this quiet time.
- Check all plant supports and make sure that tree ties are secure but not too tight.
- Remove snow from evergreen shrubs, conifers and hedges.
- Refirm any plants partially lifted by frost (this applies especially to spring bedding plants).
- Plan the vegetable garden, decide what you want to grow and order seeds.
- Inspect vegetables and fruit in store and discard any that are rotting.
- Lift parsnips and leeks as they are needed in the kitchen.

Jobs for late winter

- Prune winter-flowering shrubs as they finish blooming.
- Deciduous shrubs, trees, climbers and roses can still be planted if the ground is not too wet or frozen.
- Plant anemone corms under cloches. Lift and divide snowdrops after flowering.
- Check trees and shrubs for dead wood and prune out if necessary.
- Prune climbers, such as large-flowered clematis, wisteria and ornamental grape vines.
- Complete the planting of fruit trees and bushes.
- Broad beans and early peas can be sown if the soil is not wet.
- Plant shallots and onion sets if the ground is in a suitable state.
- Seed potatoes should be chitted (sprouted) in light, in a frost-proof place.

Trouble-shooting

Pests

What is the cause of 'cuckoo spit' and should it be controlled?

The frothy liquid seen on the young stems of many shrubs in late spring and early summer conceals the nymph stage of the froghopper. Neither the adult nor the nymph causes significant damage, but if you find it unsightly the 'cuckoo spit' can be easily dislodged with a jet of water.

How can I stop mice and voles digging up and eating crocus bulbs?

Make sure that all bulbs are firmly planted and remove dead leaves from the tops of bulbs after they die back to make it difficult for rodents to locate them. Bulbs can also be treated with rodent repellent before planting. If the problem continues, place wire mesh above the bulbs but below the soil's surface when you are planting them.

The leaves of ornamental plants in my greenhouse become mottled, then turn yellow and brittle before falling. They show a fine webbing on the underside. What causes this?

The culprit is red spider mite, a serious pest of many indoor plants, particularly in dry conditions. Increase the humidity in the greenhouse and mist the plants regularly. See pages 207 and 213 for possible controls. Remember not to use an insecticidal spray once you have introduced the biological control.

above Red spider mite damage.

Ragged holes have appeared overnight in the petals of my dahlias. What is the culprit?

Earwigs often produce this kind of damage on the flowers and leaves of dahlias and chrysanthemums. Remove dead leaves from the ground and spray on and around the infested plants with bifenthrin. Alternatively, place inverted flowerpots filled with straw on short bamboo poles close to the plants to trap the earwigs, then shake them out every morning and step on the earwigs (or move them to somewhere else in the garden).

Pansies growing in a pot have shrivelled back, and seem to have been eaten through at ground level. Can this be prevented?

It's possible that the damage was caused by woodlice, which will eat stems and leaves of seedlings and young plants that are in contact with the soil. Good garden hygiene will help – remember to wash containers before planting up and remove garden debris where they can hide. If they persist, dust hiding sites under stones and the like with an insecticide containing bendiocarb.

My hostas are frequently attacked by slugs. How can I control the damage?

Slugs are particularly fond of hosta leaves and can destroy the entire plant if they are not discouraged. They feed mainly at night, and during the day they hide under stones and in dead leaves. Remove any garden debris from around the plants. Go out at night when they are active and pick them off by hand, disposing of them as you will. In late summer, when the soil temperature is above 5°C (40°F), water the nematode *Phasmarhabditis hermaphrodita* into the ground around the hostas (see page 213). The nematodes infect slugs with a bacteria that causes their death. Avoid planting the hostas out altogether and try growing them in pots, which can have a mulch of gravel to deter slugs and snails. If you are desperate, scatter metaldehyde or methiocarb pellets around the plants, covering them with stones. Clear up the dead slugs so that you do not poison hedgehogs.

above Hoverflies prey on aphids.

Is there any way of dealing with aphids without using chemical sprays?

If you are patient, you can wait for ladybirds and hoverflies, the main predators of aphids, to come to the rescue. You can encourage hoverflies to visit your garden by planting annuals, such as *Limnanthes douglasii* (poached-egg plant), near the affected plants. The trouble is that aphids transmit viruses and exude sticky honeydew, which encourages the growth of fungus, so it is wise to control them. See pages 207 and 213 for controls.

What are the fat, white, C-shaped grubs with a brown head I found in the soil during cultivation, and do they cause any damage to plants?

They sound like chafer grubs, the larvae of the chafer beetle. The adults rarely cause serious damage, but the grubs eat the roots and bulbs of many ornamental plants and can damage lawns. The simplest control is to turn over the soil and leave the birds to eat them.

What are the tiny flies that rise up from the compost of greenhouse plants when I am watering? Are they harmful?

These are sciarid flies (fungus gnats), which lay their eggs in large numbers in potting compost, especially if it contains peat. The tiny, pale larvae feed on organic matter in the compost and frequently damage young plants. The adults cause no significant damage, but are a nuisance. Hang sticky yellow traps around affected plants to catch adults and disrupt the lifecycle. See pages 208 and 213 for methods of control.

What pest causes the pale twisting tunnels in leaves of sweet williams and how can it be controlled?

The damage is caused by leaf miners, which are the immature form of certain flies and moths. Although they affect numerous plants, including chrysanthemums, the damage is most serious to *Dianthus* species and cultivars, such as carnations, pinks and sweet williams. Remove and burn badly affected leaves and inspect plants regularly for damage, squashing the larvae in the leaves as soon as they are seen.

The edges of some leaves on a shrub rose have rolled tightly underneath on themselves. What is the cause of this and how can it be remedied?

This is caused by leaf-rolling sawfly. There are a number of different species of sawfly affecting a range of plants, but only one produces this kind of damage. The insect lays eggs in the leaf and injects a chemical that makes it roll up to protect the grub when it hatches. Hand-pick rolled leaves or spray with permethrin as a preventative.

Is it possible to discourage moles from damaging a lawn without having to resort to trapping them?

Mole smokes are quite successful, although they occasionally kill moles. A recent method that seems to be effective involves the use of a metal stake that produces a high-frequency sound. The stake is pushed into the ground along the mole run, and it periodically emits a sound that drives the moles away.

Should ants in the garden be controlled?

There are usually so many ant nests around a garden that it would be pointless to try to control them completely, particularly as they do little direct damage. On lawns the soil they excavate may form heaps, which may be spread during mowing and provide a site for weeds to establish, so brush the heaps before mowing. If they are a serious pest, apply a specific ant-killing preparation to the soil around the nests.

What are the waxy brown-red scales that have formed in clusters on the older branches of my fig tree?

These are brown scale, a type of scale insect that affects a number of woody plants, including roses. The scale you see is not the insect but a covering beneath which the insect feeds on the sap. Deciduous plants can be sprayed with tar oil wash in early to midwinter.

What control is possible for the grey-white caterpillars that completely strip solomon's seal of its leaves?

These caterpillars are the larvae of the solomon's seal sawfly, which lays eggs in the stems of the plant, in batches of up to 20. The caterpillars go on to pupate in the soil under the plant and re-emerge in late spring or early summer. To break the cycle, spray the plants with derris or permethrin as soon as you see the larvae.

In the soil around wilting herbaceous plants are a small number of creamy-brown caterpillars, about 4cm (1½in) long. Are they the cause of the wilting and how can they themselves be controlled?

These are cutworms, the larvae of various types of moth. They feed on roots and on the stems of plants at soil level and can kill the plants if they are allowed to continue. Remove and destroy the cutworms, then cultivate the area regularly to expose the grubs to their natural predators, birds. Treating the soil with an appropriate insecticide will also help.

The leaves of my geraniums have small tattered holes but I can't see a pest. Earlier in the season, however, I saw fast-moving green, winged insects around the plants. Are these the cause of the damage?

This damage is characteristic of capsid bugs. They are sap-suckers, and their feeding damages cells in young leaves and buds. When these expand, the damaged areas tear to produce tattered holes, but the bugs are long gone. Control them when noticed by spraying regularly with a contact insecticide, such as derris or permethrin. Spray the ground under the plants and the undersides of the leaves.

above Birds will eat unwanted pests.

Do crane flies cause damage in the garden?

Not in the adult form, but the larvae are a serious pest of lawns and ornamental plants, particularly in areas that are being brought into cultivation. Leatherjackets are fat, legless, greyish grubs, about 4cm (1½in) long, and they feed on roots from summer to late spring. Regular cultivation exposes them to birds. On lawns, water thoroughly at night, then cover the area with black plastic. Remove in the morning when the pests will have come up to the surface, and leave them for the birds.

What is the cause of brown scarring on the flowerbuds of Michaelmas daisies, which then go on to produce small leaves rather than petals?

The problem is caused by tarsonemid mites, which also affect cyclamen and begonias, among other plants. Lift and burn badly damaged plants of *Aster novi-belgii*, because there is no spray available that controls these pests. Try planting *A. novae-angliae* or *A. amellus*, which will flower even if infected.

Circular holes are appearing in the margins of rose leaves, but no caterpillars are present. What is the cause?

Leaf-cutter bees produce this kind of damage on roses, laburnums and lilacs. They use the leaf material to build small nests in soil, rotting wood or sometimes even in pots of compost. Damage is not usually very serious and, since the bees are such good pollinators, control is not recommended.

Diseases

Why have the shoots on the clematis suddenly died back in summer?

As long as the plant has been well fed and watered, the probable answer is clematis wilt, which is caused by a fungus. Cut the plant right back to ground level and spray the immediate area with a fungicide, following the manufacturer's instructions. Clematis that are cut right back to ground level will usually shoot again – you won't have lost anything if it doesn't – and this is the reason you are advised to plant a new clematis more deeply than it was in its original pot.

The shoots on my cotoneaster are dying back, but the dead leaves are still hanging on the plant. Is this a serious problem?

Potentially, yes. This sounds like a case of fireblight, which can affect a number of other plants in the rose family, including apples, pyracanthas and *Chaenomeles* spp. (flowering quince, japonica). Cut out all diseased wood, which will show a reddish-brown staining under the bark, and burn it. Disinfect your pruning tools thoroughly with a horticultural disinfectant.

Why have all the softwood cuttings in a cold-frame collapsed and seem to be covered with a fluffy fungal growth?

Botrytis cinerea or grey mould is common in humid conditions, particularly if there are any dead leaves present, through which the infection can enter. See page 208.

How can I control rose blackspot?

This common fungal disease appears in early summer as circular black or dark brown marks on the leaves, which fall early. In a severe case, the whole plant may lose its leaves. Rake up and burn fallen leaves on which the fungus overwinters and spray at regular intervals throughout the growing season, starting in early spring, with mancozeb or a specific rose formula, which will also help prevent powdery mildew. A foliar feed will help restore vigour. See page 203 for some resistant cultivars.

My ornamental cherry is oozing amber-coloured gum. Is it a sign of disease and is it serious?

Not necessarily, although it could be bacterial canker, which is a serious disease of all types of *Prunus*, both fruiting and ornamental. If the leaves are spotted in summer with small holes forming later, and with cankers forming in the angles of branches, it is likely to be this disease. Spray three times with Bordeaux mixture in late summer and autumn and prune in summer, when infection through cuts is less likely.

What can I do to prevent geranium cuttings turning black at the bottom and dying?

The disease known as blackleg is probably caused by a fungus, which will spread rapidly to all cuttings in a tray or pot. Always use new potting compost and clean pots, take cuttings with a clean knife and select from healthy plants. Do not overwater and remove dying leaves promptly.

What is the cause of oval black spots on the leaves of weeping willow?

Anthracnose is a fungal disease that causes serious problems to *Salix* spp. (willow), particularly in wet summers. The leaves will turn yellow and fall early, and after a few years there is likely to be serious dieback. Spray small trees with Bordeaux mixture as the new leaves emerge, and repeat the application in summer. Large trees cannot be treated, but gather up and destroy fallen leaves.

The leaves of a flowering almond have become thickened and curled, then covered in blisters, which are initially red then turn pale. These fall early in the season and the tree is not thriving. What is the remedy?

Peach leaf curl affects flowering peaches as well as fruiting types. The spores overwinter on the plant and reinfect the developing buds. Spray twice with Bordeaux mixture in mid- to late winter, and then again just before the leaves fall. Remove all the affected leaves promptly if the infection is not serious.

above Aerate your lawn with a garden fork to reduce the likelihood of red thread recurring.

What are the pink patches that appear in my lawn in late summer and autumn?

This is a fungus known as red thread. Although unsightly, it rarely causes serious damage and may last only a few weeks. The likelihood of it recurring can be reduced by aerating the lawn and applying a general lawn feed during spring and summer. Severe attacks can be treated with a fungicide such as benomyl.

What causes fairy rings on lawns and what is the best way to treat them?

Fairy rings are caused by a fungus that spreads outwards in ever larger circles. Although the outer rim is dark green, the grass inside turns brown, although it recovers in time. To speed recovery, feed the lawn and remove and burn the toadstools when they appear in summer and autumn. Mow the infected area separately, burn the clippings and disinfect the mower blades to prevent any spread.

Are the pinky-red raised pustules that appear on dead wood a danger to live plants growing nearby?

This is coral spot, a fungus that is most obvious on dead wood in damp weather. It can, however, spread to live wood and is particularly damaging to magnolias and acers, which can be killed by a serious infection to the main trunk. Cut out all the infected wood to at least 10cm (4in) below the pustules and burn the debris.

Why have the blossoms and leaves on my ornamental crabapple failed to develop, yet have remained on the tree until winter?

Blossom wilt is the fungal disease that causes this problem. Remove and burn the affected spurs and apply a tar oil wash in winter. In spring spray with benomyl or carbendazim.

If hyacinth bulbs have a light bluish fungus on the outside, is it safe to plant them?

If the infection is only slight, they may produce quite satisfactory flowers, but the risk is that the fungus may spread, killing the bulb and infecting others nearby, particularly if they are damaged in any way. Examine bulbs carefully before buying them and control slugs in the soil, which can damage the surface, allowing infection to enter.

What causes the brown marks at the tips of tulip leaves? The affected bulbs developed brown spots on the leaves and the flowers then rotted back.

The problem is tulip fire, a common but serious form of *Botrytis* fungus. Badly affected plants and bulbs should be lifted and burned, but spray every two weeks with mancozeb when the leaves are emerging until the flowers appear.

How can virus diseases be identified and how should they be dealt with?

There is a wide variety of symptoms, but one common indication is yellow blotching and mottling of leaves, which may also become distorted. Viruses are often spread by aphids and other sap-sucking insects, so controlling these pests will help prevent the spread of viruses. There is no cure for plant viruses and severely infected plants should be removed and burned.

What are the orange-red pustules on the undersides of hawthorn leaves?

This is probably rust, which is a fungus disease that affects roses, box, *Sorbus* spp. and various other plants. It can be serious and will weaken the plant. Spray with mancozeb, thiram or a similar fungicide, rake up and burn fallen leaves, and try feeding, mulching and watering your plants so that they are strong enough to withstand infection.

above Honey fungus produces tough, brown to black, bootlace-like fungal strands.

What is honey fungus and how can it be identified?

This serious disease of trees and shrubs can lead to the rapid death of affected plants. Leaves wither and discolour but do not fall and buds will fail to open in spring. There may be white, fan-shaped fungal growths beneath the bark at ground level and tough, dark brown 'bootlaces' among the roots. Remove and burn dead and dying plants, try to remove the bootlaces, which will spread the infection, and plant only annuals in the site for three to five years. See also page 209.

Branches on an azalea are dying back and the cut surface of the branch has a purple staining. What is the cause?

This is probably silverleaf, despite the fact that the leaves naturally show the characteristic silvery colour. It is also seen in cotoneasters, poplars and species of *Prunus*. It can lead to the death of the plant. Cut affected branches back to a point where no staining is visible in the wood, then cut back another 15cm (6in). Feed and water the plants to improve their vigour, but if the disease worsens the only solution is to lift and burn the plant. See also page 209.

What has caused the stems of all my sunflowers to rot with discoloured patches? This has now occurred for several years in succession.

The cause of the problem is sclerotina rot, which affects a large number of ornamental plants. It usually produces a fluffy white mass containing black resting bodies, but in sunflowers it is not so obvious. Remove and burn any stems that are discoloured or rotting.

Common problems

Lichen and moss are growing on my apple tree. Does it mean the tree is dying?

It could do. Such growths are seen on healthy plants in humid conditions, but they are more likely to appear on trees suffering from dieback. Try to encourage healthy growth in the affected tree by feeding in spring and watering throughout the season. Clear grass and weeds from around the base of the tree.

What causes the pale blisters that turn to scabby patches on the undersides of leaves on camellias grown in the greenhouse?

This is probably oedema, and it is caused when the atmosphere and soil are too moist. The plant takes up too much water but is unable to get rid of it, and this causes the damage. Do not remove affected leaves, but improve ventilation and water less.

Why do all the flowerbuds of a stephanotis fall before they open?

This problem is usually caused by dryness at the roots as the buds start to develop, but in a newly bought plant it is more likely to be the result of rapid changes of temperature as the plant is moved from one location to another. Plants don't like sudden changes in temperature, light levels and humidity, so always try to introduce plants to new positions gradually.

After years of flowering well, a clump of daffodils has failed to produce any flowerbuds at all. How can this be cured?

The name for this condition is blindness, and it usually occurs when bulbs are too small. In an established clump, the bulbs have probably divided and are now congested and starved. Lift and divide the clump, taking care to feed and water during the growing season. In double varieties, blindness can simply be caused by lack of water.

What could have caused the leaves of my snapdragons to turn silver overnight?

Low night temperatures have this effect and will also make the leaves of morning glory and sweet peas turn white. If frost is likely, protect newly planted-out specimens.

The new growth on one of my roses is distorted, with spirally twisting stalks bearing stunted, twisted, cupped leaves. I can't see any pests, and the roses have been carefully mulched, watered and fed. What is the problem?

This is probably damage caused by a hormone weedkiller, sprayed nearby on a windy day, from a sprayer that was not thoroughly cleaned out, or transported in a mulch, particularly if grass clippings have been used. Remove affected shoots and the mulch, if it is the likely culprit. Remember to spray garden chemicals only in calm conditions and keep separate sprayers for weedkillers, foliar feeds and pesticides.

I've heard that a new rose should not be planted on the same site as an old rose. Is this true?

Yes, although the reason is not fully understood. The problem is known as rose sickness or replant disease. The new bush is likely to sicken and die back, perhaps because of a build-up of pests in the soil, which attack the new young plant when the previous, established one was able to resist. You should either choose a different site for your new rose or replace the soil in the existing site to a depth of about 60cm (2ft) over the area. Roses are not the only plants to be affected in this way, and it is always sensible to replace a plant with something from a different species or to replace the soil if you want the same type of plant.

above Do not plant a rose on the same site as an old rose.

What could have caused a lack of fruit on an otherwise healthy pyracantha after a good display of flowers?

If the weather conditions were poor while the plant was in flower, pollinating insects will have been discouraged and fruit will not have set. There is no remedy for this but it occurs infrequently.

What are the blackened patches that have appeared on grass just a few days after the application of lawn sand?

This is scorch, and it has been caused by applying nitrogenous fertilizer at too high a rate. Always follow the manufacturer's instructions to the letter when you are using any garden chemical and, in this case, check the setting on the spreader before use.

How can I get rid of slippery algae and lichens from a lawn?

These dark green growths will only appear on the lawn in areas that are always damp because of poor drainage. Try to improve the drainage in the area by spiking the ground or, if the problem is really serious, laying land drains. The algae can be treated with dichlorophen.

A variegated elaeagnus is producing shoots with all-green leaves. Should these shoots be removed?

Yes – and as soon as possible. Most plants with variegated foliage are naturally occurring variants on a plain-coloured type. They will often start to revert to the plain foliage of the original species, particularly if they are grown in deep shade. Because the all-green foliage contains more chlorophyll than the variegated type, it is usually more vigorous and will grow faster. If left unpruned, the plant may revert to the all-green type. Green shoots should be removed right to the base of the plant.

What is the best way to clear a garden pond of algae?

Algae is a common problem in newly established pools and will often clear up in time. The organisms that cause the algal growth thrive in sunny conditions, so one way is to grow waterlilies and other floating plants so that about two-thirds of the surface of the water is covered. In addition, introduce some plants to oxygenate the water, because the algae need carbon dioxide to survive.

Why are the edges of the leaves of my Japanese acer turning brown?

Some acers, particularly the ones with finely cut foliage, are sensitive to cold winds and will show this kind of damage, particularly on young leaves, if they are planted in exposed positions. Remove any damaged leaves, because they might allow fungal diseases to enter the plant. Give the plant a foliar feed during the growing season to help it recover.

What is the best way to improve clay soil?

The mineral particles in clay soils are tiny and, when compacted, will not allow the free movement of air and water through the soil. This makes for a heavy soil that is slow to warm up. The best way of improving clay soil is to add coarse grit, to open up the texture, and organic matter, such as well-rotted manure or garden compost, to improve water retention and drainage. Lime can also be added, but not on soil that is already alkaline.

How can I encourage a blue hydrangea to go on producing flowers of a good blue instead of pinkish ones?

Blue hydrangeas need an acid soil to produce flowers of a true colour, while pink hydrangeas need alkaline soil. When the flowerbuds are forming, apply aluminium sulphate to blue-flowered types and ground limestone to pink-flowered types so that they maintain their true colour.

What causes a shrub rose to produce a flower stem from the centre of an open flower?

This is a condition known as proliferation, and it tends to occur more frequently on old roses than on new cultivars. It is usually caused by minor damage to the developing bud, perhaps as a result of late frost or an insect attack. If the problem keeps occurring, it may be due to a virus, in which case the plant should be lifted and burned. Otherwise, no action is required.

The seedlings raised on a windowsill have grown very long and pale. Can they be planted out and will they flower?

This etiolated growth is almost certainly caused by insufficient light. As soon as seeds have germinated, they need plenty of light and a windowsill will rarely provide that. It is worth pricking the seedlings out and providing them with better conditions to harden off.

How can I get rid of moss on my lawn?

Good lawn management to produce a healthy vigorous sward is the best defence against moss. The conditions that encourage moss include wetness; dryness – for example, on humps and ridges where the grass becomes weak; cutting the grass too short; an uneven surface that leads to 'scalping' with the mower; a soft, spongy sward with a thick fibrous layer underneath; low fertility caused by a deficiency of lime or plant food, or a shortage of topsoil; and constant shade. There is little point in using a mosskiller until you have established why it is there, because it will only return.

Why is my garden compost heap slimy and smelly? How can I turn it into a useful product?

If too much soft plant material, such as lawn clippings, is placed on the compost heap, oxygen is excluded and anaerobic rotting takes place. The result is the unappealing mess you have. Add layers of coarser matter, such as bark or shredded paper. to enable it to rot down properly. This will also help balance the chemical content of the compost, because grass is rich in nitrogen and the coarser material is usually rich in carbon. Never place diseased plants on the heap.

Do I need to carry out pH tests on my soil in more than one location in the garden?

Yes, definitely. The use to which a garden has been put in the past may affect the pH of the soil in various areas, as can the underlying bedrock, which can vary from place to place. If you are using a chemical tester, remember to use sterilized or demineralized water so that it does not affect the results.

above You can use a pH test kit to find out whether your garden has acid or alkaline soil.

Why do some of the plants in my chalky soil have unhealthy, yellow leaves?

Although a certain amount of lime in the soil is required by many plants, an excess will make some plant foods unobtainable to their root systems. Iron deficiency causes young leaves to go yellow (a condition known as chlorosis), while magnesium deficiency causes older leaves to go yellow, with the veins usually remaining green. Iron sequestrene can be used to correct the first deficiency, while Epsom salts is used to control magnesium deficiency. The remedies should be applied according to the manufacturer's instructions.

Our seaside garden is at the mercy of strong winds and sometimes even gales. What trees can I use to protect it?

The following are good, hardy trees that will help create a windbreak to shelter the garden. You will need to provide a temporary barrier between the trees and the wind for a year or two while they get established. Try *Crataegus monogyna* (hawthorn), the evergreen conifer *Cupressus macrocarpa* (Monterey cypress), *Pinus contorta* (beach pine, lodgepole pine), *Salix caprea* (pussy willow) or *Sorbus aria* (whitebeam).

Can you suggest a suitable hedging plant for my front garden, which is constantly overrun by neighbours' cats and dogs? I want the hedge to be about 1m (3ft) tall.

A strong and effective hedge can be grown from some of the barberries, *Berberis* spp., which are prickly, vigorous and decorative and should keep animals out. *B. gagnepainii* is excellent for this purpose; it has dense, upright growth, evergreen leaves and yellow, pendent flower clusters in late spring. Another good form is the purple-leaved *B. thunbergii* 'Rose Glow', whose young growth is a spectacular pink. The flowers are orange-yellow in mid-spring and the leaves develop reddish tints in autumn.

My holly bush never seems to have any berries. Why could this be?

The plants of *Ilex* spp. (holly) are either male or female, and only the female plants bear berries. What is more, they have to be pollinated by a male plant if fruiting is to be successful. You could buy a cultivar such as 'J.C. van Tol' or 'Golden King', both of which are female, and make sure you or one of your neighbours has a male plant to pollinate it.

My garden slopes in one corner to a rather wet patch where nothing except weeds seems to thrive. Are there any shrubs I can grow there?

Few shrubs will grow in this type of situation, but you could try a *Cornus* (dogwood), especially some of the cultivars of *C. alba* (red-barked dogwood), which have colourful stems in winter. *Salix* spp. (willow) will do well, too; *S. caprea* has grey leaves and woolly catkins, while *S. purpurea* (purple osier) has red-tinged stems and grey-green catkins. Some types of *Sambucus* spp. (elder) with variegated or yellow leaves are also suitable for this type of position.

I have tried to grow parsley from seeds but they didn't germinate. What did I do wrong?

Parsley is notoriously slow to germinate, and if the compost or soil dries out, the seeds may not germinate at all. If you are sowing seeds in the garden, make a seed drill and water the soil until it is just moist. Sow the seeds, then cover them with dry soil. This dry covering will prevent evaporation, so the seeds will stay moist for longer. If you are sowing seeds in pots, make sure the compost does not dry out by covering the pots with glass or a plastic bag. Make sure you plant out seedlings while they are still small to avoid too much root disturbance.

I grew sweetcorn last year and the cobs were small and patchy with few kernels. Why is this?

Sweetcorn needs a long growing season, so it is only really successful in warmer climates in a sheltered, sunny position. The plants should be arranged in a block, spaced 35cm (14in) apart, rather than in a row, because they are cross-pollinated by wind, and pollination is more successful when the plants are in a huddle. Patchy kernels are the result of poor pollination.

A lot of seeds are marked F1. What does this mean and are they worth growing?

F1 is an expression used to define cultivars obtained by a complicated and costly breeding process in which two carefully selected parent lines, which have been inbred for several generations, are crossed. The seed is, therefore, more expensive than ordinary seed, but because of its 'hybrid vigour' the plants are of exceptional quality and consistency.

Jargon-busting

Acid (soil) Soil with a pH of below 7. See also alkaline, neutral and pH.

Aerate (soil) To loosen the soil in order to allow in air.

Air layering A method of propagation in which a portion of stem is encouraged to root by making a wound and enclosing it in a medium such as damp moss.

Alkaline (soil) With a pH of over 7. See also acid, neutral and pH.

Alpine A plant that grows above the tree line in mountainous areas; loosely applied to rock-garden plants that enjoy similar growing conditions at a lower altitude.

Anaerobic A process carried out in the absence of air.

Annual A plant that completes its lifecycle within the space of one growing season.

Anther In a flower, the part of the stamen that carries the pollen.

Aquatic Any plant that grows in water. See also bog plant, deep-water aquatic, floating aquatic, marginal plant and submerged plant.

Aspect A garden position that faces a particular direction.

Bare-rooted or bare-root (plant) A plant lifted from the open ground. See also container-grown plant.

Bedding (plant) Annuals, biennials and tender perennials used for temporary garden display, usually flowering in spring and summer. Spring bedding includes bulbs and biennials planted in the autumn to flower in the spring; summer bedding includes half-hardy annuals and tender perennials planted out after the last frost for a summer display.

Biennial A plant that completes its lifecycle over the space of two growing seasons. Hardy biennials are usually sown in late spring or early summer to bloom the following spring or summer.

Biodegradable (material) A naturally derived material that can be broken down into its constituent parts by the action of micro-organisms.

Bog plant A plant that thrives in permanently damp conditions but does not grow in the water, as an aquatic does.

Bolting The premature production of flowers and seeds.

Branch A shoot from the main stem or trunk of a woody plant.

Broadcast To sow seed by sprinkling it evenly over an area rather than in rows.

Budding A method of propagation in which a growth bud from one plant is grafted onto the rootstock of another.

Bulb A plant with a modified stem acting as a storage system, like an onion. The term is sometimes used loosely to cover bulbs, corms, rhizomes and tubers – all plants sold as dormant storage organs by bulb suppliers.

Bulb scale The individual segments from which a bulb is made up. These are most obvious in lilies, where they can be pulled off and used for propagation.

Bulbil A small bulb-like organ, often borne in a leaf axil, occasionally found on a stem or in a flowerhead. See also bulblet.

Bulblet A small developing bulb produced from the basal plate of a mature bulb. See also bulbil.

Carpeting plant A low-growing plant, usually used for groundcover.

Chlorophyll Green pigment present in most plants.

Clay A fine-grained soil rich in nutrients but with poor drainage capability.

Climber A plant that climbs by clinging to other plants or objects by means of twining stems or tendrils or adhesive tendrils. More generally, any long-stemmed plant that is trained upwards.

Cloche A glass or polythene cover used for propagation, for protecting early crops raised in open ground or to warm the soil before planting. May also be used to protect vulnerable overwintering plants.

Cold-frame An unheated structure, made from wood, brick or glass, with a hinged glass or clear plastic lid, used to protect plants from the cold.

Compost (garden) Rotted organic matter.

Compost (seed or potting) A mixture of materials used as a medium for sowing seeds or potting plants, usually based on loam or peat (or peat substitute), with added nutrients.

Compost activator Material that initiates the composting process. Young nettles and comfrey can be used instead of proprietary products.

Conifers Trees and shrubs with linear or needle-like leaves. The seeds are normally borne in cones and most are evergreen.

Container-grown (plant) Also known as containerized plant, a plant grown in a pot or other container. See also bare-rooted plant.

Corm A bulb-like swollen stem or base, often surrounded by a papery tunic, that acts as an underground storage organ. Unlike a bulb, there are no distinct layers when a corm is cut in half.

Corolla The part of the flower formed by the petals.

Crocks Broken pieces of clay pot used to cover the drainage holes of pots to provide drainage and aeration and to prevent the growing medium from escaping or blocking the holes.

Cultivar A cultivated plant or group of plants distinguished by one or more characteristics, which are retained whether it is propagated sexually or asexually. Short for 'cultivated variety' and often abbreviated to 'cv'.

Cutting A leaf, shoot, root or bud that is cut off a plant in order to be used for propagation.

Deadhead To remove a dead flowerhead. This is sometimes done to extend the flowering season (because allowing a plant to form seeds may shorten the flowering period) or to improve its appearance.

Deciduous (plant) A plant that loses all its leaves annually at the end of the growing season. Evergreen plants also shed their leaves, but over a long period so they are never leafless.

Deep-water aquatic A plant that grows with its roots in the bottom of the pond (or in a planting basket there), rather than in the shallow water around the edge. Many deep-water aquatics will grow happily with about 12in (30cm) of water over their roots.

Deeply cultivated (soil) Soil dug to more than the depth of a single spade blade. The term usually implies double digging (worked to a depth of two spade blades).

Division A method of increasing plants by splitting the crown or roots into smaller pieces, each with roots and shoots (or buds that will form shoots).

Double digging A cultivation technique in which the soil is worked over to a depth of two spade blades.

Drainage The passage of excess water through the soil, or systems of drainage that are used to remove excess water.

Drill A shallow furrow made in the soil, into which seeds are sown. A drill is best taken out using a garden line or straight-edge against which the soil is removed with a stick or the corner of a hoe or rake.

Ericaceous A term describing plants of the family Ericaceae (heathers), usually lime-hating and requiring a pH of 6.5 or less, or compost with an appropriate acidity for the growing of plants that are termed ericaceous.

Erosion The process of soil being washed away or blown off the surface of the ground caused either naturally or by man's intervention.

Evergreen A plant that retains its leaves throughout the year.

Fastigiate An erect, upright form of growth with branches close together.

Filament In a flower, the fine stem that bears the anther.

Floating aquatic A plant that floats on the surface with its roots suspended in the water, from where it derives all its nutrients.

Flower The part of a plant containing the reproductive organs, usually surrounded by sepals and petals.

Framework plants The plants that form the basis or structure of the design of a garden, especially trees and shrubs.

Frost-hardy A plant that is able to withstand frost without protection.

Frost-tender A plant that will succumb to frost damage.

Genus A category of plant classification that identifies a group of related species. *Rosa* is a genus, to which many different species belong.

Germination The process by which a seed develops into a seedling.

Graft A method of propagation in which a shoot from the desired variety or cultivar is joined to a specially prepared rootstock, to which it is bound and sealed until the two unite.

Green manure A plant grown to improve the soil.

Groundcover Usually low-growing plants that cover the soil surface and suppress weeds.

Growing medium The soil mixture in which plants are grown.

Growing season The period during which a plant is actively producing leaves and flowers.

Habitat The natural home of a plant.

Half-hardy A plant that is unable to survive the winter without protection but does not require protection all year round.

Hard pan A hard, compacted layer in the soil.

Harden off To acclimatize plants raised in warmth to the cooler conditions in the garden. This is done by reducing the amount of warmth gradually, and using a cold-frame, if possible, as an intermediate environment before they are placed in the open garden.

Hardy (plant) A plant that is capable of surviving the winter in the open without protection. Not all hardy plants will tolerate cold temperatures to the same extent, however, and some are more cold-hardy than others.

Herb A plant grown for its medicinal, culinary or decorative qualities.

Herbaceous perennial A non-woody plant in which the upper parts die down to a rootstock at the end of the growing season.

Herbicide A weedkiller.

Humus The organic residue of decayed vegetable matter in the soil.

Interplant In the context of the ornamental garden, the planting of two or more different types of plants together. Forget-me-nots or winter pansies might be interplanted between tall tulips to cover the ground and fill in the gaps as well as provide an improved flowering display.

Layering A method of propagation in which a portion of stem is induced to root while it is still attached to the parent plant. After rooting, the rooted section is severed and grown on independently.

Leaching The removal of soluble substances from soil or potting mixtures by the passage of water.

Leaf mould Decomposed autumn leaves, used as a soil conditioner.

Loam This is normally soil of medium texture, easily worked, that contains more or less equal parts of sand, silt and clay. It is usually rich in humus.

Manure Bulky organic substances of animal origin (often mixed with straw) that are either dug into the soil or applied as a mulch.

Marginal plant A plant that grows partially submerged in shallow water or in moist soil at the edge of a pond.

Mixed border A border containing different types of plants, such as a combination of shrubs, herbaceous plants, bulbs and annuals.

Modules Moulded plastic or polystyrene trays divided into cells, which are filled with compost for sowing seeds.

Mulch A layer of organic or other material applied to the surface of the soil to suppress weeds and conserve moisture. Organic mulches, such as garden compost, chipped bark or cocoa shells, should be applied in a layer at least 5cm (2in) thick. Sheet mulches, such as plastics, also make efficient mulches, but in decorative parts of the garden are usually covered with a thin layer of a visually more acceptable material, such as chipped bark.

Multi-sowing Sowing more than one seed in a pot or module cell and leaving them all to grow on.

Naturalize To establish and grow as if in the wild. The term is usually applied to bulbs planted informally in a lawn or in longer grass.

Neutral Soil with a pH of 7. See also acid and alkaline.

Nitrogen An important plant food, especially used in the growth of leaves and shoots.

Non-degradable (material) One that is not biodegradable.

Nutrient A plant food.

Offset A young plant that arises from around the base of the parent plant, and is still attached to it initially. Bulbs also produce offsets, but this time smaller bulbs around the base of the original one; in time these become detached and grow into individual plants.

Organic matter Material consisting of, or derived from, living organisms, such as compost, leaf mould and farmyard manure.

Ovary The female part of a flower that contains the ovules, which develop into seeds after fertilization.

Peat The remains of partially decayed vegetation, such as mosses, laid down millions of years ago in waterlogged soil. It contains few nutrients but holds water well and improves soil structure in the short term. It is acid and therefore useful for acid-loving plants. Most gardeners prefer to use peat substitutes wherever possible. These include seed and potting composts (potting soils) made from coir or other waste plant material.

Perennial A plant that lives for at least three growing seasons.

Pesticide A chemical substance used for killing pests.

Petal A modified leaf, one part of the corolla, which is often brightly coloured to attract attention.

pH A measure of the acidity or alkalinity of the soil. The scale runs from 0 to 14, with a pH of 7 being technically neutral, with higher numbers indicating alkaline soil, and lower numbers acid soil. Soils seldom fall outside the range 4–8.5, and most plants will thrive with a pH of 5.5–7.5. Although these differences sound small, the scale is logarithmic, so pH8 is ten times more alkaline than pH7. Simple soil test kits are available to home gardeners so they can check the pH of their soil.

Phosphate A phosphorus compound.

Phosphorus One of the major plant foods, important in the germination and development of seedlings and in root growth.

Photosynthesis The process by which green plants use chlorophyll to convert carbon dioxide into carbohydrates under the influence of sunlight.

Pinching out The removal of the growing tip of a plant to encourage the production of sideshoots or flowerbuds.

Pistil The female reproductive parts of a flower, consisting of ovary, style and stigma. See also stamen.

Pollen In a flower, the male sex cells, carried on the anthers and transferred to the stigma of other flowers for the process of pollination.

Pollination The transfer of pollen to the stigma of a flower, which takes place in the process of fertilization.

Potash A potassium compound. The word potash is often used loosely to mean potassium.

Potassium One of the major plant foods affecting the size and quality of fruit and flowers. It can also increase resistance to frost, pests and diseases.

Pricking out The transplanting of a small seedling into its own pot, or into a larger tray where it is spaced out to allow more growing space.

Propagation The production of a new generation of plants by sowing seeds, by cuttings or by division.

Raceme A botanical term used to describe an elongated, unbranched flower cluster, in which each flower is attached to the main stem by a stalk. A laburnum's flowers are borne in racemes.

Resistant variety A plant variety that shows particular resistance to a pest and/or disease.

Resting body A structure produced by a fungus that remains dormant for a period before germinating.

Rhizome A horizontal creeping underground stem, which acts as a storage organ.

Rootball The roots and accompanying soil or compost that are visible when a plant is lifted.

Rooting hormone A chemical (usually a powder but sometimes a gel or liquid formulation) that stimulates a cutting to produce roots.

Rootstock The crown and root system of herbaceous perennials and suckering shrubs. In propagation terms, a young plant onto which the desirable variety of certain plants is budded or grafted. The rootstock controls the vigour of the plants, sometimes making a plant more dwarf or more suitable for certain growing conditions. Rootstocks may also be used because the variety grafted or budded onto them will not root readily from cuttings or layers.

Rotavate To use a machine with rotating blades to break up the soil.

Runner A trailing stem that grows along the surface, takes root and forms new growth at nodes or the tip.

Scooping and scouring Techniques that are used in the propagation and growth of hyacinth bulbs.

Scree A slope consisting of rock fragments, simulated in gardens as scree beds, in which drainage is particularly good.

Seed A fertilized plant ovule consisting of an embryo and its food store surrounded by a protective coat.

Seedhead A faded flowerhead that has been successfully fertilized and contains seeds.

Seedling A young plant raised from a seed.

Semi-deciduous A plant that loses only some of its leaves at the end of the growing season.

Semi-evergreen A plant that retains a small proportion of its leaves for more than one season.

Sepal One of the outermost modified leaves, behind the petals and usually green, that compose a flowerhead.

Shrub A woody plant that branches from the base with no obvious trunk.

Silt A fine deposit of mud or clay.

Soil conditioner Material that improves the structure of the soil without necessarily adding to the plant foods.

Species A group of closely related plants within a genus.

Specimen plant A striking plant, usually a tree or shrub, grown where it can be clearly viewed.

Spur A slow-growing, short branch system that usually bears a cluster of flowerbuds.

Stamen The male part of a flower, usually consisting of anther and filament and producing pollen.

Stigma In a flower, the part of the pistil that receives the pollen.

Style The part of a flower's reproductive system that lies between the ovary and the stigma.

Submerged plant A plant that is grown in the deeper part of a pond or pool.

Subsoil The layer of soil below the topsoil which is lighter in colour and lacking in organic matter, soil life and nutrients.

Taproot A strongly growing vertical root with little branching. Dandelions and carrots have taproots.

Tilth A fine, crumbly surface layer of soil, suitable for growing seeds.

Top-dress To apply a material, such as organic matter or fertilizer, to the surface of the soil around a plant.

Topiary The trimming or training of trees and bushes into decorative shapes, such as animals, birds and geometric forms lining an avenue in a formal garden.

Topsoil The upper layer of soil that is the most fertile. It contains more organic matter and nutrients than subsoil and is usually darker in colour.

Trace elements Food materials that are required by plants in minute quantities.

Tuber A swollen, usually underground organ for storing nutrients derived from a stem or root system.

Underplanting The use of low-growing plants beneath taller ones.

Variegated Marked with various colours in an irregular pattern. The word is particularly applied to leaves that have white, yellow or cream markings on the edges.

Variety Strictly, a naturally occurring variant of a wild species, but the word is also used to describe any variant of a plant with consistently reproducible characteristics.

Vegetative propagation The increase of plants by asexual methods, such as cuttings or division, usually resulting in genetically identical plants.

Water in To water around the stem of a newly transplanted plant to settle the soil around its roots.

Water table The level in the soil below which the soil is saturated by ground water.

Windbreak Any structure that shelters plants from strong winds.

Worm compost Plant material that has been converted to compost by worms.

Index

acknowledgements

Garden Picture Library/Mark Bolton 217; /Brian Carter 92 bottom; /Suzie Gibbons 221; /John Glover 135; /Juliet Greene 52 right; /Sunniva Hart 92 top; /Francois de Heel 71 top; /Marijke Heuff 58; /Neil Holmes 161 bottom; /Michael Howes 33, 124 top, 160 bottom, 219 bottom; /Jacqui Hurst 52 centre right, 134 top; /A.I. Lord 171, 210 bottom; /Mayer/Le Scanff 16 bottom, 137; /Jerry Pavia 64 top; /Clay Perry 201; /Howard Rice 60, 103 bottom, 212; /Friedrich Strauss 161 top, 218; /Juliette Wade 128 top right, 128 bottom; /Mel Watson 28, 211, 214 centre left, 223 bottom. **John Glover** 44; /RHS Wisley, Surrey 95 bottom right. **Jerry Harpur** 59 bottom, 63, 108 top; /Mr and Mrs Bradshaw 122; /The Dingle 236 top; /des: Chris Grey-Wilson 125; /des: Bunny Guiness, RHS Chelsea'94 124 bottom. **Holt Studios International**/Nigel Cattlin 206, 208 top, 210 top, 220, 242 top; /Bob Gibbons 127; /Mike Lane 243; /Rosemary Mayer 205 bottom, 214 left, 214 centre right, 216 top, 223 top. **Andrew Lawson** 29 bottom, 96 bottom left, 102 bottom left, 108 bottom, 120, 198 centre left, 204 top, 204 bottom, 216 bottom, 224 right, 238 top; des: Sir Terence Conran, RHS Chelsea'99 136 top; des: Arabella Lennox-Boyd 188 top; Ryton Organic Gardens 205 top. **Octopus Publishing Group Limited** 56 top right, 66 bottom, 77 bottom, 81 left, 81 right, 89 bottom, 94, 99, 107, 111 bottom, 146 left, 152. **/Mark Bolton** 189 bottom; des: Sharon Clarke, RHS Chelsea'01 130 top; des: Christopher Costin, RHS Hampton Court '01 230 top; des: The Courseworks Design Team, RHS Hampton Court '01 123 bottom; des: Paul Dyer, RHS Hampton Court '01 122 top; des: Jeff Groundrill, HRH Leyhill Inmates, RHS Chelsea'01 126 bottom; des: Marney Hall, RHS Hampton Court'01 11; des: Richmond Adult Community College, RHS Hampton Court '01 172 centre left, 183 bottom; des: Scotts of Thrapston, RHS Hampton Court 01 181 top; des: Paul Stone, RHS Chelsea'01 158 top; des: Topiary by Design, RHS Hampton Court '01 184 top; des: Carole Vincent, RHS Chelsea'01 174; des: Geoffrey Whiten, RHS Chelsea '01 186 right, 192. **/Michael Boys** 85 top, 95 centre left, 97 top left, 101 bottom, 103 top, 104, 105 left, 109, 110 top, 165, 240 bottom. **/Marcus Harpur** 1, 2 centre left, 2 right, 2 centre right, 10 top, 12 left, 12 right, 12 centre left, 14 top, 14 bottom, 15 top, 15 bottom, 20 top, 20 bottom, 22 left, 22 right, 22 centre left, 22 centre right, 24, 26 top, 27, 29 top, 32 top, 32 bottom, 36 top, 40 top left, 40 top right, 40 bottom right, 40 bottom left, 45 top left, 45 top right, 45 bottom right, 45 bottom left, 45 bottom centre, 57, 71 bottom, 88, 90 top, 93 bottom, 96 top right, 98 bottom left, 105 right, 106 bottom, 114 Top, 118, 126 top right, 132 top, 132 bottom, 133 left, 133 right, 144 left, 154 left, 154 centre left, 154 centre right, 157 top, 157 bottom, 158 bottom, 159 top, 160 top, 162, 163 top, 186 centre right, 186 centre left, 189 top, 193 top, 193 bottom, 194 top, 194 bottom, 196 bottom right, 196 bottom left, 197, 198 left, 200 top, 200 bottom, 224 left, 226 top, 230 bottom, 232 bottom, 244,

247, 256, Cambridge Botanic Gardens 239, East Ruston Old Vicarage, Norfolk 235, 234 top, Villa Ramsdall, Essex, MHA 228 top, Weeks Farm, Kent 114 bottom, 115 top, RHS Wisley, Surrey 231 top, 238 bottom. **/Jerry Harpur** 2 left, 18, 19, 52 left, 59 top 61 bottom, 65, 77 top, 78 bottom, 82, 83 top, 84 bottom, 87 top, 89 top, 95 top right, 100 left, 101 top, 102 top right, 112 top, 131, 143 top, 143 bottom, 148. **/Neil Holmes** 129 left. **/Andrew Lawson** 66 top, 67, 68 bottom, 69, 70, 75 bottom, 85 bottom, 86 top, 86 bottom, 87 bottom, 93 bottom, 98 top right, 100 right, 113 bottom, 115 bottom, 118 bottom, 119 top, 144 right, 147 left, 150, 153, 240 top. **/David Loftus** 147 right, 245. **/Peter Myers** 12 centre right, 17, 26 bottom, 34 centre left, 39 top left, 42, 72 top, 72 bottom, 163 bottom, 202 bottom, 208 bottom, 228 bottom. **/Sean Myers** 16 top, 34 right, 36 bottom, 37 left, 37 right, 39 top centre, 39 top right, 39 bottom right, 39 bottom left, 49, 62 top, 172 centre right, 178 top, 227 bottom, 242 bottom, 246. **/Peter Pugh-Cook** 8 bottom. **/Graham Rankin** 198 bottom, 202 top, 209 top, 226 bottom. **/Howard Rice** 7, 8 top, 10 bottom, 34 left, 34 centre left, 46, 47, 50, 62 bottom, 68 top, 74, 75 top, 76, 123 top, 129 right, 129 centre, 130 bottom, 134 Bottom Left, 154 right, 156 Top, 156 bottom left, 181 bottom, 186 left, 190, 196 top, 214 right, 219 top, 231 bottom, 234 bottom. **/Guy Ryecart** 175 bottom. **/David Sarton**, des: Mark Ashmead, RHS Hampton Court '02 175 top; des: The Bulbeck Foundry, RHS Chelsea'02 184 bottom; des: Hugh Cox, RHS Hampton Court '03 159 bottom; des: Moya Drummond, RHS Hampton Court'02 6 bottom left; des: Marney Hall, RHS Chelsea'03 140; des: Fiona Lawrenson&Chris Moss RHS Chelsea'03 56 bottom left; des: Erik de Maeijer&Jane Hudson, RHS Chelsea'03 90 bottom; des: May&Watts Garden Design, RHS Hampton Court 03 38; des: Patric McCann, RHS Chelsea'02 9; des: Shila Patel, RHS Hampton Court '02 176, 172 left, 177; des: Heather Ritter, RHS Chelsea'03 54 top; des: David Rosewarne&Maggie Gray, RHS Chelsea'02 142; des: Tollemache&Kellett, RHS Chelsea'03 188 bottom; des: Cheryl Waller, RHS Chelsea'03 122 bottom; des: Kay Yamada, RHS Chelsea'03 55, 224 centre left, 232 top. **/Mark Winwood** 6 top right, 79, 198 centre right, 207 left, 207 right, 209 bottom. **/Steve Wooster** 61 top, 83 bottom, 106 top, 136 bottom, 172 right, 178 bottom, 179, 183 top, 203, 224 centre right, 227 top, 236 bottom. **/George Wright** 15 centre right, 41, 78 top, 84 top, 97 bottom right, 110 bottom, 111 top, 112 bottom, 113 top, 116 top, 117 top, 117 bottom, 141, 143 right, 144 centre left, 144 centre right, 149, 151. **/James Young** 52 centre left, 64 bottom.

The Publishers would like to thank Robin MacDonald for modeling for this book. They would also like to thank Marjorie, Jerry and Marcus Harpur for their kind hospitality during the photo shoot.

Executive Editor **Sarah Ford**
Managing Editor **Clare Churly**
Editors **Jo Smith** and **Lydia Darbyshire**
Executive Art Editor **Rozelle Bentheim**
Designer **Lisa Tai**
Special Photography **Marcus Harper**
Illustration **Line & Line**
Picture Researchers **Christine Junemann** and **Jennifer Veall**
Production Manager **Louise Hall**